Socialism Betrayed

Also by Roger Keeran

The Communist Party and the Auto Workers Unions

Socialism Betrayed:

Behind the Collapse of the Soviet Union

Roger Keeran

and

Thomas Kenny

iUniverse, Inc.
New York   Bloomington

Socialism Betrayed
Behind the Collapse of the Soviet Union

iUniverse books may be ordered through booksellers or by contacting:

iUniverse
1663 Liberty Drive
Bloomington, IN 47403
www.iuniverse.com
1-800-Authors (1-800-288-4677)

Because of the dynamic nature of the Internet, any Web addresses or links contained in this book may have changed since publication and may no longer be valid. The views expressed in this work are solely those of the author and do not necessarily reflect the views of the publisher, and the publisher hereby disclaims any responsibility for them.

ISBN: 978-1-4502-4171-7 (sc)
ISBN: 978-1-4502-4172-4 (ebook)

Printed in the United States of America

iUniverse rev. date: 10/06/2010

Contents

Preface to the Second Edition

Socialism Betrayed was first published by International Publishers in 2004, for which we would like to extend our appreciation to International's Director, Betty Smith. That the first edition sold out was largely due to the favorable reviews and publicity the book garnered in the United States by reviewer Mark Almberg of the *People's Weekly World* and in Britain by the *Morning Star*, Ireland by the *Socialist Voice*, Canada by the *People's Voice* and *The Spark*, Australia by *The Guardian* and *Australian Marxist Review*, and Germany by *Marxistische Blaetter*. We thank the editors and reviewers of these periodicals. Though reviewers largely ignored the book in the United States, the book did gain critical notice in *Political Affairs, Science & Society*, and *Nature, Society and Thought*. Since critical notice is better than no notice, we would like to thank those reviewers as well.

Since 2004, *Socialism Betrayed* has been translated into several languages. We would like to take the opportunity of the second English edition to thank those who in various ways aided its publication abroad. Irina Malenko and Blagovesta Doncheva, have been great friends and enthusiastic and tireless advocates of the book, and their efforts were primarily responsible for the book's publication in Bulgarian and Russian. We cannot thank them enough. We are also grateful to Dr. Ivan Ivanov for the Russian translation and Algoritm Press for the Russian edition. The Persian edition of the book was due to Mohammad Mehryar and Feridon Darafshi, who took the book from the U.S. to Iran and introduced it to one of the heroes of the struggle for Iranian freedom, Mohammad Ali Amooii (sometimes spelled Amoui), who liked the book well enough to translate it himself. We owe deep debt of gratitude to all three men. In Greece, part of the book appeared in *KOMEP*, the journal of the Communist Party of Greece (KKE) edited by Eleni Bellou. She and her colleagues Kyrillos Papastavrou, Vasilis Opsimou, Babis Angourakis and Nikos Seratakis arranged for the authors to attend in December 2007 an international conference in Athens on the causes of the Soviet demise. This conference acquainted others with the book, including Francisco Melo, editor of *Vertices*. He and his colleagues, including Maria Antunes, engineered the translation and publication of the book in Portugal, where under the title, *O Socialismo Traido*, the book has gone through two printings . Aytek Alpan initiated the publication of the book in Turkey. Henri Alleg and Emmanuel Tang played a similar role in France, and through their initiative the book will be published by Editions Delga headed by Aymeric Monville. In expressing our thanks, we would point out that the considerable effort on the part of all of these people arose not from material gain but entirely from their belief that the book had value and deserved a wide readership.

The second edition of *Socialism Betrayed* is due to the generous support of the Dogwood Foundation for Socialist Education. We would like to thank the Foundation and its Director Paul Bjarnason for the confidence they have shown in our work.

Preface

In the introduction to his 1957 on the Hungarian uprising, Herbert Aptheker, acknowledged the hazards of trying to evaluate something "so recent in time and distant in space," but said he did so anyway because he "had to try to understand that upheaval." In this preface, we acknowledge the same hazard and motivation. Not only was the Soviet upheaval near in time and distant in space, but also it was outside the authors' usual area of study. One of us is an American historian and the other a labor economist. Both of us, however, were driven to understand what had happened, and we think that we have reached a reasonable interpretation and some original insights. And we desire to put these views to what Aptheker called "the ordeal of careful scrutiny."

This book would not have been possible without the generous contributions of numerous friends who read the manuscript, corrected errors, suggested sources, added ideas, qualified judgements, challenged jargon, and pared the wordiness. Special thanks goes to Bahman Azad, Norman Markowitz, Michael Parenti, Anthony Coughlan, and Betty Smith for reading the entire manuscript and suggesting editorial and substantive changes. We would also like to thank those who read all or parts of the manuscript and those who shared their ideas and sometimes their encouragement: Gerald Horne, Frank Goldsmith, Erwin Marquit, Sam Webb, Elena Mora, Mark

Rosenzweig, Gerald Meyer, Joe Sims, Lee Dlugin, Pat Barile, Danny Rubin, Phil Bonosky, Bill Davis, Evelina Alarcon, Tim Wheeler, Scott Marshall, Noel Rabinowitz, Paul Mishler, Jarvis Tyner, Esther Moroze, Marilyn Bechtell, Gerald Erickson, Constance Pohl, Jackie DiSalvo, Richard and Brawee Najarian, and Jim Miller. We would also like to thank the librarians, Mark Rosenzweig of the Reference Center for Marxist Studies and Jackie LaValle, for helping with the research, and Eileen Jamison for tracking down numerous books and articles. We also owe a debt of gratitude to Gregory Grossman for helping us find sources on the second economy. We also thank SUNY Empire State College for granting a sabbatical leave to Roger Keeran during which he did some early research and writing. We want to thank Catherine Keeran for her assistance and Alice and John Ward for providing accommodations and company, while Roger did research at the University of Texas. For their consultations on the cover and other matters, we would like to thank David Granville, Derek Kotz, Ian Denning and Charles Keller, and for technical help, John Quinn. For their camaraderie, Michael and Mary Donovan, Bill Towne, and Christina Hassinger of Flannery's Seminar in Contemporary Politics, get a grateful nod.

Finally, we would like to thank our wives, Carol and Mary, who discussed this project from beginning to end. They also patiently endured lost weekends, obsessive ravings about the importance of an unfashionable topic, book-strewn kitchen tables, seas of paper, and endless distracted hours at word processors.

Mark Twain said, "It is difference of opinion that makes horse races." He might have added it also makes politics. Among political people, the downfall of the Soviet Union generates strong and diverse views. It seemed to us that everyone who had visited a socialist country, talked to a Soviet citizen, or read a book on socialism had theories to explain and anecdotes to prove what went wrong. Many who read this manuscript had firm ideas of their own and did not share ours. Hence, we must declare with more than usual vigor that all the views, as well as the mistakes, are the responsibility of the authors and the authors alone.

1. Introduction

The story of the last Soviet power struggle is not, I believe, one that is best understood in terms of an irresistible unfolding of large historical forces and trends. On the contrary, it is in many respects the most curious story in modern history. Anthony D'Agostino, historian[1]

In awe, amazement and disbelief, the world witnessed the collapse of the Soviet Union, which swept away the Soviet system of government, the erstwhile superpower, the communist belief system and the ruling party. Alexander Dallin, historian[2]

The Soviet Union's existence was as sure as the sun rising in the morning. For, it was such a solid, powerful, strong country that had survived extremely difficult tests. Fidel Castro[3]

This book is about the collapse of the Soviet Union and its meaning for the 21ˢᵗ century. The size of the debacle gave rise to extravagant claims by the political right. For them, the collapse meant the Cold War was over and capitalism had won. It signified "the end of history." Henceforth, capitalism would represent the highest form, the culmination, of economic and

1

political evolution. Most people sympathetic with the Soviet project did not share this rightwing triumphalism. For them, the Soviet collapse had momentous implications but did not alter the usefulness of Marxism for understanding a world that more than ever was shaped by class conflict and the struggles of oppressed people against corporate power, nor did it shake the values and commitment of those on the side of workers, unions, minorities, national liberation, peace, women, the environment, and human rights. Still, what had happened to socialism represented both a theoretical challenge to Marxism and a practical challenge to the future prospects of anti-capitalist struggles and socialism.

For those who believe that a better world--beyond capitalist exploitation, inequality, greed, poverty, ignorance, and injustice--is possible, the demise of the Soviet Union represented a staggering loss. Soviet socialism had many problems (that we discuss later) and did not constitute the only conceivable socialist order. Nevertheless, it embodied the essence of socialism as defined by Marx--a society that had overthrown bourgeois property, the "free market," and the capitalist state and replaced them with collective property, central planning, and a workers' state. Moreover, it achieved an unprecedented level of equality, security, health care, housing, education, employment, and culture for all of its citizens, in particular working people of factory and farm.

A brief review of the Soviet Union's accomplishments underscores what was lost. The Soviet Union not only eliminated the exploiting classes of the old order, but also ended inflation, unemployment, racial and national discrimination, grinding poverty, and glaring inequalities of wealth, income, education, and opportunity. In fifty years, the country went from an industrial production that was only 12 percent of that in the United States to industrial production that was 80 percent and an agricultural output 85 percent of the U.S. Though Soviet per capita consumption remained lower than in the U.S., no society had ever increased living standards and consumption so rapidly

2

in such a short period of time for all its people. Employment was guaranteed. Free education was available for all, from kindergarten through secondary schools (general, technical and vocational), universities, and after-work schools. Besides free tuition, post-secondary students received living stipends. Free health care existed for all, with about twice as many doctors per person as in the United States. Workers who were injured or ill had job guarantees and sick pay. In the mid-1970s, workers averaged 21.2 working days of vacation (a month's vacation), and sanitariums, resorts, and children's camps were either free or subsidized. Trade unions had the power to veto firings and recall managers. The state regulated all prices and subsidized the cost of basic food and housing. Rents constituted only 2-3 percent of the family budget; water and utilities only 4-5 percent. No segregated housing by income existed. Though some neighborhoods were reserved for high officials, elsewhere plant managers, nurses, professors and janitors lived side by side.[4]

The government included cultural and intellectual growth as part of the effort to enhance living standards. State subsidies kept the price of books, periodicals and cultural events at a minimum. As a result, workers often owned their own libraries, and the average family subscribed to four periodicals. UNESCO reported that Soviet citizens read more books and saw more films than any other people in the world. Every year the number of people visiting museums equaled nearly half entire population, and attendance at theaters, concerts, and other performances surpassed the total population. The government made a concerted effort to raise the literacy and living standards of the most backward areas and to encourage the cultural expression of the more than a hundred nationality groups that constituted the Soviet Union. In Kirghizia, for example, only one out of every five hundred people could read and write in 1917, but fifty years later nearly everyone could.[5]

3

In 1983, American sociologist Albert Szymanski reviewed a variety of Western studies of Soviet income distribution and living standards. He found that the highest paid people in the Soviet Union were prominent artists, writers, professors, administrators, and scientists, who earned as high as 1,200 to 1,500 rubles a month. Leading government officials earned about 600 rubles a month; enterprise directors from 190 to 400 rubles a month; and workers about 150 rubles a month. Consequently, the highest incomes amounted to only 10 times the average worker's wages, while in the United States the highest paid corporate heads made 115 times the wages of workers. Privileges that came with high office, such as special stores and official automobiles, remained small and limited and did not offset a continuous, forty-year trend toward greater egalitarianism. (The opposite trend occurred in the United States, where by the late 1990s, corporate heads were making 480 times the wages of the average worker.) Though the tendency to level wages and incomes created problems (discussed later), the overall equalization of living conditions in the Soviet Union represented an unprecedented feat in human history. The equalization was furthered by a pricing policy that fixed the cost of luxuries above their value and of necessities below their value. It was also furthered by a steadily increasing "social wage," that is, the provision of an increasing number of free or subsidized social benefits. Beside those already mentioned, the benefits included, paid maternity leave, inexpensive child care and generous pensions. Szymanski concluded, "While the Soviet social structure may not match the Communist or socialist ideal, it is both qualitatively different from, and more equalitarian than, that of Western capitalist countries. Socialism has made a radical difference in favor of the working class."[6]

In the world context, the demise of the Soviet Union also meant an incalculable loss. It meant the disappearance of a counterweight to colonialism and imperialism. It meant the eclipse of a model of how newly freed nations could harmonize different ethnic constituents and develop themselves without mortgaging their futures to the United States or Western Europe. By 1991, the leading non-capitalist country in the world, the main support of national liberation movements and socialist governments like Cuba, had fallen apart. No amount of rationalization could escape this fact and the setback it represented for socialist and peoples' struggles.

Even more important than appreciating what was lost in the Soviet collapse is the effort to understand it. How great an impact this event will have depends in part on how its causes come to be understood. In the Great Anti-Communist Celebration of the early 1990s, the triumphant right hammered several ideas into the consciousness of millions: the Soviet socialism as a planned economic system did not work and could not bring abundance, because it was an accident, an experiment born in violence and sustained by coercion, an aberration doomed by its defiance of human nature and its incompatibility with democracy. The Soviet Union ended because a society ruled by the working class is a delusion; there is no post-capitalist order.

Some people on the left, typically those of social democratic views, drew conclusions that were similar, if less extreme, than those on the right. They believed that Soviet socialism was flawed in some fundamental and irreparable way, that the flaws were "systemic," rooted in a lack of democracy and over-centralization of the economy. The social democrats did not conclude that socialism in the future is doomed, but they did conclude that the Soviet collapse deprived Marxism-Leninism of much of its authority and that a future socialism must be built on a completely different basis than the Soviet form. For them, Gorbachev's reforms were not wrong, just too late.

Obviously, if such claims are true, the future of Marxist-Leninist theory, socialism and anti-capitalist struggle must be very different from what Marxists forecast before 1985. If Marxist-Leninist theory failed the Soviet leaders who presided over the debacle, Marxist theory was mostly wrong and must

5

be abandoned. Past efforts to build socialism held no lessons for the future. Those who oppose global capitalism must realize history is not on their side and settle for piecemeal, partial reform. Clearly, these were the lessons the triumphant right wanted everyone to draw.

Our investigation was motivated by the enormity of the collapse's implications. We were skeptical of the triumphant right, but prepared to follow the facts wherever they led. We were mindful that previous socialist partisans had to analyze huge defeats of the working class. In *The Civil War in France*, Karl Marx analyzed the defeat of the Paris Commune in 1871. Twenty years later Frederick Engels expanded upon his analysis in an introduction to Marx's work on the Commune.[7] Vladimir Lenin and his generation had to account for the failed Russian revolution of 1905 and the failure of Western European revolutions to materialize in 1918-22. Later Marxists, like Edward Boorstein, had to analyze the failure of the Chilean revolution in 1973.[8] Such analyses showed that sympathy with the defeated did not bar the pursuit of tough questions about the reasons for the defeat.

Within the overarching question of why the Soviet Union collapsed, other questions arose: What was the state of Soviet society when *perestroika* began? Was the Soviet Union facing a crisis in 1985? What problems was Gorbachev's *perestroika* supposed to address? Were there viable alternatives to the reform course chosen by Gorbachev? What forces favored and what forces opposed the reform path leading to capitalism? Once Gorbachev's reform started producing economic disaster and national disintegration, why did Gorbachev not change course, or why did the other leaders of the Communist Party not replace him? Why was Soviet socialism seemingly so fragile? Why did the working class apparently do so little to defend socialism? Why did the leaders so underestimate nationalist separatism? Why did socialism--at least in some form--manage to survive in China, North Korea, Vietnam, and Cuba, while in the Soviet Union, where it was ostensibly more rooted and developed, it failed to last? Was the Soviet demise inevitable? This last question was pivotal. Whether socialism has a future depends on whether what transpired in the Soviet Union was inevitable or avoidable. Certainly, it was possible to imagine an explanation that differed from the inevitability trumpeted by the right. Take, for example, the following thought experiment. Suppose the Soviet Union had fallen apart because a nuclear attack by the United States had destroyed its government and devastated its cities and industries. Some might still conclude that the Cold War was over and capitalism had won, but no one could reasonably argue that this event proved that Marx was wrong, or that left to its own devices, socialism was unworkable. In other words, if Soviet socialism came to an end mainly because of externalities, such as foreign military threats or subversion, one might conclude that this fate did not compromise Marxism as a theory and socialism as a viable system.

In another example, some have asserted that the Soviet Union unraveled because of "human error" rather than "systemic weaknesses." In other words, mediocre leaders and poor decisions brought down a basically sound system. If true, this explanation like the former would preserve the integrity of Marxist theory and socialist viability. In actuality, however, this idea has not served as an explanation or even the beginning of an explanation but rather as a reason to avoid a searching explanation. As an acquaintance said, "The Soviet Communists screwed up, but we will do better." To have any plausibility, however, this explanation needed to answer important questions: what made the leaders mediocre and the decisions poor? Why did the system produce such leaders and how could they get away with making poor decisions? Did viable alternatives exist to the ones chosen? What lessons are to be drawn?

Questioning the inevitability of the Soviet demise is a risky business. The British historian, E. H. Carr, warned that questioning the inevitability of any historical event can lead to a parlor game of speculation on "the might-have-beens of history." The historians' job was to explain what happened, not to let "their imagination run riot on all the more agreeable things that might have happened." Carr acknowledged, however, that while explaining why one course was chosen over another, historians quite appropriately discuss the "alternative courses available."[9] Similarly, British historian Eric Hobsbawm argued that not all "counter-factual" speculation is the same. Some thinking about historical options falls into the category of "imagination run riot," which a serious historian should rule out. Such is the case of musing about outcomes that were never in the historical cards, such as whether czarist Russia would have evolved into a liberal democracy without the Russian Revolution or whether the South would have eliminated slavery without the Civil War. Some counter-factual speculation, however, when it hews closely to the historical facts and real possibilities, serves a useful purpose. Where real alternative courses of action existed, they can show the contingency of what actually did occur. Coincidentally, Hobsbawm gave a relevant example from recent Soviet history. Hobsbawm quoted a former CIA director as saying, "I believe that if [Soviet leader, Yuri] Andropov had been fifteen years younger when he took power in 1982, we would still have a Soviet Union with us." On this, Hobsbawm remarked, "I don't like to agree with CIA chiefs, but this seems to me to be entirely plausible."[10] We too think this is plausible, and we discuss the reasons in the next chapter.

Counter-factual speculation can legitimately suggest how, under future circumstances similar to the past, one might act differently. The debates of historians over the decision to use the atom bomb on Hiroshima, for example, not only have changed the way educated people understand this event but also have reduced the likelihood of a similar decision in the future. After all, if history is to be more than a parlor diversion, it should and can teach us something about avoiding past mistakes.

The interpretation of the Soviet collapse involves a fight over the future. Explanations will help determine whether in the 21st century working people will once again "storm the heavens" to replace capitalism with a better system. They will hardly take the risks and bear the costs if they believe that working class rule, collective ownership, and a planned economy are bound to fail, that only the "free market" works, and that millions of people in eastern Europe and the Soviet Union tried socialism but went back to capitalism because they wanted prosperity and freedom. As the radical movement against globalism grows and the labor movement revives, as the long economic boom of the 1990s recedes, and capitalism's lasting evils-- unemployment, racism, inequality, environmental degradation, and war--become more and more evident, the questioning of capitalism's future will invariably move to the foreground. But the youth and labor movements will hardly advance much beyond narrow economic demands, moral protest, anarchism or nihilism, if they consider socialism an impossibility. The stakes could hardly be higher.

As the significance of the loss of the Soviet Union sinks in, the opportunity for dispassionate discourse on Soviet history increases. Certainly, a lot of early notions about a peaceful and prosperous post-Cold War world have turned to bitter ashes. A bipolar world was replaced by a unipolar one dominated by American corporate and military power. Globalism replaced anti-communism as the governing ideology. Globalism insists that the domination of the world by a few transnational corporations, the spread of information technology, and the free movement of goods and capital in search of the lowest costs and highest profits represents an unstoppable force before which all other interests--those of weak states, national independence movements, labor movements, defenders of the environment-- must give way. Without the Soviet Union as a viable alternative to capitalism--social welfare, the welfare state, the public sector, Keynesianism, the "third way"--have come under attack. In

9

all countries progressive and social democratic parties have staggered under the pressure of an emboldened neo-liberal right. Since 1991, world poverty and inequality have grown by leaps and bounds.

In another crushed illusion, the idea of a post-Cold War peace dividend vanished. Instead of cutting the military budget, the George W. Bush and other American leaders frantically sought a rationale for increased spending and new weapons systems. They tried using a war on drugs, rogue states, and Islamic fundamentalism as rationales. Then the attack on the World Trade Center gave them the justification they needed--an unending war against international terrorism. For many people, these post-Soviet disappointments have diminished the triumphalist interpretation of the Soviet collapse.

Equally tarnishing to the triumphalist interpretation has been the disastrous human toll brought by gangster capitalism in the former Soviet Union. What a decade ago was touted as Russia's "democratic transformation" and its rebirth as a "vibrant market economy" turned into a sick joke. A United Nations' report in 1998 said, "No region in the world has suffered such reversals in the 1990s as have the countries of the former Soviet Union and Eastern Europe." People living in poverty increased by over 150 million, a figure greater than the total combined population of France, the UK, the Netherlands, and Scandinavia. The national income declined "drastically" in the face of "some of the most rampant inflation witnessed anywhere on the globe."[11]

In *Failed Crusade*, historian Stephen F. Cohen went even further. By 1998, the Soviet economy, dominated by gangsters and foreigners, was barely half the size it was in the early 1990s. Meat and dairy herds were a fourth of their size; wages were less than half. Typhus, typhoid, cholera and other diseases had reached epidemic proportions. Millions of children suffered malnutrition. Male life expectancy plunged to sixty years, what it was at the end of the nineteenth century. In Cohen's words, "the nation's economic and social disintegration has been so great that it has led to the unprecedented demodernization of a twentieth century country."[12] In the face of the catastrophic failure of Russia's road to capitalism, smugness over the inevitable problems of socialism lost some of its traction.

Not only may more people be interested in understanding the Soviet experience than previously, but the raw material for analysis is more available than before. The first publications on *perestroika* and the collapse were dominated by the writing of Gorbachev partisans and anti-Communist war-horses. These included the memoirs and other writings of Gorbachev, Boris Yeltsin and their supporters, the memoirs of American Ambassador to the Soviet Union, Jack Matlock, the essays of such often unreliable Soviet dissidents as Roy Medvedev and Andrei Sakharov, the reports of such Western journalists as David Remnick and David Pryce-Jones, and the work of such anti-Soviet historians as Martin Malia and Richard Pipes. Since then, however, a second wave of publications has appeared. These publications included a much expanded memoir literature of secondary leaders, including Yegor Ligachev, military men and academics. It also included a great number of monographic studies on particular aspects of the Gorbachev years including *glasnost*, nationalism, co-ops, economic policy, privatization of state property, Soviet policy toward the African National Congress, and Soviet policy in Afghanistan. An American Communist journalist who was stationed in Moscow, Mike Davidow, published *Perestroika: Its Rise and Fall*, and the Marxist economist Bahman Azad published *Heroic Struggle Bitter Defeat: Factors Contributing to the Dismantling of the Socialist State in the Soviet Union*. Also, various Communist Parties, leaders and theoreticians, such as Fidel Castro, Joe Slovo, Hans Heinz Holz, and the Russian Communist Party issued statements on *perestroika* and the collapse. We have drawn on all of these in our examination.

It goes without saying that the defeat of the Paris Commune after seventy days delivered a less telling blow to socialists than the eclipse of the Soviet Union after over seventy years. It may be impossible to end our analysis with the defiance with which Engels ended his remarks on the Commune: "Of late, the Social-Democratic philistine has once more been filled with wholesome terror at the words: Dictatorship of the Proletariat. Well and good, gentlemen, do you want to know what this dictatorship looks like? Look at the Paris Commune. That was the Dictatorship of the Proletariat." Nevertheless, it is possible to acknowledge the achievements of the Soviet Union, to estimate the size and consequences of the external forces arrayed against it, to assess some of the contending political views within Soviet socialism and to venture some judgments on the policies. It will, however, take much more than this book to reach a full analysis, so that in the future, men and women of the left can struggle for a socialism confident that they are not prisoners of the past. Then they can echo Marx's words on the Commune, that the Soviet Union, too, "will be for ever celebrated as the glorious harbinger of a new society."[13]

In what follows, we argue that the Soviet collapse occurred in the main because of the policies that Mikhail Gorbachev pursued after 1986. These policies did not drop from the sky, nor were they the only possible ones to address existing problems. They derived from a debate within the Communist movement, nearly as old as Marxism itself, over how to build a socialist society. In order to explain the lineage of Gorbachev's policies before and after 1985, in Chapter 2, we discuss the two main tendencies or trends in the Soviet debate over building socialism. The ongoing debate centered around this question: under the particular circumstances pertaining at any given time, how should Communists build socialism? The left position favored pushing forward class struggle, the interests of the working class and the power of the Communist Party, and the right position favored retreats or compromises and the incorporation of various capitalist ideas into socialism. In this sense, "left" and "right" were not synonyms for good and bad. Rather the correctness or appropriateness of a policy had to do with whether it best represented the immediate and long-term interests of socialism under existing conditions. The history of Soviet politics was thus a complex matter. On the one hand, Vladimir Lenin, who fearlessly pushed forward the class struggle for socialism, at times favored compromise, as in the Treaty of Brest-Litovsk and the New Economic Policy. On the other hand, Nikita Khrushchev, who often favored incorporating certain Western ideas, at the same time favored a leftist policy of greater wage equality. In this chapter, we do not intend to provide a full history and evaluation of Soviet politics but rather a useful, if simplified, backdrop for the later argument that Gorbachev's early policies resembled the leftwing Communist tradition represented in the main by Vladimir Lenin, Joseph Stalin, and Yuri Andropov, while his later policies resembled the rightwing Communist tradition represented in the main by Nicolai Bukharin and Nikita Khrushchev. After 1985, Gorbachev's policies moved to the right, in the sense that they involved what might be called a social democratic vision of socialism that weakened the Communist Party, compromised with capitalism, and incorporated into Soviet socialism certain aspects of capitalist private property, markets, and political forms.

In Chapter 3, we discuss the underlying reasons for Gorbachev's shift in policies and their material basis. We argue that the reason for Gorbachev's shift was the development of a phenomenon overlooked by most Marxists and non-Marxists, namely the development within socialism of a "second economy" of private enterprise and with it a new and growing petty bourgeois stratum and a new level of Party corruption. The growth of the second economy reflected the problems of the "first economy," the socialized sector, in meeting the rising expectations of the people. It also reflected the laxness of the authorities in enforcing the law against illegal economic activity, and the failure of the Party to recognize the corrosive effects of private economic activity.

In Chapter 4, we explain the economic, political and international problems that troubled Soviet society in the mid-1980s, problems that gave rise to a search for reforms. We also recount the promising beginning of some of Gorbachev's reforms, and the problematic aspects of others. In Chapter 5, we explain the transformation of Gorbachev's policies in 1987 and 1988 and their deleterious consequences. In Chapter 6, we describe the unraveling of the Soviet system. In Chapter 7, we conclude with a discussion of the significance of the Soviet collapse. In an Epilogue, we critique other explanations.

2. Two Trends in Soviet Politics

Bukharin is a most highly valued and important party theoretician... but it is very doubtful if his theoretical outlook can be considered as fully Marxist. V. I. Lenin[14]

Khrushchev in essence was a Bukharinite. V. M. Molotov[15]

Andropov obviously was not on the side of Khrushchev nor on the side of Brezhnev for that matter. V. M. Molotov[16]

The crisis that came upon Soviet society [in the 1980s] was due in large measure to the crisis in the Party. Two--opposing tendencies existed in the CPSU--proletarian and petty bourgeois, democratic and bureaucratic. Program of the Fourth Congress of the Communist Party of the Russian Federation (1997)[17]

The collapse of the Soviet Union did not occur because of an internal economic crisis or popular uprising. It occurred because of the reforms initiated at the top by the Communist Party of the Soviet Union (CPSU) and its General Secretary

15

Mikhail Gorbachev. It goes without saying that problems must have existed in the Soviet Union, otherwise no need for reforms would have arisen. Gorbachev's reforms were a response to the underlying problems. In Chapter 4, we will examine the chronic problems facing Soviet society in three areas: economics, politics, and foreign relations--all of which had become more acute because of developments in the early 1980s. Since, however, the treatment of the illness rather than the illness itself caused the death of the patient, the origin and character of the treatment, that is the origin and character of Gorbachev's reforms, require our first attention.

We proceed from the simple assumption that the diagnosis of social problems, even more than medical problems, are rarely matters of certainty. The definition and diagnosis of social problems, as well as the policy responses to problems, involve politics, that is, conflicting values and interests, and this was no less the case in the Soviet Union than in the United States. Outsiders commonly assumed that because the Soviet Union had only one party, political thought was monolithic and political debate non-existent. This was far from true. Starting before the revolution, the Soviet Communist Party contained more than one tendency or trend. Gorbachev did not invent his policies out of whole cloth, but rather his policies reflected trends in the Party that had earlier been represented in part by Nikolai Bukharin, Nikita Khrushchev and others.

Just as Gorbachev's ideas did not arise in a political vacuum, neither did they arise in a socio-economic vacuum. That is, Gorbachev's political ideas reflected social and economic interests. Gorbachev's reforms after 1986 reflected the interests of those in Soviet society with a stake in private enterprise and the "free market." This sector consisted of entrepreneurs and corrupt Party officials whose numbers had increased during the previous thirty years.

Before proceeding, a word of clarification is necessary. Though a continuity existed in the approach of Bukharin,

16

Khrushchev, and Gorbachev, the problems they confronted, the social basis of their support, and the policies they advocated differed. For example, in the 1920s, the largest social group with an interest in private enterprise was the peasantry, which constituted a distinct class representing about 80 percent of the population. By the 1970s only 20 percent of the population worked in agriculture, and most of these were agricultural workers on state farms or collective farms. By then the social group with a stake in private enterprise had become the petty entrepreneurs in the second economy. Such elements had thrived under the New Economic Policy (NEP) of the early 1920s, shrank drastically with the collectivization of property under Joseph Stalin, re-emerged under Khrushchev's so-called liberalization, increased greatly in size under Brezhnev's laxness, and ballooned under Gorbachev's reforms. In another difference, the agricultural question, which was so prominent in Bukharin's championing of the kulaks, and in various Khrushchev policies, did not figure prominently in Gorbachev's program. Moreover, Gorbachev's foreign policy retreats, cultural liberalization, weakening of the Party, and market initiatives went to lengths never contemplated by his precursors.

In the politics of the Russian revolution, two poles or tendencies arose because the winners of the Russian Revolution were two classes: the working class and the petty bourgeoisie, chiefly the peasantry. In 1917 the Soviet working class was small, and in the decades after 1917, tens of millions of peasants were the human material that would make up the new, growing Soviet working class. As these two classes persisted so did two political tendencies that more or less reflected their class interests. In the 1920s, both tendencies ostensibly favored building socialism. The working class tendency, however, favored policies that strengthened the working class by rapidly building up industry and weakened the property-owning classes by collectivizing agriculture, and policies that strengthened the role of the Communist Party particularly in centralized economic planning. The petty bourgeois tendency favored building socialism slowly by maintaining or incorporating aspects of capitalism, for example maintaining private property, competitive markets, and profit incentives. Though not all political ideas fell neatly into one or the other category, nonetheless, these categories provided the poles around which the variety often pivoted. This was evident in the early debate over the New Economic Policy (NEP).

In late 1920 and early 1921, with the country freed of foreign invaders, Lenin and other leaders of the revolution turned their attention from war to peace. They needed to replace the policies of "war communism," particularly the forceful appropriation of surplus grain that had alienated many peasants. They had to grapple with acute shortages of fuel, food, and transportation, to revive industry and food production, and insure the unity between workers and peasants. In March 1921 at the Tenth Congress of the Bolshevik Party, Lenin proposed what became known as the New Economic Policy (NEP).[18] It was a "strategic retreat,"[19] a chance to regroup and lay the foundations for a future march toward socialism. Under the NEP, a tax in kind replaced the appropriation of peasant grain. Peasants could engage in free trade to sell their surplus, and various other kinds of capitalist enterprises could exist. The idea was that the NEP would encourage the peasants to produce more, and the state could use taxes on peasant produce to revive the state-owned industry. Debate soon arose. The "Lefts" called the NEP a capitulation to capitalism that would doom the Soviet project. On the other end of the spectrum, Leon Trotsky, Grigory Zinoviev, Nikolai Bukharin and others thought the NEP was too tame and advocated even more far-reaching concessions to capitalism. Lenin agreed that the NEP represented a danger. It means "unrestricted trade," he said, "and that means turning back towards capitalism."[20] Still, he thought the Party could handle the danger by limiting the retreat and keeping it temporary. Lenin prevailed.[21]

By the time of Lenin's death in 1924, the revolution had seized state power and consolidated its hold, had defeated invading imperialist armies and the domestic counterrevolution, had nationalized key industries, had distributed land to the peasants, and had revitalized industry and food production. Originally, all leading Communists thought that completing the socialist revolution in a backward, peasant country like Russia would be impossible without revolutions in the West. With the defeat of an uprising of the German workers in 1923, however, it became clear that no European revolution was on the horizon. With no European revolution to count on, what was to be done? Three solutions presented themselves: Leon Trotsky's, Nikolai Bukharin's, and Joseph Stalin's.

Leon Trotsky advocated an attempt to build socialism at home while continuing to press for socialist revolution abroad. Domestically, he urged the development of industry, the collectivization and mechanization of agriculture, and the development of economic planning. Above all, however, and with increasing stridency, Trotsky stressed the need for international revolution as the only hope for Russia to escape from what he called bureaucratic degeneration and the loss of revolutionary fervor. Trotsky and the Left Opposition were decisively defeated at the Fourteenth Party Congress in 1925, which adopted a course of rapid industrialization and self-sufficiency.[22]

Nikolai Bukharin represented a petty bourgeois or right-wing solution to socialism's way forward. Barrington Moore pointed out that unlike Lenin, Trotsky, and Stalin, Bukharin never held a high administrative post with major organizational responsibilities. As editor of *Pravda* and an official of the Comintern, he manipulated "symbols rather than men." Moreover, as a theoretician he moved from the "extreme left to the extreme right of the Communist political spectrum." By the

1920s, he was firmly on the right. He believed that Russia could not skip the stage of capitalism or even pass through it quickly. As Moore said, Bukharin's positions "strongly resembled the gradualist views of Western Social Democracy." He softened the idea of class struggle, to the idea of a peaceful contest between competing interest groups, between state industry and private industry, between cooperative farms and private farms, in which the former would gradually show their superiority. Whereas Lenin, the originator of the New Economic Policy, had frankly viewed it as a retreat, Bukharin viewed the NEP as the road to socialism. He would have continued the New Economic Policy and allowed or even encouraged private enterprise, particularly among the kulaks. Bukharin opposed rapid industrialization, the collectivization of agriculture and any coercion of the peasants. Instead, he said the peasants should be given what they wanted, and he advanced a slogan for the peasants, "Enrich yourselves." In a kind of pale imitation of Trotsky's vain hope in socialist revolutions abroad, Bukharin sought to obtain support for the Soviet Union from non-Communist groups abroad, hopes that were dashed by the failure in 1926-27 to win the support of British trade unionists, German Social Democrats, and Chinese nationalists. Bukharin and the Right Opposition were rebuffed by the Fifteenth Party Congress in 1927 that adopted a policy of promoting the collectivization of agriculture.[23] (Sixty years later, Gorbachev read a biography of Bukharin by historian Stephen F. Cohen. According to Gorbachev's close advisor, Anatoly Chernyaev, it was then that Gorbachev decided to rehabilitate Bukharin, and the re-evaluation of Bukharin "opened the sluice gates to reconsidering our whole ideology."[24])

In the course of debates with Trotsky and Bukharin, Stalin developed his own solution to socialism's way forward. It had four main components. First was the idea that socialism could be built in one country, a reiteration of Lenin's 1915 idea that "the victory of socialism" was possible "even in one single capitalist country."[25] In the 1920s, Stalin translated this idea into a program. Stalin argued that the Soviet Union could advance toward socialism without a revolution in the West, without help from non-Communist allies abroad, and without passing through developed capitalism, providing that the country industrialized rapidly. This was the second component. Industrialization required financing. Since the self-financing of industry would be slow, and financing by foreign investment was impossible, the growth of industry would have to be financed by increasing agricultural yields. Hence rapid industrialization required the development of large-scale collective farms utilizing mechanized production. This was the third component. The coordination of industrial growth and agricultural production demanded centralized planning, the fourth component.[26] British historian, E. H. Carr, called this formulation of the problem and its solution proof of "Stalin's political genius." With these ideas, Stalin defeated first Trotsky and then Bukharin. Moreover, as Carr noted, he saved the revolution: "More than ten years after Lenin's revolution, Stalin made a second revolution without which Lenin's revolution would have run out into the sand. In this sense, Stalin continued and fulfilled Leninism."[27]

Underneath the policy differences between Stalin and Bukharin resided more fundamental differences. Bukharin thought that class struggle was only needed until the establishment of the dictatorship of the proletariat. Though Stalin did not (as many have asserted) maintain that the class struggle in general intensified as socialism developed, he did argue that class struggle would intensify specifically as the country moved from the NEP toward collectivization.[28] Bukharin viewed the NEP concessions to the peasants, the market, and capitalism as a long-term policy; Stalin viewed them as a temporary expedient that the revolution had to jettison when able. During the grain crisis of 1927-28, Bukharin wanted to rely on the free market and to encourage peasants to grow more grain by offering them more consumer goods. Even with

21

the threat of impending war, Bukharin opposed speeding up industrialization if it meant adversely affecting the peasants. For Stalin, impending war provided an additional reason for speeding industrialization even if it meant exacting surplus from the peasants to finance it, and he dismissed Bukharin as one of the "peasant philosophers."[29]

The differences between Bukharin and Stalin permeated other issues besides political economy, notably the national question. One of the most striking features of Lenin's and Stalin's approach to the national question was the considerable attention they devoted to it. Lenin read dozens of books in different languages on the history and problems of various national groups, prepared hundreds of pages of notes, and wrote at least twelve major speeches, reports, or sections of books on this question.[30] Lenin made novel refinements in Marxist theory with regard to the importance of national liberation struggles and the right of nations to self-determination.[31] Stalin, too, devoted considerable attention to the national question, on which he wrote numerous speeches and reports.[32] Moreover, after the revolution, Stalin served as Commissar of Nationalities and dealt with numerous difficult national problems, on which he and Lenin occasionally disagreed. Under Lenin, Stalin presided over the creation of the Union of Soviet Socialist Republics in 1922, and over several modifications in the Union that eventually embraced fifteen republics and numerous autonomous regions. Under three decades of Stalin's leadership, the Soviet Union also used the wealth and know-how of the more advanced Russian republic in order to build up the industry, mechanize the agriculture, and raise the educational and cultural level of the outlying republics. These policies brought liberation and advancement to those who had been systematically oppressed in what Lenin called the czarist "prison of peoples."[33] None of this is to say that Lenin and Stalin solved all problems. Indeed, insofar as industrializing involved overrunning some of the outlying republics with Russian citizens and polluting some of their waterways, the policies of Stalin and his successors created new national grievances. Still, the attention that Lenin and Stalin gave to the national question contrasted sharply with the comparative neglect of Bukharin, Khrushchev, and Gorbachev.

The different importance the two tendencies attached to the national question reflected a deeper difference. As with political economy, what distinguished the left wing tendency from the right wing pivoted around struggle. For both Lenin and Stalin, Communists had to engage with nationalism as an important independent variable in the equation of revolution. The proletarian revolution faced the greatest peril if it ignored either the importance of the national aspirations of oppressed people or the danger of big power chauvinism and narrow, petty bourgeois nationalism. Between 1914 and 1919, a major dispute occurred between Lenin and Bukharin precisely on this question. Bukharin rejected appeals to nationalism as classless and unMarxist, and he consequently failed to foresee the upswing of national liberation movements after World War I. By contrast, Lenin argued that nationalism in colonial and non-colonial areas had a revolutionary potential and that if socialist revolutionaries sincerely fought for national self-determination, the mainly peasant nationalists in oppressed nations would join forces with the proletarian revolution. Bukharin's biographer Stephen F. Cohen said, "Bukharin's failure to see anti-imperialist nationalism as a revolutionary force was the most glaring defect in his original treatment of imperialism."[34] The Russian revolution's success in winning the support of oppressed nations in the czar's empire vindicated Lenin's approach and even changed Bukharin's opinion.

During the NEP, Stalin faced a different problem than had Lenin before 1919. The NEP encouraged the development of petty capitalists, or what Stalin called the "middle strata" consisting of the peasantry and "petty toiling population of the towns." These middle strata constituted nine tenths of the population of the "oppressed nationalities," and they were particularly susceptible to nationalist appeals. The development of nationalism in these strata constituted a real threat to the consolidation of the proletarian dictatorship whose basis was "mainly and primarily of the central, the industrial regions." Consequently, Stalin urged a struggle against "the nationalist tendencies which are developing and becoming accentuated in connection with the New Economic Policy." Stalin's main opposition on this point came from Bukharin, who in 1919 had made an about-face from opposing self-determination to embracing it. By 1923, Bukharin not only supported the NEP and the petty capitalists created by it but also advocated a hands-off approach toward this class' growing nationalism. Stalin noted that Bukharin had gone from one extreme to the other, from denying the right of self-determination to supporting it one-sidely.[35] What remained the same, however, was Bukharin's failure to accord nationalism sufficient importance, his failure to appreciate either its potential support of--or its potential danger to--the revolution, and his reluctance to struggle with nationalists who opposed socialist development.

Stalin went a long way toward the creation of a fair and viable multinational state, but his policies also had a problematic side. During World War II, in his determination to thwart narrow nationalism among the backward elements on the periphery, Stalin relocated entire populations, attacked Jews as "rootless cosmopolitans," and gave Russians domination of the Party and state.[36]

From the mid-1930s to Stalin's death in 1953, the policies of forced collectivization, rapid industrialization, and centralized planning through a series of five-year plans held complete sway. Certainly, the trial and execution of Bukharin and other leaders, and the imprisonment of tens of thousands of rank and file Communists, many of whom were innocent of any wrongdoing, had much to do with the comparative reticence of opposition voices. It would be wrong, however, to assume either that Stalin eliminated all diversity of thinking or that repression alone accounted for the dominance of Stalin's views. The widespread acceptance of Stalin's approach to building socialism resulted mainly from its obvious success in bringing the Soviet Union within a short period out of semi-feudal backwardness into the front ranks of the industrialized nations.

Bahman Azad gives a succinct summary of the accomplishments. In the first two five-year plans, industrial production grew at an average annual rate of 11 percent. From 1928 to 1940, the industrial sector grew from 28 percent to 45 percent of the economy. Between 1928 and 1937, heavy manufacturing output's share of total manufacturing output grew from 31 percent to 63 percent. The illiteracy rate dropped from 56 percent to 20 percent. The number of graduates from high school, specialized schools and universities jumped. Moreover, in this period, the state began providing free education, free health services, and social insurance, and after 1936 the state gave subsidies to single mothers and to mothers with many children. These accomplishments, Azad notes, were "impressive and historically unprecedented."[37]

Between 1941 and 1953, the Soviet Union defeated fascist Germany and rebuilt from the devastation of the war. By 1948 overall industrial output exceeded that of 1940, and by 1952 it exceeded 1940 by two and a half times.[38] The Soviet Union developed an atomic bomb and forced the West into a Cold War stalemate. Admittedly, problems existed, notably acute agricultural shortages, and even the achievements exacted a certain cost in terms of lives, living standards, socialist democracy, and collective leadership, but they had occurred nonetheless.

It is impossible to understand the divergence of Nikita Khrushchev's policies from Stalin's without appreciating the persistence of ideological diversity and debate in the Party. A fascinating piece of CPSU history involved the struggle between Georgi Malenkov and Andrei Zhdanov after World War II. Both men had impeccable revolutionary credentials. Before the war, Zhdanov had headed Party ideological work, and during the war he had been in charge of Leningrad's heroic resistance to the German siege. Malenkov had an equally important wartime role. As a member of the State Defense Committee in charge of the country, Malenkov was responsible for the Party and government personnel and operation. At the end of the war, though they disagreed about postwar prospects and priorities, Zhdanov and Malenkov emerged as Stalin's two top deputies. Zhdanov thought the promising prospects for international peace should govern Party policies. Winning the war had required giving priority to production and technical know-how, but with an enduring peace at hand, Zhdanov thought the Party should give priority to ideology. Moreover, the Party should emphasize improving living standards and increasing consumer goods. In 1946 and 1947, for example, Zhdanov and his allies launched a campaign against ideological weaknesses in literature and culture and a campaign against "private farming." One of Zhdanov's targets was Nikita Khrushchev, the Party leader in the Ukraine, whom Zhdanov and his supporters accused of laxness in admitting new members to the Party and of "bourgeois nationalist" errors with respect to Ukrainian histories published during his watch.

In contrast, Malenkov believed the international dangers remained real and that the Party's priorities must remain the development basic industry and military strength. Malenkov's belief in the priority of industrial development placed him solidly with Stalin and against Bukharin. (When Khrushchev later echoed Zhdanov's priorities of increasing consumer goods and raising living standards, Malenkov continued to advocate a stress on industrial development.) In 1946, Stalin sided with Zhdanov, but by 1947 after the Truman Doctrine and Marshall Plan signaled aggressive anti-Soviet course for American foreign policy, Stalin agreed with Malenkov. In 1948, Zhdanov died, his closest allies were demoted, and two of them were tried for treason and executed.[39] The policy of strengthening industry and the military remained pre-eminent. The Zhdanov-Malenkov struggle showed that serious political differences over the direction of socialism continued at the highest levels even under Stalin, and they resembled earlier polarities and tendencies.[40]

With Stalin's death in 1953, the political struggles over the direction of socialism continued. At first, Khrushchev became the head of the Party, and Malenkov became head of the government. The Party's collective leadership agreed on the need to put Stalin's repression behind them and to improve the living standards of the people. All of the Party Presidium joined with Khrushchev in a secret plan to arrest and depose Lavrenti Beria, the head of the secret police, who aspired to the top Party position after Stalin's death and whose name had become synonymous with excessive repression.[41] The Central Committee also began releasing and rehabilitating some of those who had been jailed for political offenses, particularly recent victims, such as members of the so-called doctor's plot, a group of doctors accused of conspiring against Stalin's health. The Central Committee also established a commission to give an accounting of the past repression, its extent and the degree to which it was or was not justified.[42]

In 1956 the unity of the top leaders foundered on Khrushchev's handling of the repression under Stalin. At midnight on the last day of the Twentieth Congress in February 1956, Khrushchev delivered a "secret speech," a four hour condemnation of Stalin's "cult of the individual" and the imprisonment, torture, and execution of thousands of innocent people, including loyal Party members. Even though the Central Committee voted to have this speech read to Party meetings throughout the country, some members of the CC took exception to it. Vyacheslav Molotov, Georgi Malenkov, Lazar Kaganovich, and K. E. Voroshilov thought that Khrushchev took an unbalanced approach that neither gave Stalin credit for his positive contributions nor acknowledged the legitimacy of some repression. Their misgivings were reinforced and extended to others by the uprisings in East Germany and Hungary that the speech seemingly sparked. In June, the Central Committee revealed a growing opposition to Khrushchev's approach when it passed a resolution crediting Stalin's accomplishments while condemning his abuse of power.[43] Subsequently, Khrushchev himself presented a more evenhanded view of Stalin, even telling his opponents in the leadership, "All of us taken together aren't worth Stalin's shit."[44] Opposition to Khrushchev, however, soon emerged on other issues.

Highly impulsive and sometimes inconsistent, Khrushchev represented an approach to building socialism that often resembled Bukharin and Zhdanov and foreshadowed Gorbachev. This approach cut across the entire spectrum of issues from ideology to agriculture, foreign affairs, economics, culture, and the operation of the Party. Though it is important to appreciate the continuity of certain ideas in the history of the CPSU, obviously the value of any particular policy depended upon its success in defending or advancing socialism at a particular time and under particular circumstances. Most would agree, for example, that Khrushchev's advancement of the idea of peaceful co-existence and his reduction of Soviet military ground forces represented appropriate and successful policies, whatever their lineage. Others of his ideas were more dubious. Both before Khrushchev consolidated his hold on the Party in 1957, Molotov and others opposed the main thrust of his policies, and in 1964 after forcing Khrushchev into retirement, the Party reversed many of his initiatives. Khrushchev's ideas, however, did not disappear entirely and would flower again under Gorbachev.

The best way to understand the differences between the thrust of Khrushchev's policies and those of his critics, like Molotov, (as well as Gorbachev's policies and his critics like Yegor Ligachev), was to see them as polarities even though in practice the differences sometimes amounted to matters of emphasis. For example, Khrushchev believed in a quick and easy path to communism, while his critics projected a more protracted and difficult road. Khrushchev looked for an "easing of the contest" with the U.S. and its allies abroad and "political relaxation" and "consumer communism" at home.[45] His critics saw a continuation of class struggle abroad and the need for vigilance and discipline at home. Khrushchev saw more in Stalin to condemn than to praise; Molotov and others more to praise than condemn. Khrushchev favored incorporating a range of capitalist or Western ideas into socialism, including market mechanisms, decentralization, some private production, the heavy reliance on fertilizer and the cultivation of corn, and increased investment in consumer goods. Molotov favored improved centralized planning and socialized ownership, and continuing the priority of industrial development. Khrushchev favored broadening the idea of the dictatorship of the proletariat and the proletarian vanguard role of the Communist Party to put other sectors of the population on an equal footing with workers; his critics did not.

Khrushchev was born into a peasant family and from 1938 to 1949 served as Party Secretary of the Ukraine, where he became an authority on agricultural questions and under Stalin supported the subordination of agriculture to the industrialization of the country. The Party had censured Khrushchev's leadership in the Ukraine (and on this Stalin agreed) for admitting too many people, mainly peasants, to the Party, for being lax on Party standards, and for tolerating narrow Ukrainian nationalism.[46] Even after he moved to Moscow to become its Party Secretary in 1949, Khrushchev retained his ties to farming, and as chief of national agricultural policy, he was the only member of Stalin's Politburo who visited the countryside frequently.[47] After 1954, his agricultural policies would play a prominent part in the growing Party debate.

In 1953, Khrushchev initiated a set of policies that proved to be problematical both ideologically and practically. Khrushchev encouraged the country to look to the West not only as a source of new methods of production but as a standard of comparison for Soviet achievements. He also shifted resources from industry to agriculture. To encourage agricultural production, Khrushchev reverted to NEP-type measures. He reduced taxes on individual plots, eliminated taxes on individual livestock, and encouraged people in villages and towns to keep more privately owned cows, pigs, and chickens and to cultivate private gardens. Khrushchev also came up with a brainstorm for boosting agricultural production overnight. In January 1954, he proposed a nationwide campaign to cultivate millions of hectares of so-called virgin lands mainly in Siberia and Kazakhstan. That year 300,000 volunteers joined the virgin lands campaign and plowed 13 million hectares of new land. The following year's effort added another 14 million hectares of cultivated land.[48]

Khrushchev also placed a new emphasis on raising living standards. After the wartime deprivations, no one opposed raising Soviet living standards. The questions were how to do it and at what cost. For his opponents, Khrushchev's approach had two problems. First, it required a shift in investment priorities from heavy industry to light industry, consumer goods. In Khrushchev's first year as General Secretary investment in heavy industry exceeded that in consumer goods by only 20 percent, compared to 70 percent before the war.[49] This shift in priorities flew in the face of Stalin's 1952 warning that "ceasing to give primacy to the production of the means of production" would "destroy the possibility of the continuous expansion of our national economy."[50] In the long run, shifting priorities would undermine the goal of surpassing the West that Khrushchev himself projected. Secondly, his opponents thought Khrushchev's emphasis placed the Soviet Union in competition with the United States and Western Europe over consumer goods, a race the Soviet Union could not and probably should not win. The German Communist, Hans Holz, said later that lowering socialist goals to material competition with capitalism was giving up "ideological territory."[51] The goal of catching up and surpassing the West in five or ten years resulted in "a stimulation of needs and cravings oriented around a Western style of consumption."[52] The slogan encouraged the Soviet people to the view that the "competition between social systems was not over the goals of life, but over the levels of consumption."[53] More simply, Molotov said, "Khrushchevism is the bourgeois spirit!"[54]

Molotov and others in the Presidium (as the Politburo was then known) opposed Khrushchev's policies across the board: on the handling of de-Stalinization, the de-emphasis on class struggle internationally, the encouragement of private agricultural production, the virgin lands initiative, the decentralization of industry, and the shift from heavy to light industry.[55] For example, Molotov and others thought that because of the problematic climate and the lack of infrastructure in the virgin lands, widespread cultivation invited disaster and that the country could more profitably use its resources to increase production in already cultivated areas. The opposition favored some moves to improve the standard of living but not an abrupt shift in priorities. The opposition to Khrushchev grew over a couple of years and then was precipitated into action by two events in May 1957. The first was Khrushchev's decision to decentralize industry.[56] The second was a speech in which Khrushchev called for a "spectacular leap forward" in the production of milk, meat, and butter in order to surpass the West in three or four years.[57] This became part of Khrushchev's belief that the Soviet Union could, in the words of his grandson, "dash forward to communism," an idea that late in his life, even Khrushchev regarded as an "incorrect concept."[58]

During a four-day Presidium meeting, June 18-21, 1957, and a Central Committee meeting that immediately followed, a decisive confrontation between Khrushchev and the opposition occurred. As a prelude to seeking Khrushchev's removal as General Secretary, the opposition assailed his economic policies, particularly his agricultural policies and his idea of decentralizing state planning.[59] Molotov and others opposed changing investment priorities from industrial to agricultural, rushing headlong to catch the West in consumer goods, opening the virgin lands, loosening agricultural strictures, and decentralizing economic decision-making. In their view, Khrushchev's policies were wrong in principle and would lead to economic disruption. Molotov called the virgin lands program an "adventure" and said it would take away resources from industrialization. Malenkov argued that the goal should be to surpass the West in steel, iron, coal, and oil, not consumer goods. "We Marxists," Malenkov said, "are accustomed to begin with industrialization." He called Khrushchev's program a "rightist peasant deviation," an "opportunistic" move that would make the Soviet people less interested in rapid industrialization.[60]

The opposition held a seven to three majority (with one neutral) in the Presidium. When word of the imminent repudiation of Khrushchev leaked out, however, Moscow members of the Central Committee (many of whom had been promoted by Khrushchev) besieged the Presidium and demanded the convening of the Central Committee. A hastily arranged meeting of the Central Committee that went on for six days ended by supporting Khrushchev and expelling Molotov, Malenkov, and Kaganovich from the Central Committee and the Presidium.[61]

After routing what he called the "anti-Party" opposition, Khrushchev ruled without serious resistance for the next seven years. Of Khrushchev's course during this time, two things stood out. First, in spite of some tacking and weaving, Khrushchev pursued a domestic course the main elements of which were cuts in military spending, attacks on Stalin, decentralization of planning, dismantling of state tractor stations, emulation of American agricultural methods, cultivation of virgin lands, promotion of consumer goods, some liberalization of intellectual and cultural restrictions, and an ideological de-emphasis of class struggle, the dictatorship of the proletariat, and the vanguard party. Secondly, all of Khrushchev's major domestic policies failed to produce the results intended. As his biographer, William Taubman said, "Too often Khrushchev made a bad situation even worse."[62]

At the Twenty-second Congress in 1961, Khrushchev returned with renewed intensity to his attack on Stalin. Two aspects of Khrushchev's anti-Stalinism foreshadowed Gorbachev. First, Khrushchev's treatment of Stalin was exaggerated, one-sided, and incomplete. Secondly, the denunciation of Stalin served politically factional ends. Much could be said about the distortions of Khrushchev's treatment of Stalin. For example, Khrushchev implied that Stalin emerged suddenly on the scene in 1924, when in truth Stalin had solid revolutionary credentials dating from his political work among railroad workers in Georgia in 1898. Khrushchev quoted Lenin's so-called last testament criticizing Stalin's rudeness but ignored Lenin's praise of Stalin as an outstanding leader. In 1956, Khrushchev concentrated on Stalin's alleged repression of Party leaders and claimed that half of the delegates to the Seventeenth Party Congress and 70 percent of the Central Committee were killed. Stalin's biographer, Ken Cameron, concluded that it is "difficult to believe that Khrushchev's figures are correct."[63] (Using the recently opened Soviet archives, scholars have numbered the total of executions from 1921 to 1953 at 799,455, far below the millions estimated by Robert Conquest, Roy Medvedev and other anti-Soviet scholars.[64]) Also, Khrushchev ignored the evidence of sabotage that served as the ostensible reason for the repression. Khrushchev blamed Stalin for faulty military strategy and dictatorial leadership during World War II, both of which were contradicted by the leading Soviet general, Georgy Zhukov. Most importantly, Khrushchev did not invite a thorough, searching, and balanced treatment of Stalin. Instead, he wrote Stalin out of Soviet history, and discussion of his role more or less stopped.[65] Consequently, Khrushchev left the history, in Yegor Ligachev's words, with "too many blank spots."[66]

Besides its deficiencies as history, Khrushchev's attack on Stalin served partisan ends. Having fabricated a monstrously distorted image of Stalin, Khrushchev then accused those who did not join the denunciation of wanting to revive Stalin's methods. In 1961, Khrushchev explicitly linked his attack on Stalin to the crimes of his opponents, whom he called a "group of factionalists headed by Molotov, Kaganovitch, and Malenkov." Khrushchev claimed that they "resisted everything new and tried to revive the pernicious methods, which prevailed under the cult of the individual."[67] Though Molotov and the others objected to Khrushchev's policies and the one-sided treatment of Stalin, they did not advocate a return to Stalin's repression. Just as anti-Communists use "Stalinism" to attack Communists, so Khrushchev employed the idea, if not the term, to defame his opponents.

Khrushchev's treatment of Stalin set the stage for Gorbachev. Gorbachev would capitalize on the desire to fill in the blank spots of history left by Khrushchev's incomplete treatment. Moreover, Gorbachev would open the door to even more one-sided attacks on Stalin than had occurred under Khrushchev. Finally, like his predecessor, Gorbachev would adroitly use attacks on Stalin to impugn those who did not join the chorus and to undermine those who opposed his policies. In 1988 during the Nina Andreyeva affair (see Chapter 5), Gorbachev echoed Khrushchev by accusing his opponents of wanting to revive Stalinist methods.

Nothing was more characteristic of Khrushchev's approach to building socialism than the belief that quick and easy solutions existed. This belief underpinned the policies that brought Soviet agriculture to near chaos in a decade. The virgin land campaign occupied the centerpiece of these initiatives. Lasting ten years, this campaign involved sending tens of thousands of tractors and combines and hundreds of thousands of volunteers to plow up acreage that eventually equaled the surface area of France, West Germany, and England combined. The first year of the campaign, grain production increased by 10 million tons, but the increase was largely due to greater yields in the non-virgin lands. The next year a drought occurred and production everywhere suffered. The following year, 1956, the campaign scored a triumph, when the virgin lands produced an exceptional yield, supplying half of all Soviet grain, even though much was lost due to insufficient equipment for harvesting, storing, and transporting the bounty. In no succeeding year did the harvest match 1956. In 1957, the harvest was 40 percent less than 1956, in 1958 8 percent less and in subsequent years still less, until 1963 and 1964, when the harvest was a total bust. In his monograph on the virgin land campaign, Gerald Meyer argued that the campaign failed because Khrushchev overestimated the favorableness of the natural conditions and underestimated the costs. A short growing season, insufficient and poorly distributed precipitation, high winds, and poor fallow practices in the virgin lands resulted in frequent droughts, vast land erosion, falling fertility, and soaring costs.[68] As a policy, the virgin land campaign was a disaster.

Three other of Khrushchev's agricultural initiatives also produced undesirable results. Two of them stemmed from Khrushchev's belief that quick and easy increases in production would follow the emulation of practices in the West. The corn campaign rested on the idea of boosting cattle production by following the American practice of growing corn for silage. The anti-fallow campaign involved encouraging the use of chemical fertilization instead of rotating crops or allowing fields to lie fallow. Both campaigns ignored the realities of natural and other conditions in the Soviet Union and never came close to being the panacea envisioned by Khrushchev.[69]

The third initiative, and one of the most extreme of Khrushchev's entire tenure, involved dismantling the state-run machine tractor stations that supplied tractors and other machinery to the collective farms. Collective farms that had relied on the tractor stations suddenly had to buy and maintain their own farm equipment. Ideologically, Khrushchev's move represented a repudiation of Stalin's last statement on the Soviet economy. Stalin had said that the direction of Soviet development should be toward the enhancement of the state sector (rather than the collective farms).[70] Practically, the policy produced another debacle. The change occurred with such abandon that a majority of the tractor stations disappeared within three months. Even Khrushchev sympathizers believed that the policy seriously reduced agricultural productivity, inflicted long-term damage on the economy and amounted to an unadulterated failure.[71]

With industry as with agriculture, Khrushchev faced serious problems but resorted to problematic solutions. Under socialism, central plans largely determined the size and nature of production. Planning eliminated the boom and bust cycle of capitalist markets, but it had its own challenges. Planning became more difficult as the economy became larger and more complex. By 1953, the number of industrial enterprises reached 200,000 and the number of planning targets reached 5000, up from 300 in the early 1930s and 2500 in 1940. At this time, the British economist Maurice Dobb claimed that "over-centralization" was cramping initiative and technical innovation, wasting resources, producing bottlenecks in supplies, placing a premium on "purely quantitative fulfillment" of the plan, rewarding unproductive enterprises, and punishing conscientious ones.[72] By shifting the economy toward consumer goods, Khrushchev complicated the already difficult job of planning. Alec Nove said, "Housing, agriculture, consumer goods, trade, all became matters of importance, even priority. So the task of planning became more complicated, because a system based on a few key priorities, resembling in this respect a Western war economy, could not work so effectively if goals were diluted or multiplied."[73]

Khrushchev sought an easy way out of the problems of centralized planning through radical decentralization and the application of such capitalist-oriented ideas as market competition. In May 1957, Khrushchev abolished the thirty plus central planning ministries and replaced them with over a hundred local economic councils. The result was predictable. Co-ordination of production and supplies became even more difficult than it was before, and local interests superseded national goals. The Medvedevs, who purportedly sympathized with Khrushchev, said his decentralization produced "anarchy," "duplication, parallelism and dissipation of responsibility."[74] In 1961, Khrushchev had to regroup and consolidate planning into seventeen large economic regions. Even this did not undo the damage of decentralization. The Soviet economy expanded at a slower rate in the second half of the 1950s than the first half, and expanded at a slower rate in the first five years of the 1960s than in the 1950s.[75] After replacing Khrushchev in 1964, the Party re-established twenty central planning ministries and tried to combine these with greater plant autonomy.[76]

Khrushchev's policies often sowed the seeds of later problems. Perhaps in an overreaction to previous criticisms of his laxness toward Ukrainian bourgeois nationalism, he often demonstrated a tin ear to national sensitivities as when, after a visit to central Asia, he rashly proposed consolidating all the Asian republics into one.[77] On a less extreme note, he declared that the country had solved the national question and aimed to achieve a "Soviet national identity" that would replace existing national identities as the various nations of the Soviet Union drew closer together toward "complete unity." However laudable as an ideal, the promotion of a Soviet national identity had the opposite effect of stimulating nationalist sentiments among those who valued their own national heritage. According to historian Yitzhak Brudny, Khrushchev's approach glossed over existing national problems and contributed to a rise of narrow nationalist sentiments both among non-Russian nations on the periphery and among Russian intellectuals at the center.[78]

The policy that most endeared Khrushchev to intellectuals and would serve as the precursor of Gorbachev's *glasnost* was the relaxation of censorship. Though the Khrushchev "thaw" was inconsistent and episodic, it did lead for a time to a greater openness toward modern art and films, poetry, and novels critical of the Soviet past. During the thaw, the publication of such previously banned novels as V. D. Dudintsev's *Not By Bread Alone* and A. I. Solzhenitsyn's *One Day in the Life of Ivan Denisovich* occurred.[79] This openness brought an inevitable underside in the spread of bourgeois economic ideas to Soviet academic circles. According to the Medvedevs, as early as 1953-54 "Western influence began to penetrate many areas of the economy."[80]

On many other matters including his views on international relations, the Party, the state, and communism, Khrushchev advanced ideas that caused controversy at the time and since among Communists inside and outside of the Soviet Union. It is beyond the scope of the present work to judge whether these ideas were creative applications of Marxism-Leninism to new circumstances or erroneous revisions of basic principles. What was clear, however, was that Khrushchev's ideas on these matters consistently leaned toward social democracy, sowed the seeds of later problems, and created a precedent for Gorbachev's even more extreme views and policies.

On international relations, Khrushchev stressed the policy of peaceful coexistence. He argued that, with the growth of the socialist world, the balance of forces had so shifted that the main struggle consisted of "peaceful competition" between socialism and capitalism and that a "peaceful transition" from capitalism to socialism was possible. Even though these ideas became the centerpiece of the Chinese denunciation of Khrushchev as a revisionist,[81] several things could be said in their defense. First, these ideas appeared at the height of the Cold War, when the Soviet Union was encircled by a vastly stronger United States that was justifying a bellicose anti-Soviet and anti-revolutionary foreign policy by claiming that an inherently expansionist Soviet Union was bent on worldwide aggression and subversion. In this context, Khrushchev's ideas forcefully rejoined imperialism's claims. They undercut the forces pushing for war against the Soviet Union and strengthened the international peace movement. Second, Khrushchev's ideas on this matter did not break new ground entirely. In a series of interviews before he died, Stalin himself had emphasized the policy of peaceful coexistence and rejected the idea that war was inevitable.[82] Thirdly, in practice, Khrushchev did not shrink from defending socialism abroad. He intervened against a counterrevolution in Hungary in 1956 and sent missiles to defend Cuba in 1962. Indeed, at the peak of the Cuban missile crisis, when the fate of the Cuban revolution hung in the balance, Khrushchev insisted on an American commitment not to invade the island before he withdrew Soviet missiles.[83] Moreover, Khrushchev never shrank from extending generous material aid and technical assistance to those struggling to make their own way against imperialism, including China (before the break), Egypt, and India. Historian William Kirby called Soviet aid to China between 1953 and 1957, "the greatest transfer of technology in world history." [84]

As appropriate and successful as Khrushchev's policy of peaceful co-existence was, he may have placed too great a trust in the willingness of the U.S. under President Eisenhower to give up the Cold War. The U.S. never reciprocated Khrushchev's unilateral reduction in the size of military spending and the Soviet armed forces nor his desire to disengage from the war in Vietnam.[85] Moreover, Khrushchev later acknowledged that his idea of peaceful cooperation was seriously undercut in 1960, when just before a planned four-power summit, the U.S. sent a

U-2 spy plane over Soviet territory and then denied having done so, until the Soviets produced the downed pilot, Gary Powers. "Those who felt America had imperialist intentions and that military strength was the most important thing," Khrushchev said, "had the evidence they needed."[86]

Khrushchev introduced two new ideas about the Party and the state: the idea that the CPSU had changed from the vanguard of the working class to the vanguard of the "whole people," and that the dictatorship of the proletariat had become the "state of the whole people." At some point in the development of socialism, some such transition would surely be in order, but the question was whether the Soviet Union had reached that point. The writer Bahman Azad suggested that these ideas had long-term corrosive effects because they fed illusions about the transcendence of class struggle and about the reliability of certain social groups, such as state bureaucrats.[87] Certainly, these ideas de-emphasized the separate interests of the working class. Since socialism supposedly served the interests of the working class, these ideas might have obscured an important standard for measuring socialism's progress. Moreover, these ideas accompanied other troublesome policies such as leveling of wages, that is reducing the wage differentials. At a certain level of socialist development, wage leveling was appropriate, but as things stood, such leveling tended to sap incentive and productivity.

Khrushchev made several changes in the way the Party operated that diluted its leadership role. In 1957, following the precedent of his years in the Ukraine, he opened the doors of the Communist Party to mass recruitment leading to a vast expansion in membership. This related to his idea that class distinctions were disappearing and that the "overwhelming majority" of Soviet citizens "reason like Communists."[88] Khrushchev also introduced a requirement that a third of Party officials be replaced at each election, a kind of Soviet term limits. The General Secretary also divided the Party into agricultural and industrial sections, a kind of incipient two party system. Though ostensibly aimed at reinvigorating the Party, such moves as mass recruitment, term limits, and Party division weakened the Party in various ways and generated much opposition. After Khrushchev, the Party abandoned these pet ideas.[89] Later, Gorbachev entertained similar ideas, such as splitting the CPSU into two, before deciding to weaken and disestablish it altogether.

In 1964, the Khrushchev period came to an end when the collective leadership forced him to retire. The ideas about economic liberalization and political democratization that Khrushchev came to symbolize did not, however, end with him. Rather, they continued to find expression in what historian John Gooding calls the "alternative tradition." In the 1960s and 1970s, this alternative tradition found its champions in the editor of *Novy Mir*, Alexander Tvardovsky, and such economists, sociologists, physicists, historians and playwrights as V. Shubikin, Nicolai Petrakov, Alexander Birman, Roy Medvedev, Andrei Sakharov, Valentin Turchin, and Tatyana Zaslavskaya, and Mikhail Shatrov. For the most part, these intellectuals remained in the Communist Party, admired Lenin, and continued to believe in socialism, but at the same time, they advocated a socialism imbued with aspects of capitalist markets, management, and political formations. Rather than attacking the current system, they believed in achieving their ends by winning the ears of Communist leaders, an effort that they eventually realized with Gorbachev.[90]

Meanwhile, Leonid Brezhnev soon emerged as the top Soviet leader and remained so until 1982. For Gorbachev and his partisans, Brezhnev became the scapegoat for everything wrong in the Soviet Union. They ridiculed his poor health, expensive tastes, personal vanity, and political weakness. Brezhnev became the symbol of stagnation and corruption. Though this view of Brezhnev lacked balance, it did have a basis. According to the Soviet historian, Dmitri Volkogonov,

Brezhnev wanted above all else "peace and quiet, serenity and an absence of conflict." Brezhnev was "terrified of reform." Replacing Khrushchev's office rotation policy with a "stability of cadre" policy, Brezhnev even resisted changes in personnel. At each of the four Party congresses at which he presided, Brezhnev acknowledged shortages, but he resisted bold solutions. Moreover, many in his leadership suffered from advanced age and disability. No one manifested these weaknesses more than Brezhnev himself, who after 1970 was debilitated by ill health. In 1976, he suffered a serious stroke, and between then and his death in 1982, he had several heart attacks and more strokes. In the last five years of his life, he was so sick and enfeebled that he played no active part in state or Party life. In the last years, Brezhnev could not speak without a written text in front of him and without slurring his words.[91]

Though much of the criticism made of Brezhnev was deserved, it obscured the simple truth that most of the problems the Soviet Union experienced under Brezhnev had their origins under Khrushchev. Moreover, though Brezhnev did little to reverse Stalin's mistreatment of certain nationalities or to denounce earlier violations of socialist legality, he did reverse some of the more extreme of Khrushchev's policies. Centralized planning returned. "Cadre stability" replaced term limits. A unitary party organization replaced the division into industrial and agricultural forms. Stricter Party admission standards replaced mass recruitment. The "state of all the people" and the "party of all the people" remained but acquired a different meaning. Pravda explained that these terms did not mean that the CPSU "loses it class character....[Rather,] the CPSU has been and remains a party of the working class."[92] Furthermore, Brezhnev's policies showed a firm commitment to international solidarity. He achieved military parity with the U.S. and aided the socialist countries in Eastern Europe and Cuba, the revolutionary struggles in Vietnam, Nicaragua,

Angola, Afghanistan and elsewhere, and the anti-apartheid movement in South Africa.

Ideologically, Brezhnev wove along an intermediate path between the two traditional poles or tendencies of Soviet politics. The Soviet writer Fedor Burlatsky said that Brezhnev "borrowed" from Stalin and from Khrushchev.[93] Stephen F. Cohen likewise places him in the middle of the contending trends in the Party:

> At least three movements had formed inside the Communist party by the time Khrushchev was overthrown in 1964: an anti-Stalinist party calling for more far reaching relaxation of controls over society; a neo-Stalinist one charging that the Khrushchev policies had gravely weakened the state and demanding that it be rejuvenated, and a conservative party mainly devoted to preserving the existing post-Stalin status quo by opposing further major changes either forward or backward. During the next twenty years these multiparty conflicts were waged in various largely muted and subterranean ways. The conservative majority headed by Brezhnev ruled the Soviet Union with some concessions to the neo-Stalinists for almost two decades. The reform movement barely survived, but in 1985 along with Gorbachev it came to power.[94]

In spite of Khrushchev's erratic and failed policies and Brezhnev's reluctance to tackle problems, the Soviet economy continued to show much vitality. In the 1950s the Soviet Union developed at twice the rate of most advanced countries. Between 1950 and 1975, the Soviet industrial production index increased 9.85 times (according to Soviet figures) or 6.77 times

43

(according to CIA figures), while the U.S. industrial production index increased 2.62 times.[95] The Soviet Union employed one fourth of the world's scientists, and the launch of Sputnik symbolized its scientific accomplishments. Wages and living standards rose steadily. The workweek was set at forty hours a week for most jobs, and thirty-five hours for the heaviest work. A universal pension system was instituted. Consumer goods became increasingly available, and "the gap in the level of economic and social development between the Soviet Union and the USA was rapidly closing." By the mid-1980s, the Soviet Union produced 20 percent of the world's industrial goods, up from 4 percent of a much smaller total at the time of the revolution. The Soviet Union led the world in the production of oil, gas, ferrous metals, minerals, tractors, reinforced concrete, wool goods, shoes, sugar beets, potatoes, milk, eggs, and other products. Its production of hydroelectricity, chemical products, machinery, cement and cotton was second only to the U.S.[96] The annual rate of increase of industrial productivity went up from 4.7 percent in 1960-65, to 5.8 percent in 1965-70, to 6.0 percent in 1970-75.[97]

In large measure, the economic gains were made possible by the concentrated investments in natural resources and heavy industry initiated by Stalin. Unquestionably, this growth was also aided by the availability of vast amounts of cheap natural resources, particularly oil, gas, coal, and iron ore. In the 1970s, however, both objective and subjective problems eroded economic performance. Three objective problems stood out: first, the relative exhaustion of natural resources, which made the extraction of gas, oil, and coal more expensive; second, the demographic consequences of World War II that had dramatically reduced the size of the workforce; three, the challenge of adopting new computer technology, particularly in the face of defective computer chips deliberately sold to the Soviet Union by the U.S. Even more important than these objective problems were the subjective ones: the problems of policy, particularly the shift of investment from heavy industry to consumer goods; the wage leveling; and the lack of sufficient attention to problems of planning and incentives in the last years of Brezhnev. As a result, while the annual growth rate of industrial production remained positive between 1973 and 1985 (according to some, even stronger than that in the U.S., 4.6 percent compared to 2.3 percent),[98] signs of trouble appeared. Between 1979-82, the production fell for 40 percent of all industrial goods. Agricultural output in this period did not reach the 1978 level. "Indicators of efficiency in social production slowed down." In the 1976-85 period, oil extraction in the Volga fell, as did the extraction of coal in the Don Coal fields, timber from the Urals, and nickel from the Kola Peninsula. According to some, the standard of living stopped rising.[99]

Brezhnev's attitude and policies toward the national question reflected his intermediate position. In some respects, Brezhnev evinced complacency akin to Khrushchev. Brezhnev praised the building up of the backward republics and the fostering of "Soviet patriotism." "The Soviet nations," he declared, "are now united more than ever."[100] The General Secretary took a decidedly non-struggle approach toward many republics, where he allowed corruption and nepotism to abound. In Uzbekistan, for example, the Party leader had fourteen relatives working in the Party apparat, and bribery, arbitrariness, injustice, and "heinous violations of the law" reportedly ran rampant.[101]

In other respects, Brezhnev's approach resembled Lenin's and Stalin's willingness to deal sharply with reactionary nationalists, while trying to win others to socialism. For example, Brezhnev replaced leaders in the Ukraine and Georgia who were fanning nationalist and anti-Russian sentiments. He also adopted what historian Yitzhak Brudny called a "politics of inclusion" toward Russian nationalists. While some viewed this as an unMarxist pandering to Great Russian chauvinism, others viewed it as a legitimate effort to win the support of some Russian nationalist intellectuals on the basis of a shared aversion to Khrushchev's liberalization and market reforms, and the intrusion of Western influence. This initiative resembled Stalin's effort to broaden and deepen support for the war by appealing to Russian patriotism. Brudny concluded that Brezhnev's policy of inclusion ultimately failed to win lasting support because it tried to give the nationalist intellectuals "a material stake in the system without satisfying their principal [ideological] concerns."[102] Thus, Brezhnev's national policies and their results were a mixed bag. At their best, they showed a willingness to engage nationalists--either combating backward national sentiments or trying to win over the Russian nationalist intellectuals--that was lacking in Bukharin, Khrushchev, and later Gorbachev. Moreover, however flawed, Brezhnev's policies never produced the open ethnic warfare that occurred under Gorbachev.

By the late Brezhnev era, many economic, social, political, and ideological problems had accumulated. It would be misleading, however, to see the situation as consisting of reformers who saw the problems and Brezhnev "conservatives" who did not. Though not everyone gave equal weight to the problems, a general agreement existed among Party leaders and outside experts that productivity and economic growth were matters of concern. The Brezhnev leadership addressed these issues at the end of the tenth five-year plan in 1979.[103]

Recognizing problems on the one hand and explaining their origin and devising their solution on the other hand were of course two entirely different matters, and matters on which Communists disagreed. In general, the analysis of the economic problems fell into the two traditional camps: the camp with ideological links to Bukharin and Khrushchev and the camp with links to Lenin and Stalin. The former saw the problems as due to over-centralization, and for it the solution was decentralization, the use of market mechanisms, and the allowance of certain forms of private enterprise. Writing in 1975, Moshe Lewin said, "It is astonishing to discover how many ideas of Bukharin's anti-Stalinist program of 1928-29 were adopted by current reformers."[104] Soviet economists of this mind represented only a minority, but they dominated three of the four leading academic institutes.[105] A leading economist in this camp was Abel Aganbegyan, who later became a key advisor to Gorbachev.

The majority of economists believed in reforming and modernizing the centralized planning system. For them the problems of growth and productivity had arisen because planning and management methods had not kept pace with the development of the productive forces. In some respects, the problems resulted not from centralization but from insufficient centralization. In construction, for example, the excessive time to complete projects and the profusion of unfinished projects occurred because central planners failed to prevail against local authorities that launched projects for which insufficient resources existed for timely completion. Insufficient coordination between engineers, industrialists, and builders also delayed the completion of projects.[106]

Productivity was often impaired by antiquated management methods and payment systems.[107] Some mainstream economists wanted to use wage incentives to increase productivity. For them, the Soviet wisecrack, "they pretend to pay us and we pretend to work," was not a product of Stalin's incentive system, where productive workers could earn big wages, but of the later wage leveling. In 1980, Victor and Ellen Perlo described other debates among mainstream economists over the ways to increase production and productivity. Noting that immediately after Khrushchev the Soviet Union had faced and overcome falling productivity, the Perlos said, "Again, as in the early 1960s, there are broad discussions underway in the USSR, heading up to a further modernization and improvement in the methods of economic planning and management.... Past experience gives reason to believe that the problems facing the Soviet economy will be solved."[108]

47

The Soviet Union had excellent chances to tackle these problems after the death of Brezhnev, when Yuri Andropov became the General Secretary of the CPSU. Andropov had admirable personal qualities, a solid grounding in Marxist-Leninist theory, rich leadership experience, a broad grasp of the problems facing the Soviet Union, and clear and forceful ideas about reform. One thing that Andropov did not have was time. Three months after taking office, Andropov developed serious kidney problems, and in fifteen months he was dead. Nevertheless, the "Andropov Year" (1983) unveiled a promising reform path completely different from the ultimately disastrous one chosen by Gorbachev.

Andropov was born in 1914 in Stavropol. His father was a railroad worker. Andropov left school at sixteen and worked as a telegraph operator and boatman on the Volga. Beginning in 1936, Andropov held a series of positions in the Komsomol (Young Communists), becoming First Secretary of the Komsomol in the Karelo-Finnish Autonomous Republic (Karelia) that bordered Finland. During the war, the Germans occupied Karelia, and Andropov joined the partisan movement against them. After the war, he became Second Secretary of the CP of Karelia. In 1951, Andropov went to work for the Central Committee in Moscow. In 1953, he became Counsellor to Hungary and in 1954 Ambassador to Hungary. From 1957 to 1962, Andropov worked for the Foreign Affairs Department of the Central Committee, where he dealt with other Communist countries. In 1962, he became Secretary of the Central Committee. In 1967, Andropov became Chairman of the KGB, a post he held for fifteen years.[109]

The details of Andropov's career were even more impressive than the résumé. On his way up, Andropov worked with three of the great figures of the CPSU. While in the Karelo-Finnish Republic, Andropov became the protégé of the old Bolshevik, Otto Kuusinen. Kuusinen had been a comrade in arms with Lenin since 1905, was the founder of the Finnish Communist

Party and the First Secretary of the CP of Karelia, when Andropov was Second Secretary. Kuusinen, who remained an important figure in the CPSU until his death in 1964, doubtlessly helped bring Andropov's abilities to the notice of others. As Ambassador to Hungary, Andropov worked under the Foreign Minister, the old Bolshevik, Molotov. As Ambassador to Hungary, Andropov also developed a close relationship to Mikhail Suslov, who became his second mentor after Kuusinen. Suslov's career in the Party stretched back to 1918, when he had joined the Young Communists. Suslov was a serious student of Marxism-Leninism and a leading ideologist of the Party under Stalin, Khrushchev and Brezhnev. Some commentators believed that Andropov modeled himself after Suslov, since Andropov's austerity, intellectuality, and work ethic resembled that of the older Suslov. When Suslov died in 1982, Andropov replaced him as the Party's leading ideologist.[110]

Andropov's career was studded by occasions that demanded great courage, calmness, and tough-mindedness. First was his war work as a partisan. Then came the Ambassadorship to Hungary. Andropov's actions in Hungary remain somewhat uncertain and the testimony of others is often contradictory, yet it was clear that he navigated successfully through extremely troubled waters. The Hungarian Communist Party was trying to build socialism in a predominantly peasant, Catholic country that had just emerged from twenty-five years of a fascist dictatorship that included an alliance with Nazi Germany during World War II. At the time of Andropov's arrival in 1954, the Hungarian Communists faced numerous problems including internal divisions and popular unrest. At the end of October 1956, the Hungarian uprising occurred, in which fascist gangs took advantage of popular discontent to assassinate, beat, and lynch Communists and their supporters. It ended only after the Soviet military intervened early in November.[111]

During the height of the crisis, Andropov operated out of the Soviet Embassy in Budapest, along with Moscow representatives,

Anastas Mikoyan and Suslov. These three men, along with Marshall Georgii Zhukov, handled the Soviet response, advising Hungarian Communists and eventually directing Soviet troops. During the crisis, as divisions sapped Communist unity, and the Prime Minister Imre Nagy increasingly capitulated to rightwing pressure, Andropov apparently persuaded the popular Communist Janos Kadar to take over the leadership of the Hungarian party. In the following two decades, Kadar became the most reform-minded leader in Eastern Europe. He introduced decentralization, profit-sharing, and cooperative farms, allowed various kinds of private enterprise, and re-established popular confidence in the Communist Party. How Andropov, who left Hungary in March 1957, assessed the Hungarian reforms remained a mystery. Nonetheless, during the crisis itself, Andropov's wisdom in favoring Kadar and his coolness under fire apparently increased Suslov's admiration of Andropov.[112]

After Hungary, Andropov handled other tough assignments. In 1963, he joined a delegation headed by Suslov that engaged in tense negotiations with the Chinese in an unsuccessful attempt to heal the recent breach between the Chinese and Soviet parties. Later, as head of the KGB, Andropov took responsibility for the crackdown on dissident intellectuals, like Alexander Solzhenitsyn. Andropov's willingness to defend these actions openly and to withstand the criticism of Western commentators and such Soviet intellectuals as Yevgeny Yevushenko, strongly suggested that Andropov would have avoided Gorbachev's blunder of turning the media over to anti-socialist elements. As head of the KGB, Andropov also showed courage and conviction by investigating corruption in high places. On his KGB watch, the entire Party Presidium and government of Azerbaijan were dismissed for corruption, bribery, and embezzlement. Moreover, in 1981, Andropov's deputy exposed and arrested some of the "black market-ridden dolce vita crowd" that included Brezhnev's daughter and son-in-law. Even investigating crime in the General Secretary's family did not daunt Andropov.[113]

Andropov had other equally impressive personal characteristics. Though his formal education did not go beyond some work at the Rybinsk technical school and the Higher Party School, Andropov unquestionably possessed a first class mind, informed by wide reading and broad cultural tastes. While Ambassador to Hungary, he learned Hungarian and studied the history and culture of Hungary, feats that endeared him to his hosts. Through his daughters, Irina, who was married to a famous actor of the Moscow theater, Alexander Filipov, and a second daughter, who was an assistant editor of a music magazine, Andropov had links to the world of artists and entertainers. He learned English, read American newspapers, magazines, and novels, and liked Glenn Miller and Miles Davis. In travel, while Gorbachev preferred the West, Andropov confined his visits to socialist countries -- Hungary, Vietnam, North Korea, Outer Mongolia, Yugoslavia, China, and Albania. In habits and demeanor, Andropov inspired confidence. He was quiet, well-spoken, calm, controlled, and sincere. Moreover, under Brezhnev, when old age, infirmity, and laxness eroded "Leninist norms" among many at the top, Andropov lived modestly and gained a reputation as a workaholic.[114]

Communists took hope in Andropov's grasp of the problems, his ideas for reform, and his decisive implementation of changes. The American scholar, Stephen Cohen, said that Andropov was the "most reform-minded" of Brezhnev's Politburo and the only PB member that the orthodox Communists trusted to handle reform wisely.[115] Yegor Ligachev said, "Andropov possessed the rare, true leader's gift of translating general tasks into the language of concrete jobs." Ligachev said that Andropov had "a clear vision of the prospects of the country's development," and unlike Gorbachev, he "disliked improvisation and hit-or-miss approaches." At the same time, Andropov "planned the renewal of socialism, understanding that it needed some deep, qualitative changes."[116]

Andropov's analysis of the Soviet Union's problems and his policy proposals occurred in three speeches that he delivered to the Central Committee in November and December 1982 and June 1983, and in an article he wrote in 1983 to mark the centenary of Marx's death. Unsurprisingly, Andropov concentrated on economic problems. The year 1982 not only set the worst record in Soviet history for labor productivity and economic growth, but also represented the fourth year in a row of poor harvests.[117] In his first address to the Central Committee as General Secretary, Andropov laid out a plan of reform that would guide his short tenure in office. Entitled "The Better We Work, the Better We Will Live," the speech outlined the main economic problems facing the country: inefficiency, waste, poor productivity, a lack of labor discipline, slow growth in living standards, and an insufficient quantity and quality of some consumer goods and services--particularly in housing, health care, and food. In defining the problem of consumer goods, Andropov distinguished his approach from Khrushchev's. Andropov stressed that the living standards did not reduce themselves to simple competition with the West for greater incomes and more material things. Rather, socialist living standards meant much more: "the growth of the consciousness and cultural level," "reasonable consumption," "a rational diet," quality public services, and "a morally and aesthetically adequate use of free time."[118]

According to Andropov, poor planning and outmoded management, the failure to utilize scientific and technological innovations, reliance on extensive rather than intensive methods of production, and the lack of labor discipline caused the economic shortcomings. Andropov called for the "acceleration [uskorenie] of scientific and technological progress." Andropov visualized a modernization of production through the application of computer technology. Beyond this, he called for standing commissions on energy that would correct the "uneconomical use of resources."[119]

Andropov also advocated attacking the economic problems by "a radical improvement of planning and management" at the top of Soviet society and by an improvement of discipline and incentives at the bottom.[120] In many cases, management needed to become smaller and simpler.[121] Andropov recognized that current planning and management methods often discouraged efficiency and the introduction of computers, robots, and flexible technology, since the adoption of new production methods could delay the fulfillment of an industry's plan. A change in "planning methods" and "material incentives" had to insure "that those who boldly introduce new technology do not find themselves at a disadvantage."[122] Andropov acknowledged that some experts thought that the economic problems occurred because of too much centralization and that a solution demanded granting greater independence to enterprises and collective and state farms. From personal experience, with decentralization under Khrushchev and Kadar, Andropov knew that it could lead to parochialism and inequality. Andropov did not reject decentralization outright, but he opposed the course Gorbachev would later embrace, a rash plunge into decentralization. Rather, Andropov said it was necessary "to act with circumspection, to experiment if need be, and to weigh and consider the experience of fraternal countries." Most importantly, any extension of independence must be combined with "greater responsibility and with concern for the interests of the entire people."[123]

To improve productivity and the quantity and quality of goods and services, Andropov proposed greater discipline and better incentives. In particular, Andropov launched a campaign against poor work, absenteeism, drunkenness, moonlighting, and irresponsibility. Those so guilty would have to pay in a "direct and inexorable way" by lost wages, reduced positions, and diminished "moral prestige."[124] In "Operation Trawl" in early 1983, the authorities "flushed out absentee workers in shops, bars, and steam baths."[125] The media joined the campaign for greater discipline, and Andropov personally took the campaign to a Moscow machine shop.[126] Andropov proposed punishment for public drunkenness and for such offenses as leaving work to shop or go to the baths. According to Zhores Medvedev, Andropov's efforts, particularly to reduce waste, brought "immediate and striking" results. Newspapers began openly criticizing inefficient farms and incompetence in the food industry.[127]

Andropov vigorously opposed wage leveling, such as had occurred under Khrushchev, as a violation of the fundamental socialist principle of "to each according to his work." He believed that unless productivity increases accompanied wage increases, greater wages would stimulate a demand that could not be fully satisfied and thus would produce shortages and other "ugly consequences," like the black-market. Properly conceived, incentives could do more than reward good work; they would stimulate quality work and an involvement in the activities and plans of the collective and of the entire people.[128]

In foreign affairs, Andropov had no taste for the kind of retreats and unilateral concessions that would mark Gorbachev's foreign policy. Andropov upheld the policy of peaceful co-existence and the avoidance of war, but he insisted that the principle of class struggle still prevailed internationally.[129] In the 1970s, he repeatedly warned that by raising issues of "dissidents" and "human rights" and by increasing the broadcasts of Radio Free Europe and Radio Liberty, the imperialists were actually intensifying their ideological and psychological warfare against the Soviet Union.[130] In his first speech as General Secretary, Andropov said Soviet foreign policy would remain "exactly as it was."[131] At that moment, Afghanistan represented the fulcrum of international struggle, and on it Andropov did not waver. Months before becoming General Secretary, Andropov said that the CPSU remained faithful to its international duty and would do everything it could to strengthen "solidarity and cooperation with its class brothers abroad."[132] Within days of becoming General Secretary, Andropov told the President of Pakistan to stop pretending that it was not a partner with the U.S. in the war against Afghanistan and assured him that "the Soviet Union will stand by Afghanistan."[133]

Andropov tried to improve the prospects for peace with the United States, but he did not have a lot of room for new initiatives. He took office at the nadir of Soviet-American relations, in the middle of what Soviet ambassador to the U.S., Anatoly Dobrynin, called the "new Cold War" that began under Carter and worsened under Reagan.[134] After Reagan called the Soviet Union the "evil empire" and announced plans for the Strategic Defense Initiative, Soviet-American relations reached a state of what Andropov called "unprecedented confrontation."[135] Andropov grounded his approach to the United States in the conviction "that peace cannot be obtained from the imperialists by begging for it. It can be upheld only by relying on the invincible might of the Soviet armed forces."[136] Consequently, Andropov rejected Reagan's lopsided "zero option" proposal (later acceded to by Gorbachev), under which Western European medium range missiles would remain, but the U.S. would refrain from installing medium range missiles in Europe, if the Soviet Union would withdraw all its existing European-based medium range missiles. Andropov had no interest in what he viewed as unilateral concessions. The Soviet Union's "entire experience," Andropov said, showed that "one cannot go to the imperialists, hat in hand, and hope to win peace."[137] Instead, Andropov made a number of disarmament proposals based on strict parity, while making it clear the Soviet Union would settle for nothing less.

In his short time in office, Andropov showed flexibility and initiative in his dealings with the U.S. He managed to restart high level discussions with Washington after a complete absence of nearly two years. When Reagan met for the first time with Dobrynin and raised only one substantive issue, the granting of exit visas to Pentecostals who had taken refuge in the American embassy in Moscow, Andropov agreed to act and allowed the Pentecostals to leave. Even though Andropov believed Reagan hoped to achieve military superiority and even contemplated a first nuclear strike, the Soviet leader instructed his arms negotiators to stop threatening to withdraw from the talks, and he re-opened the confidential communications channel that had been shut down since Carter. Andropov also instructed Dobrynin to be alert to any signs of Reagan's willingness to improve relations. In the end, Andropov's efforts to open a dialogue with the U.S. came to little. In September 1983, when a Soviet aircraft mistakenly shot down a Korean passenger plane and Reagan spokesmen reacted with a rhetorical rampage, any chance of improving relations vanished.[138]

In his brief tenure, Andropov also addressed problems related to Party standards, personnel, democracy, ideology, and the national question. He made clear that the Party would not tolerate corruption, bribery, or embezzlement. He insisted on a restoration of "Leninist norms." According to Ligachev, after Andropov became General Secretary "everyone went from an abbreviated workday to a longer one."[139] Andropov also abolished Brezhnev's "stability of cadre" policy and forced out the old and incompetent and brought in new and effective Party and state officials. One of his first moves was to replace the head of the Transport Ministry, which had been a source of persistent bottlenecks in the economy.[140] To improve democracy, Andropov attacked the excessive formalism of Party meetings and demanded an end to their scripted character.[141] He demanded the removal of obstacles to initiatives in the workplace, and according to Ligachev, introduced "the practice of holding preliminary discussions of Party and government decisions in work collectives and factories."[142] In June 1983, Andropov devoted a plenary meeting of the Central Committee to a discussion of the improvement of ideological work.[143]

Unquestionably, Andropov understood the problems facing the Soviet Union and the CPSU and undertook serious reforms. Some writers in the West suggested that the Soviet leader was a closet liberal, but they were wishing to make it so.[144] Nothing in Andropov's words or deeds showed the slightest interest in the path that Gorbachev would follow after 1987. It was not simply that Andropov quoted Marx and Lenin and hewed to the Party line. The Party expected no less of any Party leader. Rather, Andropov distinguished himself, as his speeches between 1964 and 1983 show, by the creative application of Marxist-Leninist ideas to immediate problems, the bold defense of tough policies, and the ability to rebut Western criticism with strength and sophistication. In precisely those areas, where Gorbachev would exhibit the most vacillation, Andropov showed the greatest steadfastness.

Similarly, Andropov took a more tough-minded approach to socialist democracy, nationalism, and the second economy than Gorbachev would. Andropov scored Stalin's breaches of socialist legality and Party democracy, but proclaimed the revolution's right and need to defend itself with force.[145] Andropov also had no sympathy whatsoever for manifestations of the second economy. No aspect of Soviet life drew more of Andropov's censure than "money-grubbing," "the plundering of the people's property," and the use of public posts for "personal enrichment."[146] Personal acquisitiveness could not be harnessed or encouraged for the benefit of socialism. It reflected a bourgeois value that socialism had to transcend. In what may have been his last article, Andropov said, "The turning of 'mine' into 'ours'...is a long and multifaceted process which should not be oversimplified. Even when socialist production relations have been established once and for all, some people still preserve, and even reproduce, individualistic habits, a striving to enrich themselves at the expense of others, at the expense of society."[147]

On the national question, Andropov took a tack that differed from the complacent optimism of previous General Secretaries and from the later indifference of Gorbachev. Far from assuming that socialism had solved these problems, Andropov asserted that national distinctions lasted much longer than class distinctions and that national self-awareness actually increased with economic and cultural progress. National problems, Andropov said, were "still on the agenda of mature socialism."[148] He called for the rectification of past and present policies that injured national sensibilities but insisted on an intolerance of national arrogance, conceit, or exclusiveness.[149] Andropov specifically called for a kind of "affirmative action" to "insure the proper representation of all nationalities" in all Party and government bodies.[150] Such a call by a Communist leader might seem entirely ordinary, but it contrasted sharply with Gorbachev's abrasive bumbling of national problems. Indeed, the eruption of nationalist sentiment that occurred in the mid-1980s served as much as a measure of Andropov's prescience as of Gorbachev's blindness.

There is every reason to think that Andropov's approach to reform would have worked. As a Communist leader, he had everything going for him except his health. Such cynics as the historian Dmitri Volkogonov asserted that Andropov's course was "ineffective." In all fairness, however, Andropov accomplished a great deal in his fifteen months, which in any case was a very short time to reform an entire society. His accomplishments were all the more impressive considering that illness consigned him to a hospital bed for half of this time and his successor lacked the capacity to continue what Andropov had started. Volkogonov acknowledged that the next General Secretary, Konstantin Chernenko, was "a total mediocrity, hardly educated, without any of the vision needed by a leader of Party and state."[151]

Some of Andropov's economic experiments did continue after him, but other reform ideas remained on the drawing board. Others barely got started. Most of them withered on the vine during Chernenko's two years in office. Consequently, most of the problems of the economy, Party, and foreign relations that had worsened under Brezhnev remained. When Gorbachev assumed the office of General Secretary in 1985, other Communists knew he favored reform but the path Gorbachev would choose remained a mystery, most likely even to the new General Secretary himself.

3. The Second Economy

The USSR's shadow economy and the rest of its underground--misappropriation, corruption, organized crime--in the end contributed to the system's collapse....[It] culminated in subornation of much of the formal apparatus of rule and control within the party-state hierarchy and in the severance or fraying of vertical lines of communication and authority, as it reoriented the nomenklatura's private (or group) interests and loyalties toward the new, nonofficial sources of wealth and power--with dire consequences for empire, union, system, and economy. --Gregory Grossman[152]

The emergence and rapid growth of the second economy since the mid-1960s contributed to the deepening economic crisis of the late 1980s and the ultimate disintegration of the Soviet economy. --Vladimir G. Treml and Michael Alexeev[153]

61

The shadow economy alleviates shortages in the consumer markets and, at the same time, provokes their growth....The presence of shortages produces the growth of organized criminal economic groups and the latter lead to socio-economic and political destabilization of the society.--Tatiana Koriagina[154]

What accounted for the persistence of two political tendencies within the CPSU? To some extent, of course, ideas have a life of their own and because of tradition and sentiments persist after the evaporation of their original purpose. More to the point, as long as capitalism and socialism existed side by side, ideas from one system were bound to penetrate the other. In the 1970s and 1980s, the extreme free market ideas of Milton Friedman of the University of Chicago and Jeffrey Sachs of Harvard enjoyed a worldwide resurgence, and the leaders of such diverse countries as Chile, Bolivia, Argentina, Britain, and Poland adopted them as a cure-all for inflation and stagnation. At the same time, some in the Soviet Union became attracted to these ideas. Such free market thinking within the Soviet Union dovetailed with the social democratic trend that had long existed.

In order for such ideas to persist in Soviet society and in the Communist Party, more than tradition, sentiment and external forces must have been at work. A section or stratum in Soviet society must have had more than an intellectual stake in those ideas. For the early decades of Soviet history, the class with such a stake was the peasantry, supplemented as well by those from a peasant background and former capitalists, so-called NEP-men, who hoped to regain their pre-revolutionary status. As the Soviet Union transformed the peasants into agricultural workers on state farms and collective farms and created a huge working class by industrializing, the peasant basis for quasi-capitalist ideas declined. The following figures reflected this transformation: the peasantry represented 83 percent of the population in 1926, but 20 percent in 1975. The workers in industry, building and transportation represented 5 million people in 1926 and 62 million in 1975.[155]

After 1953, a new economic basis for bourgeois ideas began growing within socialism. This basis was the population engaged in private economic activity for personal gain, in a so-called second economy that existed beside the first, socialist economy. At first, the very existence of a second economy was disguised by its interpenetration of the first or socialized economy. The second economy usually did not involve a separate class of people, but rather workers and farmers in the primary economy who spent time making money on the side in legal or illegal, private activity. Increasingly, however, in the post-war years, the second economy embraced more and more people and accounted for more and more of their income and in effect re-created a petty bourgeois stratum. The most corrosive product of the Khrushchev and Brezhnev eras resided precisely in this second, private economy and the stratum that benefited from it. Private economic activity never totally disappeared under socialism, but after being restrained under Stalin, it emerged with new vitality under Khrushchev, flourished under Brezhnev, and in many respects replaced the primary socialist economy under Gorbachev and Yeltsin. The second economy had profound and widespread negative effects on Soviet socialism. It created, or re-created, private sources of income and systems of distribution and production. It led to widespread corruption and criminality. It spawned ideas and sentiments to justify private enterprise. It became a source of funds for critics and opponents of the system. It provided a material basis for social democratic ideas.

Before detailing the consequences of the second economy, it is first necessary to define it, discuss its treatment in socialist literature, describe its various manifestations, recount its history, and estimate its size. We define the second economy as economic activity for private gain whether legal or illegal. There are two good reasons for including both legal and illegal private moneymaking. First, this is the definition used by Gregory Grossman and other students of the second economy, and hence using a consistent definition will reduce confusion when referring to their studies.[156] Second, private economic activity fosters relations, values, and ideas that are different from collective economic activity. As such, it can pose a danger to socialism. The Soviets recognized this during the NEP period, as have the Cubans in relationship to the foreign investment and private activity allowed during the so-called Special Period. Because of this, widespread private economic activity, whether it is legal or illegal, can pose a problem for socialism.

Including legal and illegal activity in the definition does not imply, however, that they were equally dangerous. Because the socialized sector could not realistically assume responsibility for every small repair, service, and petty exchange of goods, private economic activity occurred in every socialist country. Kept within bounds, private activity occupied a natural and unthreatening place. This was the case with most legal economic activity in the Soviet Union. Between 1950 and 1985, legal private economic activity actually diminished in size relative to the socialized sector. The opposite was true of illegal activity. As we shall discuss, it corroded socialism in a number of ways, not least of which was the way it often compromised legal activity. Moreover, in the period from 1950 to 1980, illegal, private economic activity expanded greatly.

The illegal aspect of the second economy, or black market activity, did not, of course, occur only in socialist societies. Under capitalism, illegal economic activity took such forms as prostitution, working off the books to avoid taxes, and selling outlawed drugs and bootleg liquor. During Prohibition, American black market activity assumed large dimensions in the sale of illegal alcohol and during World War II in the sale of tires, sugar and other rationed products. Because socialism prohibited a greater range of private economic activity than did capitalism, black market activity represented a greater potential problem. Moreover, since socialist revolutions have occurred in economically developing societies where the needs of capital investment and national security required limiting the investment in consumer goods, the demand for some consumer goods invariably exceeded the supply. This in turn led to a system of distribution that required lines and/or ration coupons. The greater the number of proscribed economic activities and the greater the shortage of consumer goods, the greater was the temptation to circumvent the law. To counter this temptation, socialist societies have used vigorous educational campaigns and rigorous law enforcement.

Even though black markets have been endemic to undeveloped socialism, the existence and growth of a second economy in the Soviet Union may come as a surprise to Marxists and others. If so, the surprise may be due to the failure of economists to give the second economy proper recognition. Popular Marxist treatments of the Soviet economy contained virtually no discussion of the second economy. In *Soviet Economic Development Since 1917*, published in 1948 and enlarged and revised in 1966, the British Marxist, Maurice Dobb, said nothing about legal or illegal, private enterprise, aside from two references to the black market in the 1920s.[157] Until 1980, with the exception of the Soviet economist, T. I. Koriagina, most Soviet economists ignored the second economy.[158] No discussion of it occurred in such standard Soviet texts as L. Leontyev, *Political Economy: A Condensed Course*; G. A. Kozlov, editor, *Political Economy: Socialism*; G. S. Sarkisyants, editor, *Soviet Economy: Results and Prospects*; P. I. Nikitin, *The Fundamentals of Political Economy* and Yuri Popov, *Essays in Political Economy*.[159] In his last discussion of the economic problems of the Soviet Union published in 1952, Joseph Stalin referred to the persistence of private commodity production in the countryside but made no mention of the danger of illegal, private enterprise (probably because of its negligible size at that time).[160] Similarly, in a pamphlet on the Soviet economy published in 1961, the American Marxist economist, Victor Perlo, devoted a short section to the black market in foreign currency but clearly saw this as a temporary and limited phenomenon. Perlo quoted Anastas Mikoyan, the First Deputy Premier, who called the black market "a handful of scum on the surface or our society," that represented "no trend among our people."[161] Even as late as 1980, in a book on the Soviet economy with a frank and informative discussion of its problems, Victor and Ellen Perlo had no discussion of a second economy.[162]

Though most Marxist economists, and for that matter most bourgeois economists, ignored private economic activity within socialism, some American, Western European, and Soviet scholars, as well as the CIA, became alert to this phenomenon in the 1970s and studied it thereafter. Indeed, the Soviet second economy spawned a cottage industry of academic work in the United States. In 1985, Gregory Grossman of the University of California--Berkeley and Vladimir Treml of Duke University began publishing the Berkeley-Duke Occasional Papers on the Second Economy in the USSR. Between 1985 and 1993, the Berkeley-Duke project published fifty-one papers by twenty-six authors on this topic. Over half of these papers dealt with the Brezhnev era and many were based on surveys administered to 1,061 households that had left the Soviet Union between 1971 and 1982.[163] In addition, the Berkeley-Duke project compiled a bibliography of 269 studies in major Western languages on the second economy in the USSR and Eastern Europe.[164] For a number of scholars, the second economy loomed large.

In terms of the law, Soviet socialism prohibited most private economic activity. The law proscribed the employment of others (except for household help), the selling or reselling of goods for profit, trading with foreigners, possessing foreign currency, and plying most crafts and trade for private gain. Consequently, the legal exploitation of labor did not exist. Nevertheless, within strict legal boundaries, Soviet socialism permitted certain kinds of private economic activity. A substantial amount of private gainful work remained legal, even though it sometimes shaded into illegal activity. Soviet law permitted private agricultural plots limited to three-quarters of an acre for those employed on collective or state farms and even for some people not so employed. In 1974, according to some estimates, private plots accounted for almost a third of all hours expended on agriculture and almost a tenth of total man-hours in the whole economy. The private plots also accounted for more than a fourth of Soviet agricultural output. To sell the products of private plots, so-called collective farm markets developed. Though legal, this growing and selling invited illegal abuses such as the diversion of socialized property (seeds, fertilizer, water, fodder, equipment, and transportation) to support the private plots and bring the produce to market.[165]

Soviet law also permitted private housing. According to Grossman, in the mid-1970s half of the Soviet population, and a quarter of the urban population, still lived in private housing. Legal, private housing often involved some illegality--subletting for illegal rent, the hiring of illegal construction or repair help, the diversion of building materials from the socialized sector, the bribery of officials and so forth. In other sectors, such professionals as doctors, dentists, teachers, and tutors could legally sell their services. Craftsmen could engage in home repair in rural areas, and certain craftsmen could work at a few limited and unimportant trades. Private prospectors could mine, providing they sold their ore to the state. The law also permitted the sale of used personal items.[166] By itself, legal private activity did not present a big problem. It steadily declined as a percentage of GNP until Gorbachev. Grossman estimated that it represented 22 percent of GNP in 1950 and 10 percent in 1977. Of course, Soviet GNP had grown greatly between 1950 and 1977, so legal private economic activity remained significant.[167]

After 1953, illegal money-making presented a much greater problem than legal activity. Illegal activity eventually assumed an astounding array of forms, eventually penetrated all aspects of Soviet life, and was limited only by the boundaries of human ingenuity. The most common form of criminal economic activity took the form of stealing from the state, that is, from work places and public organizations. Grossman said, "The peasant steals fodder from the kolkhoz to maintain his animals, the worker steals materials and tools with which to ply his trade 'on the side,' the physician steals medicines, the driver steals gasoline and the use of the official car to operate an unofficial taxi." Variations on this theme included the diversion of goods into the private market by truck drivers and the use of state resources to build a summerhouse, renovate an apartment, or repair a car.[168]

At times stealing from the state occurred in wholesale and systematic ways. This included "well-organized gangs of criminals capable of pulling off daring and large-scale feats." It included the practices of managers reporting the loss or spoilage of goods in order to divert them to the black market. It embraced a common practice in state stores of salespeople and managers laying aside rare goods in order to secure tips from favored customers or to sell them in the black market. Consumer durable goods like automobiles for which waiting lists existed presented "considerable opportunity for graft," as well as for "speculation," that is, for resale at higher prices.[169]

Repairs, services and even production constituted other avenues of illegal gain. This included household repair, automotive repair, sewing and tailoring, moving furniture, and building private dwellings. This work, illegal in itself, often involved material and time stolen from regular employment. Private production even took the form of full-blown, underground capitalists in the full sense of the word--

investing capital, organizing production on a large scale, hiring and exploiting workers, and selling commodities in the black market. According to Grossman, the products usually consisted of consumer goods--"garments, footwear, household articles, knickknacks, etc." Moreover, "large-scale private operations such as these commonly take place behind the protective façade of a state-owned factory or a collective farm--naturally, with appropriate payoffs to those who provide the cover."[170] Konstantin Simis, a prominent Soviet lawyer who represented many underground businessmen in the 1970s, subsequently described his experiences in a book subtitled, *The Secret World of Soviet Capitalism*. Simis said "a network of private factories is spread across the whole country," tens of thousands of them, manufacturing "knitwear, shoes, sunglasses, recording of Western popular music, handbags, and many other goods." The owners ranged from the owners of "a single workshop" to "multimillion-ruble family clans that own dozens of factories."[171]

Taken together, a variety of monographs provided a kaleidoscopic view of the second economy during the Brezhnev years. Private food vendors sold goods valued at 35.5 billion rubles a year.[172] Soviet barbers in state-owned barbershops customarily collected "very high" tips "in effect transporting the transaction into the SE [second economy]."[173] The home production of grape and fruit wine and beer, the illegal resale of state beverages, and the sale of stolen ethanol accounted for as much as 2.2 percent of the Gross Domestic Product in 1979.[174] By the late 1970s, the black market sale of gasoline by drivers of state-owned cars and trucks allegedly accounted for between 33 and 65 percent of all gasoline sales in urban areas.[175] Privately rented housing brought illegal landlords an estimated 1.5 million rubles in 1977.[176] Tips, bribes, and payments for private services (such as religious ceremonies) associated with funerals involved more than four times the amount of money spent on official funerals.[177] Prostitution and illegal drug sales constituted another part of the second economy.[178]

The researcher, Marina Kurkchiyan, provided a detailed description of the way the second economy worked in the transportation system of Soviet Armenia, which she regarded as "typical." Even though a bus driver made more than average wages, he made more money from his customers than from his state wages. The driver collected fares directly from customers and turned over only part of the receipts to the state. Out of his own pocket, the driver paid for cleaning, parts, maintenance and fuel. In the end, a bus driver's total income, after expenses, amounted to two to three times the size of his official state salary. Kurkchiyan concluded that by the end of the 1980s, partly as a result of Gorbachev's policies and economic hardships, "everybody" was engaged in the second economy, and it had become "the dominant force in the allocation of goods and services."[179]

How big was the second economy? All kinds of methodological problems bedevil an attempt to measure its size and growth. Experts have challenged each other's figures, as well as official Soviet figures issued after 1989. Nonetheless, all experts agreed that for over thirty years the second economy grew at an increasing rate. For certain regions of Russia and the Ukraine, Vladimir G. Treml and Michael Alexeev analyzed the relationship between earned, legal income on the one hand and the amounts spent on goods and services or saved on the other hand. They discovered that between 1965 and 1989 the correlation between income and expenditures/savings became weaker and weaker until it disappeared. In other words, the total amount of money spent or saved increasingly exceeded the amount of income earned legally. They surmised that illegal income accounted for the difference. They provided no figures for the size and growth of the second economy, but concluded that "the second economy was growing rapidly between 1965 and 1985."[180] Another researcher, Byung-Yeon Kim, using

Soviet statistics that became available after 1991, similarly concluded, "The absolute size of the informal economy had indeed increased from 1969 to 1990."[181]

The leading Soviet specialist on the second economy, T. I. Koriagina of the Economic Research Institute of the USSR State Planning Commission (which favored legalizing at least some of the second economy), also attempted to measure the growth of the second economy. In one study, Koriagina used a methodology similar to Treml and Alexeev's. She compared the amount of legally, earned income per month with the total amount spent and saved. Her figures likewise showed not only a large size for the second economy, but also a steady expansion.

The Growth of the Monthly Salary of Workers
Compared with the Growth of the Total Size
of Money Spent on Goods and Services
and Saved in Savings Banks[182]

	1960	1970	1975	1980	1985	1988
Monthly Salary in Billions of Rubles	80.6	122	145.8	168.9	190.1	219.8
Percentage of 1960		152	180	210	236	273
Total Spent and Saved in Billions of Rubles	103.2	223.2	329.9	464.6	590	718.4
Percentage of 1960		216	320	450	572	696

Using statistics for the whole Soviet economy, Koriagina estimated that the second economy was growing even faster than in the selected areas above. Moreover, the second economy was growing faster than the first economy. According to Koriagina, official national income and the value of retail goods and services had increased four or five times between early 1960s and late 1980s, while the second economy had grown eighteen times.[183]

Though the second economy grew, its actual size is difficult to measure. Both American and Soviet economists of all ideological viewpoints admit it is hard to estimate the size of the second economy of the USSR in relation to its total economy. One difficulty involves varying definitions of the "informal economy," the "shadow economy," the "second economy," the "private economy," the "underground economy," the "black market economy," and so forth. For some scholars, the important measure is legal and illegal, private economic activity, for others the measure is only illegal activity. Even if a definition could be agreed upon, all estimates involve assumptions that may be more or less realistic. One economist has compared the measurement of the Soviet second economy to the determination by physicists of Pluto's orbit by studying the oscillation of its planetary neighbors. All of these caveats aside, the estimates are nonetheless highly revealing.

Based on macroeconomic figures, Koriagina estimated that the annual value of illegal goods and services grew from approximately 5 billion rubles in the early 1960s to 90 billion rubles in the late 1980s. If the value of the Soviet national income (net material product) in current prices was 145 billion rubles in 1960, 422 rubles in 1988, and 701 billion rubles in 1990, then the value of second economy was approximately 3.4 percent of national income in 1960, 20 percent in 1988 and 12.8 percent in 1990.[184] (By 1990, some previously illegal activity was now legal.) In 1988, Koriagina estimated that the total accumulated illegally attained personal wealth amounted to 200-240 billion rubles, or 20-25 percent of all personal wealth.[185]

Koriagina's figures represented only income from illegal economic activity. To get a sense of the total size of private economic activity, one would have to add to her figures the size of legal private activity. In other words, the size of all private activity would presumably be at least 10 percentage points higher for a total of 30 per cent in 1988 or 30 to 35 percent of accumulated personal wealth in 1988.

If such adjustments to Koriagina's figures were made, her figures would be comparable to those of the leading American authority, Gregory Grossman, whose estimates came from microeconomic data gleaned from interviews with over a thousand Soviet emigrants. Grossman found that in the late 1970s the urban population (which constituted 62 percent of the total population) earned about 30 percent of its total income from nonofficial sources, that is to say, from either legal or illegal, private activity.[186]

Research using the Soviet archives after 1991 has reinforced these estimates of the size of the second economy. In 2003, Byung-Yeon Kim, an economist at the University of Warwick, England, estimated the size of the second economy on the basis of official Soviet Family Budget Survey Data (FBSD). Between 1969 and 1990, the Soviet government collected data from a sample of 62,000 to 90,000 families on income and expenditures. Respondents reported both official income and "informal" income and expenditures, that is to say, income (not necessarily illegal) derived from private activity and expenditures in private transactions. Such informal income included income in kind, income from the sale of agricultural animals and products, and income from individuals. Informal expenditures included the consumption of self-produced goods and money paid to individuals for goods. Kim noted that one would naturally expect these respondents to be less willing to reveal income and expenditures involving illegal activity than the émigré respondents used by Grossman. At the same time, it is likely that Grossman's respondents were more disaffected with socialism and hence more involved in private undertakings and were more apt to exaggerate their importance than Soviet citizens who did not emigrate. In any event, one would expect estimates of the second economy based on Kim's data to be smaller than Grossman's. This indeed was the case. Kim estimated total income from the second economy as 16 percent, while Grossman estimated total income from the second economy as 28-33 percent. Correcting for the possible reporting bias on both sides would mean the true figure was probably some where in the middle.[187]

In another study, Grossman found that the second economy assumed larger dimensions in areas on the periphery of the Soviet Union than in Russia:

Grossman's Estimates of the
Size of the Soviet Second Economy
Compared to the First Economy

Brezhnev Era (1977)[188]

Russia (RSFSR)	29.6%
Belorussia, Moldavia, and Ukraine	40.2%
Armenia (ethnic Armenians only)	64.1%
'Europeans' residing in Transcaucasia or Central Asia	49.7%

Grossman noted that while 30 percent of urban income derived from the second economy by the late 70s, the second economy had relatively greater strength in the south (the Northern Caucasus regions and the Transcaucasian republics of Georgia, Armenia, and Azerbaijan, and Central Asia) than in the north (central Russia, the Baltics, and Siberia). It was also large in certain border regions like Odessa and in territory joined to the USSR after 1917, such as Moldavia, the Ukraine and Belarus. Because of regional and ethnic variations, in some areas the people averaged as much income from illegal, private activity as from regular, legal employment. In some areas, people averaged twice as much from illegal as legal sources.[189] Kim's study based on Family Budget Survey Data confirmed the conclusions of Grossman and others that the second economy was smallest in Russia, Estonia, and Latvia and largest in Uzbekistan, Georgia, Azerbaijan, Kirghizstan, Tadzhikstan, and Armenia.[190]

How many people did the second economy involve? Most scholars agreed that by the 1980s the second economy reached into every nook and cranny of the society and touched almost everyone. In a reference to private money-making, Brezhnev himself remarked, "No one lives on wages alone."[191] What was important, however, was not petty pilfering or the purchase of black market goods, but the emergence of a layer of people who depended upon private activity for all or a substantial portion of their income. Some people became exceedingly wealthy and acquired the name, the "Brezhnev new rich. "[192] Such people could rightly be considered a nascent class of petty bourgeoisie.

Some scholars have attempted to assign a number or percentage to those involved in the second economy, particularly to those who derived a substantial income from illegal, private enterprise. According to Vladimir Treml, the underground, or illegal, economy in the late 1970s involved 10 to 12 percent of the labor force.[193] Koriagina estimated that the number of people involved in the illegal parts of the second economy grew from less than 8 million people in the early 1960s to 17-20 million (6 to 7.6 percent) in 1974 to about 30 million (roughly 12 percent of the population) in 1989.[194] Grossman summed up the extent of the second economy in the mid-1980s:

> And so during the last three decades of the Soviet era, illegal economic activity penetrated into every sector and chink of the economy; assumed every conceivable shape and form; and operated on a scale ranging from minimal or modest for the mass to the substantial for

the many, to the lavish and gigantic, as well as elaborately organized, for some.[195]

The large amount of wheeling and dealing that occurred outside the official socialized economy contributed mightily to the Soviet downfall. First, it created or exacerbated the economic and political problems the Soviet Union faced in the 1980s that gave rise to the need for reform. Secondly, it provided an economic basis for the ideas and policies that Gorbachev eventually adopted that doomed Soviet socialism.

On the surface, it might have seemed that the second economy served a benign, even stabilizing, function. The second economy met some consumer appetites not satisfied by the first economy and thus drained off a certain amount of discontent over the quantity and quality of socialist goods. It also offered a remunerative outlet for individual initiative that otherwise might have been turned directly against the system.

Perhaps such beliefs accounted for the failure of Soviet authorities to pay much attention to the second economy and to crack down on its crimes. As noted earlier, Soviet economic texts ignored the second economy. Valery Rutgaizer, who headed Gosplan's Scientific and Research Economic Institute (where Koriagina did her studies) said the first publications on the second economy in the Soviet Union did not appear until the beginning of the 1980s.[196] More importantly, Soviet authorities made no concerted effort to suppress it. Grossman said:

> By 1960 the Soviet shadow economy was already institutionally mature and of notable scope and size. In the early 1960s it was the target of a fierce campaign by Khrushchev to the point of reintroduction of the death penalty. In the event, this campaign, like all others against 'economic crime' before and since, did little to set back the steady, rapid rise of illicit

activity. Instead the shadow economy spread out, grew, and prospered--under Brezhnev (1964-82), thanks to benign neglect if not tacit encouragement.[197]

An indication of this benign neglect appeared in the almost complete absence of prosecution of clearly illegal economic activity. In the early 1980s, crimes of speculation (buying to resell at a higher price) accounted for only 2 percent of all reported crimes. According to one estimate, the actual amount of speculation was a hundred times greater.[198] In retrospect, few other mistakes of the Soviet leadership did so much harm as the indifference toward illegal economic activity.

Whatever small and temporary benefits Soviet society may have reaped from the second economy, the costs far outstripped them. Most important, the second economy damaged the first economy. If the second economy satisfied some consumer appetites and deflected some discontent, it simultaneously stimulated these appetites and increased discontent. Koriagina said, "The second economy alleviates shortages in consumer markets and at the same time, provokes their growth." Shortages then encouraged even more criminal economic activity, and this led to the "socio-economic and political destabilization of the society."[199] Moreover, the larger the illegal economy became, the more it interfered with the performance of the legitimate economy. Since the second economy involved stealing time and material from the socialist sector, it impaired socialism's efficiency. Alexeev said, "Diverting inputs and outputs to the black market must have lowered the official performance of at least some enterprises."[200] Furthermore, the second economy undermined economic planning. If an enterprise compensated for a misallocation of resources by resorting to informal purchases or trades, the planners had no reason to correct future allocations. By weakening or destroying the feedback mechanism, the second economy forced planners to "direct the

Soviet economy with a highly distorted map of the economic situation."[201] Finally, private moneymaking increased income inequality and its attendant jealousies and resentments. In all of these ways, the second economy either caused or exacerbated the Soviet Union's economic problems.

How did the second economy influence the Communist Party? In one word, the answer was corruption. Corruption of some cadres more than anything else explained why the Party that had rebuffed Bukharin and Khrushchev (though not without some damage) did not overcome Gorbachev. The peasantry that provided a class basis for Bukharin's ideas did not require the corruption of the Party for its existence, but the entrepreneurs of the second economy did. Simply put, to exist and thrive, illegal producing and selling required the bribery of some Party and state officials, and the more organized and widespread this producing and selling became, the more corruption they required. Simis said, "No underground enterprise could be created without the venality of [some in] the state administration; it would not last a month."[202]

In 1979, Grossman reported that corruption, namely the bribery of Soviet officials, was "extremely widespread" and reached "up and down nearly all levels of the formal hierarchy." At the lowest level, in an actual case recounted by a former Soviet prosecutor, it might involve the director of a vegetable storage warehouse being forced "on pain of dismissal to pay regular graft to several of the Party and government chiefs of the given district."[203] At the highest levels, it led to scandals such as the so-called cotton fraud of the 1970s and early 1980s, in which top Party and government officials in Uzbekistan and elsewhere "boldly and deftly padded" the size of the cotton crop to harvest billions of rubles. In the process "thousands were bought off," including Brezhnev's son-in-law.[204] The rackets varied by area: in Azerbaijan caviar, in Georgia wines and precious stones, in the Baltics fish, and in Kirghyzia meat, and invariably they required the corruption of the Party.[205]

Venality reached the highest levels of the Party. Frol Kozlov, Khrushchev's right hand man, Deputy Premier and Secretary of the Central Committee, retired in disgrace after the authorities opened the safe of a deceased Leningrad official and discovered packages belonging to Kozlov that contained precious jewels and bundles of money. These were payoffs in part for Kozlov using his influence to stop the criminal prosecution of illegal businessmen.[206] Eventually, corruption reached the very top. After Chernenko's death in 1985, officials of the Central Committee found "desk drawers stuffed with banknotes. Banknotes also filled half of the General Secretary's personal secret office safe."[207]

Alexander Gurov, a top police official in the USSR, related the development of Party corruption from the time of Khrushchev to Gorbachev directly to the development of illegal economy and organized crime:

> It [organized crime] was bound to happen as soon as our system opened up and that was in the so-called thaw of the 1960s when Nikita Khrushchev was in power....It was impossible to imagine powerful organized crime groups under Stalin.... What we got after that in our society was the moral code of the plunderer. And of course it was run totally in the interest of the [Party] bureaucracy. For example, we had a so-called trade mafia in Moscow with representatives in top Party bodies as early as 1974. If I or anyone else had tried to warn people about the danger of the shadow economy then, liberals would have laughed and the government would have called us crazy. But that was how it started. And the government allowed it to happen, for reasons that ought to make us think. It began under Khrushchev and

developed under Brezhnev. But the Gorbachev era was the period in which organized crime really became powerful in our country.[208]

The political problems of the Communist Party were intimately related to the corruption. Even if the cause and effect were not all in one direction, low Party standards, ideological weakness, formalism, cynicism and other political weaknesses were intertwined with corruption. Corruption gave some Communist Party and state officials a material stake in private enterprise. These officials may not have been directly involved in private trade or production, but they were in fact engaging in their own form of illicit money grubbing.

If the second economy greatly contributed to the problems of Soviet socialism, it had an equally corrosive effect on the attempt to solve those problems. As bad as the problems were, they did not bring down socialism; Gorbachev did that, and his thinking increasingly reflected the interests of the second economy entrepreneurs. The course that Gorbachev followed after 1986 stemmed directly from the second economy in two respects. First, for all the reasons given above, the second economy had created and fed a great cynicism about the efficiency of socialism, the effectiveness of planning, and the integrity of the Communist Party. Increasingly, Gorbachev exploited and even fanned this cynicism, until it spun out of control. Secondly, by creating a nascent petty bourgeoisie, the second economy had created a stratum within socialism whose personal interests lay outside of socialism. It served as a ready-built constituency for Gorbachev's pro-market and pro-private property policies.

Too often Party leaders underestimated this stratum's ideological danger. Some even denied that such a danger existed. In this respect, the aforementioned Frol Kozlov rang the bell for complacent hypocrisy. At the very time Kozlov was secretly lining his pockets protecting would-be capitalists, he brazenly assured the Twenty-second Congress of the CPSU "that in Soviet society there no longer exists a social basis on which any opportunist trends could thrive in the party."[209]

In the society at large, illegal, private moneymaking promoted petty bourgeois values and undermined socialist legitimacy. On the one hand, the underground economy served as a training ground for entrepreneurs, shaped a public consciousness favorable to markets, and "helped create a consensus for market reforms."[210] On the other hand, the underground economy and everything that went with it created what some called a "demoralization crisis." The prevalence of illegal activities, pilfering, time-stealing, bribery, and corruption, the ubiquitous blat or the "economy of favours,"[211] and the growing inequality undermined some people's faith in the ultimate fairness of the system. The diversion of the highest quality goods into the black market and the shortages aggravated by the black market cast doubts on the system's efficacy. The second economy thus cut two ways--it slashed at socialism's worth, while it carved an altar for money. Grossman said, "The prevalence of economic illegalities and corruption casts doubt on the ability of the Soviet system to provide minimal material benefits to its population or to administer its own socialist economy according to its own principles and rules." Meanwhile, "it elevates the power of money in society" to rival that of the governing Party.[212]

Some Communists who noticed the development of anti-socialist ideas and values within socialism did not go very far in diagnosing its origin or prescribing a solution. Georgy Shakhnazarov, later a key aide to Gorbachev, wrote a futurological essay in 1978 in which he warned of the growing "philistine, petty bourgeois mentality," the true source of which was "the scrimmage for riches and the accompanying advantage." Shakhnazarov noted that inequality and classes still existed and "so long as the problem [of classes] is not radically settled, relapses of petty bourgeois mentality are possible. And relapses mean epidemics, not isolated cases of the malaise, often affecting whole social groups."[213]

If Shakhnazarov could point to a petty bourgeois mentality in the 1970s, by the early 1980s this mentality was crystallizing into interest groups with their own agendas. That is to say, the second economy began to serve as the material basis for social structures and ideologies at variance with socialism. One was the world of organized crime. Another was the world of "political dissidents, ethnic and religious activists, refuseniks, opters-out, non-conformist writers and artists, and samizdat publishers." The second economy and the West furnished these alternative social structures "much material support, especially in the pre-Gorbachev years." Inscribed on their banners was the petty bourgeois watchword--freedom: freedom to promulgate religion, freedom to emigrate, freedom not to work, freedom to make money, freedom to exploit others, freedom to write and publish anything. Historian S. Frederick Starr said, "Unsanctioned informal groups and networks sprang up in many fields. Tens of thousands of them were in existence by the mid-1980s, some founded only to provide voluntary services but others existing to influence public policy." These groups did not arise to promote class struggle, sacrifice, civic virtue, or international working class solidarity. Rather, they promoted freedom, individualism and acquisitiveness, and as Starr noted, "All of this ferment began prior to Gorbachev's rise to power in 1985."[214]

A striking example was the organization, In Defense of Economic Freedom, formed in 1981 and led by V. Sokirko. In Defense of Economic Freedom waged an open campaign for the legalization of the second economy. In particular, it conducted agitation for the repeal of Article 153 of the Russian Soviet Penal Code that outlawed private entrepreneurial activity. The group appealed to the USSR Supreme Soviet's Committee on Legal Affairs to abolish the article. The organization compiled the records of cases brought under this article and published a journal exposing what the editors regarded as unfair convictions. The group also conducted show trials based on actual cases, where the juries generally acquitted those whom the authorities had convicted. According to Valery Rutgaizer of Gosplan, In Defense of Economic Freedom's campaign "managed to create an atmosphere of public censure of Article 153" even to the point of stopping prosecutions.[215]

Before Gorbachev came to power, the ideological influence of the second economy made itself apparent within the Communist Party and the Soviet government. Two distinct approaches toward the illegal economy developed in the early 1980s. One approach predominated in two research institutes that Andropov set up to study the second economy--one institute in the USSR Procurator's Office and the other in the USSR Interior Ministry. For these two institutes, individual labor activity fell into one of two categories, that which was legal and beneficial to the society, and that which was illegal and resulted in unearned, illegitimate income. Both institutes viewed the latter, the "shadow economy," as incompatible with socialism. Its growth had resulted from "legal shortcomings"--a failure to enforce the law. It needed to be combated by "stepping up control and monitoring of the individual labor activity."[216]

The other approach found expression in Gosplan's Scientific and Research Economic Institute headed by Valery Rutgaizer. This approach, which Gorbachev eventually embraced, viewed most of the shadow economy as legitimate and useful. This institute aimed at "transforming the economic system" so as to legalize much previously illegal, private economic activity. Early on the members of this institute argued for using leasing and cooperative arrangements to legitimate parts of the second economy, a course of action Gorbachev would follow. These arrangements became a way station on the road to privatization and marketization.[217]

In the early 1980s, as at other times in the past, the Communist Party faced a variety of economic, political and foreign policy problems. As in the past, some saw the way forward as involving some kind of accommodation with capitalism or incorporation of capitalist ideas. By the 1980s, however, this approach had acquired hidden reserves. Those reserves were embodied by the stealthy growth of a petty bourgeois stratum and a corrupt section of the Party and state that likewise favored a move toward capitalism, toward free markets, private property, free enterprise, and other bourgeois "freedoms." In this sense, Gorbachev's move to the right in 1987 and the subsequent unraveling of Soviet socialism can best be understood as the product of a conjunction of the historic Bukharin/Khrushchev tradition and the emerging petty bourgeois of the second economy.

However important the second economy was in providing a basis for bourgeois ideas, this stratum did not exist in isolation. It floated on a larger sea of potential discontent. The very success of socialism had created a vast urbanized and educated intelligentsia in the Soviet sense of white-collar, non-manual workers. Some of this intelligentsia felt disadvantaged by the wage equalization that had occurred since the 1950s. For example, doctors, teachers, engineers, and administrators typically earned less than skilled workers did. Moreover, increased travel and communication had made the intelligentsia aware that they enjoyed a lower standard of living than their counterparts in the West. By the 1980s, this intelligentsia, by the way, had a disproportionate influence at the top. At least half the members of the Communist Party, and an even greater proportion of leaders, came from this sector.[218]

In 2001, a member of the Central Committee of the Communist Party of the Russian Federation (CPRF), Victor Trushkov, offered an analysis of the Soviet collapse that complements the one presented here. Trushkov said that capitalist restoration in the Soviet Union remained a danger as long as "exploiters on a world level" continued to exist, but "external pressure" only became a mortal threat when forces developed "inside the socialist system" with "an interest in restoring capitalism." To understand how such forces could develop, Trushkov said, one must appreciate that "the picture of Soviet society as a practically classless one in the 80s," was "far from reality."

Trushkov pointed to the development of two quasi-bourgeois strata. In the first place, "a system of small-scale retail trade," emerged. This trade was "barely legal" and depended on the misuse of resources that belonged to the state. Nevertheless, "between the moonlighting bricklayers and taxidrivers and the sales of the product of smallholdings it meant that this retailing was relatively important." In the second place, a "private wholesale trade, which existed in the form of a parallel economy" emerged. "Its economic power was even greater [than retail trade]....Some research workers state that its turnover was comparable to that of the state." In 1987-88, when Gorbachev began legalizing this retail and wholesale trade, those active in these areas sought "political means of protecting their interests," hence the pressure for even more marketization and privatization. These moves in turn began an erosion of the state sector. "When the Gorbachev-Yakovlev tandem started to introduce the bourgeois system," Trushkov said, "an important part of the [state] apparatus discovered it had competitors in those acting in the already existing forms of private property and expressed the will to preserve its privileged status (the privileges of power) by themselves appropriating state property."[219] In these ways, the second economy and Gorbachev's reform sparked a dialectic of socialist betrayal.

4. Promise and Foreboding, 1985-86

Gorbachev's first days and months were electrifying. His speeches and person-to-person talks with Leningrad workers put the first cracks in the ice of stagnation. Mike Davidow [220]

A struggle still lies ahead for the party. Khrushchev was no accident. We are primarily a peasant country, and the right wing is powerful. Where's the guarantee to prevent them from getting the upper hand? The anti-Stalinists in all probability will come to power in the near future, and they are most likely to be Bukharinists. V. M. Molotov [221]

In place of the old corrupt elements that for decades had been festering in the body of the Communist Party and the society at large, suddenly, in the space of a year or two, came even more horrible and more absolutely corrupt forces that stifled the healthy start made in the Party and the country after April 1985. Yegor Ligachev [222]

The policies of Mikhail Gorbachev occupy the center of any explanation of the collapse of Soviet socialism. In 1985, Gorbachev took over a country facing longstanding problems and in short order exacerbated the situation into a system-wide crisis. The kindest judgment that could be made of Gorbachev's policies is that they failed. *Perestroika* did not produce its ostensible ends--a democratic, productive, and efficient socialism. Instead, it destroyed the Soviet Union as a state and left in its place a set of balkanized countries dominated by oligarchic and lawless capitalism that after a decade had impoverished the majority of the population. Whatever Gorbachev may have hoped to achieve, it was unlikely that he wanted this. Nor was it likely that he want to become a politician without a party, a president without a state, and a socialist without socialism.

Gorbachev and his defenders said that he inherited a society in crisis. This was false. In any conventional sense, the Soviet Union had not sunk into the throes of a crisis. In 1985, its economic problems did not approach the inflation and instability of Germany in the 1920s or the depression in the United States in the 1930s. Moreover, its political problems fell far short of a crisis of legitimacy. Complaints about shortages, waiting lines, and the quality of consumer goods occurred, but little popular discontent with the system itself existed. Oleg Kalugin, a high ranking KGB officer who served in Leningrad from 1979 to 1986, said he never encountered serious opposition to the system.[223] As Michael Ellman and Vladimir Kontorovich point out that discontent arose as a product, not a cause, of the reform. Personal consumption of Soviet citizens had increased between 1975 and 1985. Even though the Soviet standard of living reached only one-third to one-fifth of the American level, a general appreciation existed that Soviet citizens enjoyed greater security, lower crime, and a higher cultural and moral level than citizens in the West did. Moreover, empirical studies in the mid-1980s revealed that Soviet and American workers expressed about the same degree of satisfaction with their jobs. As late as 1990, only a small minority favored a transition to a capitalist system. Barely 4 percent of Soviet citizens favored the removal of price controls, and only 18 per cent favored the encouragement of private property.[224]

The absence of an acute economic crisis and mass discontent did not mean that all was well. Soviet society faced manifold problems in economics, politics, and foreign affairs. A failure to address them might have eventually produced a crisis. Even such Communists as Yegor Ligachev and Gennady Zyuganov, who became strong critics of Gorbachev, acknowledged the severity of the problems that led to the reforms. Ligachev recalled that he "like many other provincial Party secretaries was impatient for change, [and was] uncomfortably aware that the country was headed for social and economic disaster."[225] Similarly, Zyuganov recalled, "The need for reforms had been obvious to everyone."[226]

The most threatening domestic problems of all were economic. In his first policy speech to a plenum of the Central Committee on November 22, 1982, Yuri Andropov provided a useful summary of the economic problems. Andropov mentioned the quantity and quality of consumer goods, the shortage of certain foods, the waste of energy resources, the poor performance of transport, and the failure of iron and steel enterprises to meet their targets. What linked many of these problems for Andropov was the failure to employ the discoveries of science and technology. This failure was reflected in unsatisfactory progress in increasing productivity, intensifying production methods, and economizing material resources. These failures were in part traceable to a planning system that placed too much emphasis on the achievement of quantitative production goals. Since improving products and production methods could temporarily reduce or slow production, there was a built-in disincentive to innovate.

Abel Aganbegyan, who headed the Institute of Economics and Industrial Organization of the Siberian branch of the Academy of Sciences from 1967 until 1985, when he became Gorbachev's key economic advisor, described numerous economic problems. Though overstating the case, Aganbegyan expressed the thinking of Gorbachev's inner circle. Aganbegyan traced most of the economic problems to over-centralization. These included waste and inefficiency, a lack of worker motivation, an absence of initiative, a weakness in productivity increases, and a poor diffusion of technological innovations. Because of a weak connection between producers and consumers, the system produced more tractors and shoes than consumers needed, but fewer quality items than consumers wanted. Consumer dissatisfaction fostered the black market and corruption. For various reasons, some of which had to do with the depletion of cheap natural resources and the demographic shortage of workers due to World War II, the rate of economic growth began to suffer. Though the economy grew between 1975 and 1985, the rate of growth slacked off in terms of national income, real per capita income, productive capital investment, number of workers in production, and productivity of labor.[227] According to Aganbegyan, at the end of the 1970s and early 1980s, "stagnation had occurred in the economy."[228]

The dissatisfaction with the slow improvement of living standards was no doubt amplified by the increasing ease with which Soviet citizens could make invidious comparisons with the West. As détente, travel, and communication brought greater awareness of how citizens lived in the West, the gap in living standards challenged the claims that socialism was leading to a better life. Fred Halliday said, "Once the living standards gap became evident then the residual legitimacy of the communist political system was swept away and that of the alternative system, the Western variant of pluralism, was enhanced."[229] Public opinion polls contradicted Halliday's exaggerated claims, yet Halliday may well have captured the fears of Soviet leaders over where a growing gap in living standards might lead.

If economic problems provided the major backdrop of *perestroika*, political problems ran close behind. The problems within the Party itself had deep roots. World War II had denuded the Party of millions of dedicated cadre who had died at the front defending socialism and the homeland. Khrushchev further weakened the Party by opening wide its doors to millions of non-workers and lowering Party standards. Leonid Brezhnev's "stability of cadre" doctrine turned Party positions into sinecures, kept Party leaders in office long past their prime, and deprived the Party of fresh blood and ideas. Moreover, as the second economy grew, it increasingly enmeshed and corrupted elements of the Party. Under Brezhnev, corruption- -according to one historian--"flourished to a fabulous extent," reaching even Brezhnev's own family.[230] In many places, nepotism, patronage, protectionism, and sycophancy prevailed. Party meetings became top-down, routine, and formal. Ideology became formulaic, and more and more intellectuals and even Party members refused to take it seriously.

Nothing symbolized the political and ideological ossification more than the senescence, illness, and death in office of the three leaders that preceded Gorbachev. The Politburo's elevation of Gorbachev, its youngest member, to the post of General Secretary reflected a widespread concern over the perceived decrepitude of the Party leaders. Gorbachev was well aware of this. He later noted that "people were sick" of having a Politburo whose average age was around seventy and many of whose members had held their posts for twenty or thirty years and were too ill to function.[231]

A third problem in the backdrop of reform had to do foreign relations. Though the Soviet Union had never been free of imperialist pressure, this pressure increased under President Jimmy Carter and increased even more under President Ronald Reagan. Between 1981 and 1986, the Reagan administration launched a "full court press"[232] against the "evil empire" designed to shrink its foreign influence and damage its economy. This campaign involved support for the Solidarity movement in Poland and the counterrevolutionary guerillas in Afghanistan, an effort to diminish Soviet gold reserves by driving down the price of oil, an increased propaganda offensive, diplomatic moves to reduce Soviet access to Western technology, the disruption of the Soviet economy by exporting faulty equipment, and an effort to bankrupt the Soviets by initiating a military build-up spearheaded by the Strategic Defense Initiative, Star Wars.[233]

A few details suggest the scope and results of this campaign. The United States was giving $8 million a year to the Polish opposition group, Solidarity, and supplying it with sophisticated communication equipment, computers, fax machines, printing equipment, and intelligence information. U.S. sanctions against Poland required the Soviet Union to send the country $1 to $2 billion a year in aid. Led by the efforts of CIA chief William Casey, the administration trained Afghans, sent them artillery and rockets, and induced the Egyptians, Saudis, and Chinese to send them aid. The Soviet military effort to protect the Afghan revolutionary government against the American-supported war lords cost the Soviets $3 to $4 billion a year.[234]

The American government worked systematically with the Saudis and OPEC to lower the price of oil on the world market, a move that aided the American economy while devastating the Soviets, who depended on oil sales for the bulk of their hard currency. The Reagan administration agreed to sell advanced military planes and Stinger missiles to the Saudis in return for greater oil production and lower prices. In 1983, under U.S. pressure, the Organization of Petroleum Exporting Countries (OPEC) cut the price of oil from $34 to $29 a barrel. In 1985, the Saudis increased their oil production from less than 2 million barrels a day to 9 million barrels. Within five months, the price of oil fell to $12 a barrel. As writer Peter Schweizer noted, "For

Moscow, over $10 billion in valuable hard currency evaporated overnight, almost half its earnings."[235]

The Reagan administration also engaged in technological warfare. Beginning in December 1981, Reagan instituted an embargo of American gas and oil equipment to the Soviet Union. In June 1982, he extended the sanctions to American licensees and subsidiaries abroad. In November 1982, Reagan signed the National Security Decision Directive NSDD-66, whose principal author described it as "a secret declaration of economic war on the Soviet Union." Among its goals was to deny high technology to the Soviet Union and reduce European imports of Soviet gas and oil. By 1983, American high-tech exports to the Soviet Union were valued at only $39 million compared to $219 million in 1975. This economic warfare did not stop with denying the Soviets access to high-tech; the U.S. also sabotaged the goods the Soviets did receive. In 1984, for example, the U.S. supplied the Soviet Union with faulty blueprints for gas turbine components and through middlemen sold the Soviet Union defective computer chips. Such moves cost the Soviet Union untold time and money.[236]

Part of Reagan's destabilization effort involved an escalation of the ideological warfare waged by Radio Free Europe and Radio Liberty. Between 1982 and 1986, both stations increased the number and sophistication of their foreign-language broadcasts, as well as the number of their listeners. As *glasnost* reduced and then eliminated jamming in 1988, Radio Liberty reached 22 million Soviet listeners a month. Both stations fomented nationalism, stirred up outrage over the Chernobyl disaster, encouraged opposition to the Soviet war in Afghanistan, provided a platform for pro-market advocates like Yeltsin, and aired unsubstantiated corruption charges against the Party leader, Yegor Ligachev, after he opposed Gorbachev.[237]

The most serious part of the U.S. strategy called for increasing the military pressure on the Soviet Union, a strategy that some American analysts called "spending them into bankruptcy."[238]

In his first news conference as president, Reagan declared the Soviet Union would "commit any crime," would lie and cheat to achieve its goal of world domination. Shortly thereafter, Reagan began "the largest peace-time military buildup in American history." This meant a military expenditure of $1.5 trillion in five years and plans to develop a Stealth bomber, to build hundreds of MX missiles, Multiple Independently-Targeted Re-entry Vehicles (MIRVed missiles), cruise missiles, and new B-1 bombers, and Trident submarines. The keystone of this ratcheting up of military pressure would be a fabulously expensive and futuristic missile defense system. On March 23, 1983, in a speech on national defense, President Reagan announced that he had decided to embark on the research and development to build such a system. Two years later, Reagan asked Congress for $26 billion to launch the Strategic Defensive Initiative.[239]

The Reagan policies cost the Soviet Union billions of dollars of income because of falling oil and gas prices and lost oil and gas sales. It cost extra billions for aid to Poland and Afghanistan and to compensate for unavailable technology and sabotaged technology. Though some Soviet experts dismissed SDI as a bluff, others thought it, along with the other American moves, represented a real threat.[240] According to Roald Z. Sagdayev, who headed the Soviet Space Research Institute, after 1983 the Soviet Union spent tens of billions of dollars responding to Star Wars. Gorbachev's predecessor, Chernenko, said, "The complex international situation has forced us to divert a great deal of resources to strengthening the security of our country."[241]

In March 1985, when Mikhail Gorbachev became General Secretary of the CPSU, he quickly established himself as a leader who was willing to confront problems and undertake bold, new initiatives. At first, Gorbachev resumed the course charted by Andropov. Gorbachev's initiatives met with some success and were enthusiastically greeted at home and abroad, including by the Soviet Communist Party, where in spite of some grumbling that he was either going too far or not far enough, no determined opposition arose. Before his first two years were over, Gorbachev began departing from Andropov's style and substance and started adopting policies that resembled Khrushchev's.

Gorbachev was born in Privolnoye, a farming village of 3000, located in the southern agricultural *krai* (region) of Stavropol, 124 miles from the city of Stavropol. This area of the Caucasus grew wheat and sunflowers and contained mineral spas and resorts. In the early 1930s, Stavropol participated in the collectivization of agriculture, in which Gorbachev's grandfather had played a role. During the war, in which seven of Gorbachev's relatives died, the Germans occupied and destroyed much of Stavropol. The destruction was still visible from the train that Gorbachev took to Moscow to attend Lomonosov State University in 1950. The Red Banner of Labor that Gorbachev achieved as a combine operator aided his acceptance at the university, where he studied the Western intellectual tradition and public speaking and obtained a law degree. Gorbachev would become the first General Secretary since Lenin with a college degree. While a student, Gorbachev joined the Communist Party, and according to one who knew him, "venerated"[242] Lenin. Also, while a student, Gorbachev married Raissa, a philosophy student.

After graduation, Gorbachev returned to Stavropol, where he remained for the next twenty-three years. Instead of practicing law, Gorbachev undertook the life of a Party professional and became known for his devotion and hard work. Through correspondence courses, he attained a second degree in agronomy. A Czechoslovak friend from college, who kept in touch with Gorbachev, reported that Gorbachev sympathized with the Czech leader, Alexander Dubcek, whose reforms led to the Soviet intervention in 1968. Such views did not impede Gorbachev's steady rise. In 1970, at the age of thirty-nine,

Gorbachev became the first secretary of the Stavropol region, a position roughly equivalent to the governor of a state of 2.4 million people. At the same time, he was elected to the Supreme Soviet. The following year, Gorbachev became a member of the Central Committee. In these posts, Gorbachev gained respect as an authority in agriculture. In 1978, partially through the influence of Andropov, who also came from Stavropol, Gorbachev gained appointment as the head of the Central Committee's agricultural department, a position that brought him to Moscow. The next year, he became a member of the Politburo, where his youth, vigor, hard work and long hours made him stand out.

At the time of his selection as General Secretary, Gorbachev had considerable assets. Along with being educated, charming, and energetic, he had training and talent as a public speaker. When widespread concern existed about the vitality of the Soviet leadership, he had the advantage of being the youngest member of the Politburo. He was married to an intelligent and stylish woman. As early as 1983, he had made it clear that he favored reform. In December 1984, in a speech to an ideological conference of the Central Committee, Gorbachev called for *glasnost* (openness) in public communications and *perestroika* (restructuring) of the economic system.[243] Nonetheless, Gorbachev seemed to be a cautious and reliable team player. He had particularly acquitted himself well during Chernenko's sickness, when according to Andrei Gromyko, he had chaired Politburo meetings "brilliantly."[244]

Still, Gorbachev had manifest weaknesses that became more glaring over time. All bureaucracies rely to some extent on patronage for advancement, and Gorbachev's rise proved no exception. It depended less on original accomplishments, even in his chosen field of agriculture, than on the fortunate attention of well-positioned patrons, like Andropov. His acquaintance with many national Party leaders who vacationed at the spas in Stavropol probably aided Gorbachev's advancement as well.

Moreover, his education notwithstanding, Gorbachev had little experience with Soviet life outside of agriculture and the Party. Before becoming General Secretary, he had traveled more widely in Western Europe and Canada than in the outlying republics of the Soviet Union, and unlike every previous Soviet leader, he lacked any experience living or working in the non-Russian parts of the country.[245] He also lacked experience with the military, foreign affairs, industry, science, technology, and the trade unions.[246] Though he liked to toss out quotations from Lenin, he lacked a deep knowledge or understanding of Marxist theory and Soviet history, both of which he distorted to suit his purposes. Historian Anthony D'Agostino said that a skeptic might well have noted that Gorbachev "was a lawyer who had never practiced law, who had spent a long career in agriculture, who knew nothing of foreign affairs, who had got the attention of his superiors because he was First Secretary in a resort area, whose qualifications were rather like those of Prince Rainier of Monaco or the mayor of Las Vegas."[247]

Moreover, Gorbachev suffered from the contradictions of an educated provincial. For most of his life he had been a big fish in a little pond. This helped make him vain, condescending, and ruthless to subordinates but deferential to the powerful and worldly. It also gave him a taste for fine wine, good food, and the other trappings of a cosmopolitan lifestyle. Several incidents revealed his arrogance. Even though Andrei Gromyko, the senior member of the Politburo, nominated Gorbachev as General Secretary, four years later Gorbachev did not attend his funeral.[248] Similarly, Gorbachev condescended to other Politburo members, all of whom were his senior, by addressing them in the familiar but belittling thou (ty) form. Gorbachev's ruthlessness was on full display on November 11, 1987, when he ordered his critic, Boris Yeltsin to leave a hospital bed, where he was having chest pains, and attend a meeting of the Moscow City Party Committee that berated him for hours and then removed him as Moscow Chair.[249]

As General Secretary, Gorbachev initially followed Andropov's policies. Like Andropov, Gorbachev called for an acceleration of scientific and technological progress, the improvement of management, and an increase in discipline. In foreign affairs, particularly in terms of relations with the U.S., Andropov had been constrained by hostile circumstances not of his making. Nonetheless, he had shown a desire to reduce tensions with the U.S. and to make progress on nuclear disarmament, and had shown flexibility in hopes of advancing toward these goals. Soviet Ambassador Dobrynin believed that in a more favorable international situation than the one he inherited, Andropov "would have been ready for serious agreements with Washington, especially in limiting nuclear arms. In this he somewhat resembled Mikhail Gorbachev, who was his protégé."[250] In tackling political stagnation, Andropov had called for a restoration of Leninist standards: collective leadership, self-criticism, discipline, modesty, honesty, and hard work--standards to which he had held himself. Andropov had started to rid the Party of time-servers, corruption, formalism, and cynicism, to revive an interest in ideology, and to elevate such honest and diligent local leaders as Yegor Ligachev and, supposedly, Gorbachev.

Addressing the Central Committee for the first time as General Secretary in March 1985 in a speech entitled, "Our Course Remains Unchanged," and a second time in April 1985, Gorbachev invoked Andropov's name and slogans. He called for social and economic acceleration, transferring the economy onto "the rails of intensive development," and quickly attaining "the most advanced scientific and technical positions." He also called for "strengthening discipline" and perfecting "the entire management system." Gorbachev advocated the elimination of wage leveling. In a swipe at the illegal parts of the second economy and corruption, he called for a struggle against "unearned incomes" and all "phenomena that are alien to the socialist way of life." In foreign policy, Gorbachev reaffirmed such traditional Soviet positions as the support of national liberation, peaceful coexistence, and cooperation with the West on "principles of equality." He gave special emphasis on ending the arms race and freezing nuclear arsenals. In politics, Gorbachev proposed "strengthening" and "heightening" the leading role of the Party, a "strict observance of the Leninist style of work" and the elimination of "false idealization" and formalism in Party meetings. Gorbachev spoke of the need for *glasnost*, or "greater openness and publicity" about the work of the Party, state and other public organizations.[251]

In deeds as well as words, Gorbachev resembled Andropov. In 1985, Gorbachev's economic policies had two thrusts. The first was to improve the "human factor" through the promotion of new cadre and through increased "discipline." The second was to move from "extensive" to "intensive" growth by changing investment policy in order to retool and modernize existing factories. Gorbachev encouraged discussion on ways to improve discipline and restructure the economy.[252] In May 1985, to improve work discipline, Gorbachev launched a campaign against alcohol consumption, a serious social problem that for years had eroded family life and health, as well as reduced labor productivity. Andropov had increased the penalties for public drunkenness; Gorbachev went further. He slashed the production of vodka and limited the hours of vodka sales.[253] In June 1985, Gorbachev devoted a plenary of the Central Committee to the scientific and technological revolution. This resulted in the creation of twenty-three new technical research complexes.[254] In October, Gorbachev changed the five-year plan in order to increase investment in machine-building and raise the technical level of production.[255] Gorbachev accompanied these moves with an explicit rejection of market reforms. In May, Gorbachev said, "Many of you see the solution to your problems in resorting to market mechanisms in place of direct planning. Some of you look at the market as a lifesaver for your economics. But, comrades, you should not think about life-savers but about the ship, and the ship is socialism."[256]

Gorbachev made two other economic moves that resembled Andropov's. In order to raise the quality of industrial goods, nineteen enterprises initiated quality control measures similar to those that worked effectively in the armament industry. In early 1986, the Council of Ministers created a state quality control body (*gospriemka*) with the authority to regulate the quality of production at the most important enterprises, including those producing consumer goods. Gorbachev also launched an attack on wage leveling, a practice that had reduced the differential between the wages of an industrial specialist and an average worker from 146 percent in 1965 to 110 percent in 1986. Under the new system, the wages of industrial specialists and of workers in research, development, education, and health care would increase more than the wages of other workers.[257]

During his first year, Gorbachev tried to break the logjam in American-Soviet relations. The situation he faced was daunting. Soviet-American relations had deteriorated since 1979, when the United States began arming the counterrevolutionaries in Afghanistan, and the Soviets had responded to the Afghan government's call for help by sending troops. To punish the Soviet Union, President Carter ended arms negotiations and imposed an agricultural boycott. Thereafter, for six years, not a single meeting of the U.S. and Soviet high officials had occurred.

In the spring of 1985, Gorbachev reaffirmed the traditional elements of Soviet foreign policy while initiating some new moves. He repeated the Soviet commitment to peace and peaceful co-existence on the basis of a military and strategic balance with the West. He underscored the Soviet Union's solidarity with socialist states and with peoples fighting for their freedom and independence. Gorbachev supported the new revolutionary government of Nicaragua.[258] He intensified the Soviet military effort in Afghanistan.[259] He increased the Soviet support of the African National Congress (ANC), including the military training of ANC activists.

At the same time, Gorbachev took steps to improve the international atmosphere with the U.S. and Western Europe. In May, he accepted a proposal from President Reagan for a summit. In July, he announced a unilateral moratorium on nuclear testing. In September, he proposed a 50 percent reduction in strategic nuclear warheads. In October, while visiting France, Gorbachev announced a unilateral reduction in Soviet intermediate-range missiles directed at Europe.[260] In November in Geneva, Gorbachev and Reagan held the first summit meeting in years. Though no substantive agreements emerged, a frank and friendly exchange of views occurred. At this time, Gorbachev told Reagan some accommodation might be possible on Afghanistan.[261] Gorbachev's actions in 1985 produced a palpable relaxation of international tensions.

Gorbachev also took steps that looked like efforts to address the political stagnation, corruption, and ideological weaknesses of the CPSU, though in many cases they simply involved promoting his supporters. At the top, Eduard Shevardnadze replaced Gromyko as Foreign Minister. N. I. Ryzhkov replaced Nikolai Tikhonov as premier. Boris Yeltsin was appointed head of the Moscow Party. While criticizing the "personal loyalty, servility, and protectionism" that marked the operation of the Party in many republics, Gorbachev replaced officials in Latvia, Lithuania, and Byelorussia. Moves against corrupt local officials occurred in Uzbekistan, Azerbaijan, and Kirghizia. The shakeup was far-reaching. Within a year, Gorbachev replaced over 50 percent of the full and candidate members of the Politburo. He replaced fourteen of the twenty-three heads of Central Committee departments, five of fourteen heads of Republics, and 50 of 157 first secretaries of *krais* (regions) and *oblasts* (districts). Gorbachev replaced 40 percent of the ambassadors, shook up many ministries, and removed fifty thousand managers. In the Ministry of Instruments (in charge of computers and electronics), Gorbachev had a thousand personnel replaced.[262]

Serious Communists especially welcomed Gorbachev's early treatment of ideology. Not only did Gorbachev recognize the preeminent role of ideology, but also he recognized that over the years the Party's ideology had become ossified and formulaic, and parts diverged from reality. In particular, Gorbachev modified two ideas that had gained a new meaning under Brezhnev. The first was the idea that capitalism had entered a period of general crisis, and the second was the idea that the Soviet Union had entered the period of "developed socialism." Earlier, Andropov had recognized the inadequacy of these concepts. He asked how it could be that under capitalism in crisis workers were living better than under developed socialism. In a similar vein, Gorbachev said, "Divergence of words from reality dramatically devalues ideological efforts."[263] While not discarding the concepts of the general crisis of capitalism and developed socialism, he changed their meaning. Gorbachev pointed out that the general crisis of capitalism did not imply that capitalism was not still growing and mastering science and technology. More importantly, Gorbachev demoted the idea of developed socialism by saying that its realization was dependent upon the acceleration of economic and social progress. Moreover, he said that the idea of developed socialism had shifted over time giving rise to unwarranted complacency. Under this idea, he said, "things were not infrequently reduced to just registering success, while many of the urgent problems... were not given due attention. Willy-nilly, this was a peculiar vindication of sluggishness in solving remaining problems. Today when the Party has proclaimed and is pursuing the policy of accelerating socio-economic development, this approach has become unacceptable."[264]

Gorbachev also ushered in a style or culture of Party life that seemingly drew inspiration from both Lenin and Andropov. He called on the Party "to build a bridge to Lenin, to connect Lenin's ideas, Lenin's approach to the problems of those years and the issues of our own day."[265] He adopted a style of speaking forthrightly and bluntly about problems. At Party meetings, he dispensed with the practice of everyone speaking on every question and of everyone routinely praising Party leaders. He called on Communists to struggle systematically "against ostentation, arrogance, eulogies, and bootlicking."[266] He asked editors of newspapers and magazines to stop "personal adulation."[267] Gorbachev called for Communists to become political leaders and not just officials and administrators. Following his own advice, Gorbachev traveled around the country and met with workers on collective farms, factories, and markets. He invited intellectuals, cultural figures, and media representatives to the Kremlin. His public appearances with his wife, informal meetings with foreign leaders, and interviews with foreign editors and reporters signaled a modern, assertive, and open style that was long overdue and breathtakingly fresh. The American Communist correspondent, Mike Davidow, who was stationed in Moscow, said, "Gorbachev's first days and months were electrifying. His speeches and person-to-person talks with Leningrad workers put the first cracks in the ice of stagnation."[268]

Gorbachev's early initiatives evoked nearly universal approval. In the West, Communist Parties, the peace movement, liberal politicians, and common citizens hailed his call for new thinking about peace. Gus Hall, head of the Communist Party of the United States, praised the Soviet leader's "new thinking" for having reduced anti-Sovietism, lessened world tensions, and shrunk the danger of nuclear war.[269] At home, enthusiastic crowds greeted Gorbachev's visits to markets and workplaces. In 1985, Soviet citizens sent 40,000 letters a month to the Kremlin, and in following year 60,000 a month, most of which supported what Gorbachev was saying and doing.[270] Even though Gorbachev removed many people from their positions in the Party and ministries, his support remained solid. In the face of new demands, some griping and inertia in the bureaucracy inevitably occurred, but no organized opposition. Even Yegor Ligachev and Boris Yeltsin, who would become Gorbachev's leading critics on the left and the right, fully supported *perestroika*. Before 1987, when Gorbachev alluded to the opponents of reform, he was largely engaging in a pre-emptive strike rather than responding to any real threat.

The widespread support for Gorbachev was quite under-standable. He was addressing problems that were perceived as central to the Soviet system by academic researchers, Party professionals, and the man and woman on the street. His moves on disarmament began to address the economic drain of the arms race. His replacement of cadre, exposure of corruption, and calls for greater openness and criticism attacked the political stagnation that had become so pervasive.

If Gorbachev initially followed a reform path that resembled Andropov's, he eventually would adopt a different path--adopting market solutions and private property, weakening the Communist Party, abandoning international solidarity, and making unilateral concessions to the West. When and why did Gorbachev change his course? Neither question is easy to answer. When the move began is difficult to specify because the rhetoric and the policies of reform sometimes moved in contradictory directions at once. Still, as we shall see, some clear signs of a move against socialism became evident within the first two years of Gorbachev's tenure, though it would not become dominant until after January 1987. Why Gorbachev changed is also hard to answer because fathoming anyone's motives is problematic. Consequently, the best we can provide is a plausible explanation.

Before examining the first signs of change, let us suggest three hypotheses as to why this shift occurred. We will argue that the first two hypotheses are flawed and that only the third provides a plausible explanation. The first hypothesis is that Gorbachev was always a social democrat or a Communist with

104

capitalist sympathies and that his early Andropov-sounding rhetoric and policies just represented political gamesmanship to keep his opponents off balance until he had the strength and opportunity to push his real agenda. The second hypothesis is that Gorbachev turned to market-oriented and Party-weakening reforms because the Andropov-type reforms proved ineffective. In other words, Gorbachev turned to capitalist economic ideas because improving the economy within the boundaries of Soviet socialism proved too difficult. He began weakening the Party because he saw the Party as an obstacle to far-reaching economic reforms.

The third hypothesis, the one advanced here, is that Gorbachev turned away from socialism and toward capitalism because he lacked the strength and sense of purpose to withstand the anti-socialist interests unleashed by the reform process. These interests had developed for years in those parts of the society and the Party enmeshed in illegal, private economic activity, but they had remained more or less dormant until the upheaval of reform. The second economy had exacerbated the chronic problems of Soviet society, had eroded confidence in socialism and the Communist Party, and had created a sizable, confident and growing social base of would-be capitalists. Hence, even before 1985, the second economy had created conditions favorable to anti-socialist and pro-capitalist ideas and policies. Gorbachev's early reforms galvanized this sector's demands for "freedom" and legitimacy. Theoretically weak, inexperienced, impulsive, and ambitious, Gorbachev vacillated and then capitulated. His desire for quick, painless, short-term success and for the adulation and political security this would bring led him to throw his lot with the growing stratum of bureaucrats and petty entrepreneurs tied to the second economy and their defenders and sympathizers among the intelligentsia.

Many who hate Gorbachev for destroying socialism, as well as some who applaud him for doing so, find the first hypothesis appealing. To be sure, some evidence supported the idea that Gorbachev had social democratic sympathies even before he became General Secretary. For example, two of his friends before 1985 were Alexander Yakovlev and Edward Shevardnadze, two of the most extreme social democratic elements in his administration. Other evidence suggested that Gorbachev held private objectives that went beyond his public views. Yakovlev said that as early as the fall of 1985, Gorbachev expressed secret sympathy with the idea of dividing the Communist Party in two but warned that such a move was premature. The present state of knowledge makes it impossible to say with absolute certainty that Gorbachev was not dissembling when, for example, he declared his fealty to Lenin and socialism. Even more information might not reveal Gorbachev's true thoughts and motivations, which are always difficult to know of anyone.

Yet, to believe that Gorbachev held social democratic or pro-capitalist views before becoming General Secretary confronts some intractable questions and stubborn facts. If Gorbachev did not adopt these ideas after becoming General Secretary, just when did he adopt them? How was it possible for someone with these views to conceal them so successfully and rise to the top while holding them? Gorbachev himself never claimed to have had a calculated and coherent plan to destroy the Communist Party and institute a free market and private property. Moreover, Ligachev and others who worked closely with the Soviet leader did not suspect him of harboring a secret revisionist agenda. This idea does appear in the writings of such outsiders as the economist Anders Aslund, who asserted that as early as 1984 Gorbachev had "a clear idea" of market-oriented economic reform. On close inspection, however, Aslund's evidence showed no more than that early on Gorbachev advocated an eclectic mix of reform ideas. He entertained some ideas like cost accounting and increased competition that vaguely foreshadowed his later embrace of the market, but he mainly proposed ideas pioneered by Andropov such as a changed investment policy to promote new technology and new measures to enhance discipline and crack down on unearned incomes.[271] Ellman and Kontorovich are nearer the mark than Aslund, when they note that Gorbachev's economic contributions in 1982-84 revealed not only no plan but also no coherence.[272]

What was true was that Gorbachev's background and experience made him uncommonly sympathetic to the second economy and susceptible to pro-capitalist ideas. For one thing, Stavropol, his home base, had a highly developed private or second economy with its attendant petty bourgeois mentality.[273] Moreover, he had traveled more widely in the West than many other Soviet leaders, and he may well have been influenced by Italian Eurocommunism, whose ideas later echoed in his speeches.[274] Thirdly, early on Gorbachev surrounded himself with advisors who held pronounced social democratic views. For example, he relied on such market-oriented intellectuals as Tatyana Zaslavskaya and Abel Aganbegyan.[275] In 1986, he hired as a consultant the philosopher, Alexander Tsipko, a self-admitted anti-Marxist, who later claimed that Gorbachev's idea of elevating "universal human values" over class values came from him.[276] Gorbachev's path would soon resemble the one Shevardnadze had followed in Georgia, the republic with "the largest second economy in the USSR," where Shevardnadze had tried to co-opt the second economy "by making the official economy more market-oriented."[277]

The hypothesis that from the start Gorbachev had a secret agenda to destroy Soviet socialism and move toward a Western European model is a hard sell. At best one could say that some things in his background might have predisposed him to move in that direction. After his initial reforms shook things up, Gorbachev--who lacked any plan--succumbed to this predisposition and abandoned Andropov's path because his own weakness and inexperience made him ill-equipped to deal with the forces released by change, because he hoped to buy time and obtain resources by giving in to pressure from U.S., and most importantly, because doing so won him the passive support of those disaffected with the system and the active support of the ascendant stratum of entrepreneurs and corrupt Party officials tied to the second economy.

The second hypothesis involves the assumption that the problems of the Soviet economy stemmed from socialism itself. It assumes that the economy could not be improved while retaining socialized property and central planning. This hypothesis appeals to Gorbachev supporters who see him tragically driven to an extreme and ultimately disastrous course by the immutability of both the economic system and the Party. This hypothesis also has the appeal of common sense. Common sense would say that if Gorbachev's initial efforts had revitalized the economy, Gorbachev would have had no need for stronger medicine. Therefore his initial efforts must have failed either because of the inherent constraints of the economic system or because of their undoing by those in the Party opposed to reform. History, however, does not always follow the logic of common sense, and history's truth is often counter-intuitive. Only an examination of the actual history can provide an answer.

When and why Gorbachev began moving to the right, toward capitalism, pivots on the answer to three questions: 1. What were the results of Gorbachev's early efforts at economic reform? That is, were the results a failure, and did they reveal the impossibility of moderate reform? 2. What was the Party's response to the economic problems? Did it resist reform? 3. Did Gorbachev's first rightward moves involve the economy? Only if the answers to these questions clearly showed that the moderate reform failed that the Party resisted economic reform, and that Gorbachev's first moves to the right concerned the economy could the second hypothesis be true. In all three areas, the truth was far different.

The hypothesis that Gorbachev turned to the right because moderate economic reform did not work could be true only if the initial economic reform failed. This was not true. The economic changes brought about by Gorbachev's early policies were not an unalloyed success, but they brought definite signs of improvement. In 1985 and 1986 both production and consumption increased.[278] Economic growth went up 1 to 2 percent in the early reform period. Productivity increased from 2-3 percent to 4.5 percent. In 1986 in the machine industry alone, capital investment increased by 30 percent, more than in the preceding five years. The same year agricultural production grew by 5 percent.[279] The consumption of goods and services increased by 10 percent in 1985 and 1986, about one and a half time greater than in the preceding years. Improvements in health care and other areas increased life expectancy for the first time in twenty years and lowered infant mortality.[280]

Gorbachev also registered some notable failures, particularly when he acted rashly. This happened with the anti-alcohol campaign. Gorbachev slashed alcohol production and sales, but this spawned rampant bootlegging. The production of illegal vodka depleted the stores of sugar and drained billions of rubles in tax revenue from the state budget. Had he based his policies on experiences elsewhere, Gorbachev would have realized that reducing the production of alcohol was bound to lead to illegal production and sales, just as Prohibition did in the United States. A campaign based on consumption taxes, education, counseling, and rehabilitation would have held greater promise. Within two years, Gorbachev abandoned the anti-alcohol campaign.[281] Similarly, Gorbachev's policy of accelerating production simply led to the increased production of shoddy goods. When Gorbachev countered with a system of state inspectors, the amount of goods rejected as substandard was so great that an outcry arose among workers who found their income reduced. Gorbachev had to abandon the inspectors just as he abandoned the anti-alcohol campaign.[282] These failures involved impulsive measures aimed at quick returns. They were not representative of the economic reforms of the first year, which yielded positive results.

The hypothesis that Gorbachev turned to the right because the other Party leaders opposed any economic reform is also false. It was far from the case that Party leaders resisted efforts to improve the economy. Ellman and Kontorovich, who based their study of economic reform on interviews with Soviet insiders, said that their interviews "provide no evidence of resistance to reforms."[283] The very reverse was true. The economist Aslund, who lived in Moscow in the 1980s and was himself a partisan of market reforms, nonetheless acknowledged that "all the new Soviet leaders want change." Even the Brezhnevites on the Politburo--Gaidar Aliev, Viktor Grishin, Dimukhamed Kunaev, Vladimir Shcherbitski and Nikolai Tikhonov--supported economic changes to move the Soviet economy toward the model of the German Democratic Republic (GDR). Moreover, Aslund identified three other economic reform currents among Soviet leaders that were more far-reaching than the Brezhnevites but still short of the marketization and privatization later advocated by Gorbachev's group. One group led by Prime Minister Nikolai Ryzhkov saw the solution to economic problems as residing in greater efficiency and the intensification of production. This group advocated such measures as the better utilization of scientific results, a new investment policy concentrated on machine building and experimentation with self-financing at enterprises. Another group led by Lev Zaikov, who became Central Committee Secretary for the military-industrial complex in July 1985, supported changes in investment policy to encourage machine building and scientific and technological progress, as well such measures as quality inspection, wage differentials, and the promotion of shift work. This group, however, was less enthusiastic than Ryzhkov's about self-financing or anything that smacked of markets and competition.[284]

A third group led by the Party's second in command, Ligachev, put its major emphasis on improving discipline. Ligachev favored the anti-alcohol campaign, and moves against consumerism, the second economy and corruption. Ligachev favored wage differentials, and he favored strengthening and streamlining centralized planning and increasing the efficiency and responsibility of individual enterprises. He supported, for example, experiments in self-financing, better enterprise accounting, and collective contracts but adamantly opposed any moves toward private property and a market economy. Ligachev endorsed changes in the economy outlined at the scientific and technical conference in June 1985 but added that the changes would occur "within the framework of scientific socialism, without any aberrations whatsoever in the direction of 'market economy' and private enterprise."[285]

The receptiveness of Party leaders to economic reform was reflected in the widespread economic experimentation at the regional and local level that began under Andropov and continued under Chernenko and Gorbachev. For example, in 1983, the Central Committee and Council of Ministers began what was called the "large-scale economic experiment," which involved reducing plan indicators and using bonus systems in five ministries. The experiment was no panacea, but it did lead to improvement in the delivery of goods and to greater labor efficiency. Eventually, the experiment expanded to embrace twenty-one ministries by 1985 and half of industrial production by 1986. In 1985 two experiments in self-financing began at the VAZ plant in Togliatti on the Volga, a car manufacturer, and in the Frunze plant in Sumy in the Ukraine, a manufacturer of natural gas equipment. This experiment involved simplifying the payment transactions between the firms and the state to a simple "tax" based on profits and correlating wage increases with productivity increases. Both experiments produced impressive results in terms of profits and productivity. Other experiments were under way in the service industry and in agriculture.[286]

The point to be made is that in the period 1984 to 1986 a great receptivity to economic reform existed and a great deal of economic experimentation was occurring. Such debate and experimentation was occurring within the boundaries of socialism and had hardly reached a dead-end when Gorbachev began introducing more extreme ideas. The economist Aslund explained this paradox this way: "[For the reform economists around Gorbachev] the actual economic results [of these experiments] were of little interest, while their political impact was everything. Many experiments were designed to perfect the system, while leading Soviet economists and the Gorbachev camp wanted to replace it with a more market-oriented system."[287] In other words, certain economists and advisors in the Gorbachev camp were already committed to market reforms and privatization, and they used the experiments within the existing framework mainly to provide arguments for going further. In 1987, the main opposition to the first economic reforms came not from Party leaders, but from the economists around Gorbachev who were eager to push onward to expanded markets and private property.

The third underpinning of the hypothesis that Gorbachev turned to the right because of the failure of the initial reform and Party opposition is as lacking as the first two. Gorbachev's first moves to the right did not arise in the economic arena. Rather, they occurred in politics, ideology, and foreign policy. In these areas as well, Gorbachev's policies bore the most problematic results.

The Twenty-seventh Congress of the CPSU meeting in February 1986 provided an early sign that Gorbachev was taking the reform process in a new, untried direction. This first occurred less as a new policy than as a new ideology of reform itself. Instead of continuity with the past, Gorbachev started stressing a break with the past and referring to the

Brezhnev years as a period of stagnation. He said in both domestic and foreign affairs, developments were at a "turning point" and that "truly revolutionary change" was necessary. He replaced Andropov's term, "acceleration of scientific and technological change" with the vaguer, broader, and potentially more troublesome term, "acceleration of economic and social development." In case anyone missed the shift in meaning, Gorbachev stressed that he was not confining change to the economic field, but envisaging changes in methods of work and political and ideological institutions. At this time, Gorbachev began replacing, *uskornie* (acceleration), with the words, *perestroika* (restructuring) and *glasnost* (openness),[288] while infusing these old terms with new meanings. In April, Gorbachev said *perestroika* meant total change. In June, he said it meant the change of all of society. In July, he said it meant revolution. This broadening gave the concept of *perestroika* dramatic appeal, but it also contained real danger. Namely, these changes in terminology robbed reform of the clear goals it had had under Andropov. *Perestroika*'s meaning became redundant, restructuring for the sake of restructuring; the goal of reform became circular, change for the sake of change.[289] These changes undermined the unity and purpose of the Party that was supposed to lead the change. Inside and outside the Party, the door was thrown open to a variety of interpretations of the ultimate reform goal. For some, the goal remained the perfection of socialism, but for others the goal was national separatism, social democracy, market socialism, capitalism or simply personal enrichment.

Gorbachev also subtly changed and expanded the meaning of *glasnost* in ways that undercut the traditional role of the Party and the function of criticism and self-criticism. During his first year in office, Gorbachev used *glasnost* as Andropov had, to mean greater openness and publicity on the part of the Party, government, state, and other public organizations and more exposure of corruption and inefficiency. In April

1985, for example, Gorbachev called for the release of more administrative information to the public. Soon, Gorbachev transformed *glasnost*'s meaning from openness by the Party and other bodies, to open criticism of the Party and its history. In June, the General Secretary met with media officials and urged them to support the reform effort by making "open, specific, and constructive" criticisms of shortcomings. Soon after, the newspaper *Sovetskaya Rossiya* criticized the Moscow Party head, Viktor Grishin. Gorbachev then replaced him with Boris Yeltsin, a presumed ally.[290]

The full extent of the problems caused by Gorbachev's version of *glasnost* would not become evident until 1987. The basis for these problems, however, occurred in the moves Gorbachev made as early as the fall of 1985. In short, Gorbachev began to encourage intellectuals and the media to criticize the Party and Party history, while simultaneously diminishing the role and authority of the Party over the media. Indeed, he did not simply diminish the Party's oversight of the media, he actually turned the media over to people who were hostile to the CPSU and socialism. While some moves toward the relaxation of censorship and a more relaxed approach to publications and culture were overdue and would have been widely supported in the Party, it nonetheless was a transition that demanded a delicate handling if it were not to lead to instability. Like so much else, Gorbachev's approach to *glasnost* was rash and reckless and would ultimately prove to be extremely foolhardy and destructive not only for the Party and but also the whole society.

In his memoirs, Gorbachev disingenuously claimed, "*Glasnost* broke out of the limits that we had initially tried to frame and became a process that was beyond anybody's control."[291] This is not accurate. By word and deed, Gorbachev himself fostered the very excesses about which he acted helpless. He was enamored with the media and intellectuals, sought their help and approval, met with them frequently, relied on them to build him a base of support outside the Party, incited them to criticize the Party and Party history, and then refused to exercise any restraint whatsoever. At the Twenty-seventh Party Congress, Gorbachev opened the door to criticism without limits. "It is time for literary and art criticism to shake off complacency and servility...and to remember that criticism is a social duty."[292] The next month, Gorbachev and Ligachev met with representatives of the mass media, and Gorbachev said that "the main enemy is bureaucratism, and the press must castigate it without backing off."[293] A truly anomalous situation thus emerged. The General Secretary, who was the leader of the Party and who had the power to reform the Party and government, was inciting attacks from the outside on those very entities, as if he were a mere bystander, not ultimately responsible for them.

This was certainly a major revision of Communist practice. At the very least, it implied that the traditional way of dealing with Party and government weaknesses through collective criticism and self-criticism lacked the force to revitalize the Party. Gorbachev turned to outside criticism as a first rather than last resort. No evidence existed of Gorbachev trying and failing to undertake criticism of the Party, or of his encountering any notable opposition. Yet, in June 1986, Gorbachev told a group of writers that they must function as the "loyal opposition." It was as if the Soviet leader was invoking an old-fashioned, idealized image of the role of the media in liberal democracy--this time as a guide to socialist reform. "We have no opposition [party]," Gorbachev said. "How then are we going to control ourselves? Only through criticism and self-criticism; but most importantly through *glasnost*."[294] Even more consequential than these words were Gorbachev's deeds. While instigating an opposition, Gorbachev systematically reduced the Party's control of the mass media and placed it in the hands of anti-socialists.

Two bodies exercised control of the mass media. The Central Committee's Department of Agitation and Propaganda

(*Agitprop*) that dated from 1920, had ultimate authority over editors and the press. *Glavlit*, a body created in 1922, exercised censorship and approval over every publication and broadcast. In 1985, Gorbachev named Alexander Yakovlev the head of *Agitprop*.[295] In this position and as one of Gorbachev's closest advisors, Yakovlev would wield the most powerful and pernicious influence of anyone on the entire reform process.

Born in 1923, Yakovlev joined the Communist Party while serving in the navy during World War II. After the war, he attended a pedagogical institute and then became a full-time worker for the Party in Yaroslavl.[296] Yakovlev attended the Central Committee's Academy of Social Sciences from 1956 to 1960 and spent the academic year 1958-59 as a graduate student at Columbia University in New York. After graduation, Yakovlev worked for the Propaganda Department of the Central Committee, and by the mid-1960s had become the head of the radio and television section. In 1965 he became first deputy director of the Propaganda Department, a position he held until 1973, when a revealing episode led to his removal.[297]

During the so-called intellectual thaw that occurred under Khrushchev, Russian nationalism grew in popularity particularly in literary circles, a development that under Brezhnev caused a debate within the Party, in which Yakovlev played a prominent part. In 1973, Yakovlev upbraided a Party journal for not being more critical of Russian nationalism. Yakovlev claimed to be upholding Marxism against the danger posed by nationalism, but in actuality, his rigid rejection of national appeals sounded more like Bukharin than Lenin. Moreover, Yakovlev's argument betrayed a pronounced attraction to the West. He argued that Russian nationalism fostered hostility to the West, while he held that Russian development could not be separate from the West.[298]

Meanwhile, Yakovlev's views alienated the Brezhnev leadership and resulted in his transfer abroad. He requested a posting to an English-speaking country and was granted the post of ambassador to Canada. Yakovlev served in this capacity for ten years, which would give him more experience in the West than any other Politburo official.[299] In 1983, Gorbachev visited Canada and spent a week with Yakovlev. Within a month of this trip, Gorbachev helped get Yakovlev appointed director of the prestigious Institute for International Relations and the World Economy (IMEMO) in Moscow.

Thereafter, Yakovlev's rise was meteoric. In 1984, Yakovlev became a corresponding member of the Academy of Sciences. In 1985 Gorbachev appointed him head of the Central Committee's Department of Propaganda (*Agitprop*). The next year, Gorbachev promoted him to Secretary for Propaganda. By then Yakovlev not only exercised authority over the media and cultural affairs, but also enjoyed great influence in foreign policy.[300]

As head of *Agitprop*, Yakovlev worked on several fronts to bring about a total transformation in leading personnel and procedures. He urged the creative unions of writers and filmmakers to adopt a liberal approach to culture, and he pushed some partisans of Gorbachev into leadership positions. For example, at the December 1985 meeting of the Russian Republican Writers' Union, Yakovlev encouraged the poet Yevgeny Yevtushenko to call for a loosening of restrictions on the publication of banned works. In April 1986, at the Congress of the Film Makers Union, Yakovlev personally nominated an ally, Elem Klimov, as First Secretary, and Klimov was elected. Yakovlev also successfully supported the election of Kiril Lavrov as head of the Theater Workers' Union. (Yakovlev's similar attempt to name the head of the Russian Writers' Union failed.)[301] Yakovlev also undoubtedly helped effectuate a major change in *Glavlit*. Some time in late 1985 or early 1986, without any apparent discussion in the Politburo, *Glavlit* relinquished its traditional oversight of publications, and this power fell to the editors of publishing houses and journals.[302] As editors gained new authority over the content of publications, Yakovlev began appointing new editors of major newspapers and journals and new cultural officials who were partisans of fast and far-reaching changes and critics or opponents of the Party. These included the editors of *Novy Mir* (the leading literary monthly), *Znamya* (a journal), *Ogonyok* (a mass circulation weekly), *Moskovskie Novosti* (a newspaper), *Sovetskaya Kultura* (a newspaper), and *Voprosy Literaturny*. He made Yury Voronov head of the Central Committee's Department of Culture and Vasily Zakharov Minister of Culture.[303] Yuri Afanasyev, soon a partisan of Boris Yeltsin, became head of the Moscow State Historical Archives. These men soon took leading roles in criticizing Stalin and the Party and pushing the most rapid and extreme reform measures.

Gorbachev and Yakovlev had a direct hand in determining the direction of *glasnost*. Their actions and sometimes their words implied that they thought *glasnost* editors and intellectuals could best aid the reform effort and put potential opponents on the defensive by attacking Stalin and criticizing the government and Party. As early as late 1985, Yakovlev had permitted the publication of Anastas Mikoyan's memoirs with their criticism of Stalin's wartime policies.[304] In September 1986 in a speech in Krasnodar that was broadcast nationwide on television, Gorbachev went further than ever before to invite attacks on the government and the Party. He identified the enemy of reform as the bureaucracy in the ministries and conservatism in the Party. He said that the "Party is at the service of the people and its managing role does not represent a privilege. To those who have forgotten this, I am now reminding you." For the first time, he called for "democratization." According to Roy Medvedev, this speech caused a "sensation."[305] It opened the floodgates of criticism, particularly criticism of Stalin. Just as in the West, criticism of Stalin was often a cover for attacks on Lenin and socialism.

In 1986 previously banned works that were critical of Stalin began to appear. Tengiz Abuladze's 1984 film *Pokayaniye*

(*Repentance*) about the repression of the thirties opened to limited audiences in Moscow. According to Roy Medvedev, the showing of this film, which Gorbachev liked, marked a "political, not merely a cultural, turning point."[306] Also, in Moscow, Mikhail Shatrov's anti-Stalinist play, *Diktatura Sovesti* (*The Dictatorship of the Conscience*) opened at the Leninisk Komsomol Theater.[307] Over objections by Ligachev, Gorbachev personally approved the publication of Anatoliy Rybakov's *Children of the Arbat*.[308] Over the objections of the head of the Writer's Union, *Novy Mir* announced that in 1987 it would begin publishing Boris Pasternak's *Dr. Zhivago*.[309] In another signal, Gorbachev personally ended the internal exile of the dissident, Andrei Sakharov.[310] While many in the West were hailing these moves, Mike Davidow, a Communist journalist stationed in Moscow, rued, "Never in history did a ruling party literally turn over the mass media to forces bent on its own destruction and the state it led, as did the leaders of the CPSU."[311]

After the Twenty-seventh Congress, Gorbachev also veered from Andropov's path with regard to Party reform. As with *glasnost*, Gorbachev's turn with regard to Party reform first occurred at the level of rhetoric, the full implications of which would not become clear until 1987. According to the historian Graeme Gill, a consensus existed inside and outside the Party that the organization had some serious problems--corruption in some republics and cadre policies based on loyalty, servility, and protectionism. Following Andropov, Gorbachev had initially called for exactingness, transparency, and discipline. The Congress adopted new rules providing for more openness, criticism and self-criticism, accountability, and collectivity. Gorbachev, however, failed to implement these decisions, but instead, in September 1986 he lurched off in a new direction by calling for the Party to "restructure itself." Whereas the Congress had called for restructuring society and strengthening the Party, Gorbachev shifted the focus to the restructure and "democratization" of the Party. The first rumblings of discontent in the Party leadership occurred at this point.[312]

Meanwhile, parallel to what was occurring with ideology and politics, Gorbachev began dubious moves in foreign policy. In this area, as in the others, no sharp break would occur in terms of Soviet support of national liberation struggles until 1987 or even later, but moves in this direction occurred. In this area, as in the others, the first sign of a change in direction came rhetorically. Lenin had defined the essence of right opportunism as sacrificing fundamental principles, particularly the principle of class struggle, for immediate gain and as making unnecessary compromises with the class enemy in hopes of finding a quick and easy advance toward socialism. This sounded a lot like the path Gorbachev began to follow. In April 1985, before he changed, Gorbachev had blamed "imperialism" for creating international tensions and for stepping up its subversion against socialist countries. By the fall of the year, however, the words, imperialism, capitalist countries, and national liberation, began disappearing from Gorbachev's discourse, though not from the world.[313] In his speech to the Twenty-seventh Congress, imperialism only appeared once, in reference to Afghanistan.[314] Eventually, Gorbachev would argue that "new thinking" required the de-ideologization of foreign affairs, that is, the replacement of class-based ideas with ideas about the priority of eternal, human values of peace and cooperation.[315] Meanwhile, this rhetorical re-orientation subtly began to manifest itself in policy.

Gorbachev had begun by making bold, new initiatives for peace and disarmament. He had unilaterally stopped Soviet nuclear tests and reduced the number of intermediate range missiles aimed at Europe. He had helped end the freeze in American-Soviet relations by meeting with Reagan in Geneva. He had forwarded such new proposals as the cutting of strategic arms by 50 percent. While these moves reduced international tensions and won Gorbachev international acclaim, they had a disturbing underside, noted by few outside of the Kremlin. Namely, Gorbachev showed a troubling tendency to make concessions to the United States while getting nothing in return. This tendency assumed a new form in early 1986. Since 1981, the Reagan administration had drastically increased military spending while putting forth a novel disarmament proposal known as the zero option. Under the zero option, the U.S. expected the Soviets to dismantle their expensive European-based missiles in return for the U.S. not deploying missiles in Europe in the future. In truth, the zero option reflected the Reagan administration's complete lack of interest in disarmament. It was a preposterously one-sided idea that demanded real reductions on the Soviet side but no reductions of existing weapons by Americans or Europeans. It was designed to convince world opinion that the Reagan administration was interested in peace while offering nothing to the Soviets. To the astonishment of the Reagan administration, Gorbachev reversed the previous Soviet rejection.[316] In an address on January 15, Gorbachev proposed the complete elimination of nuclear weapons by the year 2000 and agreed to the zero option.[317] If Gorbachev had limited his concessions to these, and they had opened a new stage of arms talks or led to concessions on the American side, then he would have gained something. Instead, Gorbachev's concessions produced no reciprocal compromises on the American side. Nine months after the dramatic reversal on the zero option, Gorbachev met with Reagan in Reykjavik, Iceland, in a summit in which Reagan offered nothing but empty promises and refused to budge on SDI.[318]

At the end of 1985 and early 1986, Gorbachev also began a retreat from the Soviet commitment to Afghanistan, even though a complete capitulation was two years away. Soviet military involvement in Afghanistan began in 1979, after the People's Democratic Party of Afghanistan (PDPA) that had seized power the previous year made repeated requests for Soviet help to repel attacks by CIA-backed warlords. While attempting to modernize one of the poorest and most backward lands on earth, the PDPA had redistributed land, promoted religious freedom, given greater freedom to women, and initiated a literacy campaign aimed at the 90 percent of the population that could not read. Almost immediately, the government had faced armed resistance from local warlords, who began a counterrevolution by assassinating the rural teachers of girls.[319] The warlords soon gained money and arms from the CIA, whose aid predated and intentionally provoked the Soviet intervention. Zbigniew Brzezinski, President Carter's National Security Advisor later said, "We knowingly increased the probability that they [the Soviets] would [intervene]."[320] This CIA support eventually amounted to its largest covert operation since World War II.[321] The Brezhnev, Andropov, and Chernenko governments viewed the Soviet aid to Afghanistan as international solidarity against the "hand of imperialism."[322]

When Gorbachev assumed office in April 1985, he intensified the Soviet military effort in Afghanistan, a sure sign that he initially viewed the war as neither immoral nor unwinnable.[323] In the fall of 1985, however, Gorbachev began to back away from the Soviet commitment, first by signaling Reagan at Geneva that some accommodation on Afghanistan was possible. [324] Then in February 1986 at the Twenty-seventh Congress, while blaming imperialism for the Afghan conflict, Gorbachev sounded a new, defeatist note. Instead of viewing Afghanistan like past leaders as a victim of imperialism, the General Secretary referred to the country as "a bleeding wound."[325] Still, the real turning point in Gorbachev's thinking apparently did not occur until after the Reyjavik summit in October 1986, when Gorbachev and his advisors decided that any favorable response by the U.S. on arms control required a Soviet retreat from Afghanistan. According to Sarah Mendelson, who studied the Soviet archives, the decision to withdraw resulted neither from public pressure at home nor from defeats on the battlefield. Rather, the real reason for Soviet decision was

Gorbachev's belief that the success of *perestroika* required a cooperative international environment, the price of which was the abandonment of Afghanistan.[326] At a Politburo meeting on November 13, 1986, the General Secretary said, "We have been at war in Afghanistan six years already. If we don't change our approach we will be there another 20-30 years."[327] After November a debate began in top Soviet circles. The next month, Gorbachev told Afghan leader, Najibullah, that the Soviet Union would begin recalling its troops in 1988, though at this time the assumption was that the Soviet action would be accompanied by some reciprocal abatement of American interference and some guarantees of Afghan neutrality. According to Yakovlev, soon after this meeting, Gorbachev decided to use *glasnost*, that is to say journalistic coverage of the war, to counter the opposition to withdrawal on the part of some Soviet leaders.[328] As Mendelson makes clear, however, neither morality, nor defeat, nor popular pressure motivated the change in Soviet policy. Instead, it was Gorbachev's willingness to sacrifice international solidarity on the altar of *perestroika*.

Even though signs of a move in new directions on domestic and foreign policy began as early as the fall of 1985, the ultimate danger they represented were more apparent in hindsight than they were at the time. In 1985, where Gorbachev was heading was unclear. The signs were contradictory. After all, Gorbachev still spoke of reinvigorating Leninism and perfecting socialism. He said that he was neither revising nor abandoning socialist ideology, just adapting it to new global circumstances. Even as he signaled a retreat in Afghanistan, he actually increased the Soviet support of the African National Congress.[329]

Though the cutting edge of Gorbachev's moves to the right first occurred subtly and hesitatingly in ideology, politics, and foreign policy, where he could act with the greatest independence, by 1986 moves consistent with these also occurred economic policy. The problematic aspects of Gorbachev's economic ideas resided in the weakening of centralized planning and state ownership. These were the notes Gorbachev sounded at the Twenty-seventh Congress. Gorbachev advocated autonomy for enterprises, saying they should become totally responsible for running their own affairs on a profitable basis. The central economic bodies should get out of the business of day-to-day management and concentrate on long-term planning and scientific leadership. Enterprises should have the right to sell products that exceeded plan requirements to other enterprises. Enterprises should be responsible for their own wage fund, which should be dependent on their sales. As central planning receded, republic, regions, cities, and districts should assume a greater role in planning. As radical as these changes sounded, Gorbachev assured the Congress that innovations meant no sacrifice of "the unquestionable priority of the interests of the whole people" and no "retreat from the principles of planned guidance," only a change in "methods."

In his speech to the Congress, Gorbachev also opened the door to non-state property and even private enterprise. He said that "cooperative property" had "far from exhausted its possibilities in socialist production" and that the "utmost support should be given to the establishment and growth of cooperative enterprises." This may have been true about genuine cooperatives, but what Gorbachev meant by "cooperative enterprises" turned out to be private enterprises, most likely not what his listeners had in mind. Gorbachev even expressed sympathy with private enterprise in the second economy by saying, "We must not permit any shadow to fall on those who do honest work to earn a supplementary income."[330] Nevertheless, Gorbachev tempered these remarks by a condemnation of the "unearned income" of those who stole from the socialist economy, took bribes, and developed a "distinct proprietary mentality." He stressed that "the consolidation of socialism in practice should be the supreme criterion" of reform.[331] Gorbachev thus masked new initiatives favoring private property by duplicitous language and contradictory intentions.

Following the Congress, the contradictions in Gorbachev's approach to economic reform persisted. On the one hand, Gorbachev supported a law to penalize unearned incomes and supported the formation of a new state control agency to improve the quality of goods. On the other hand, and more importantly, the General Secretary initiated three steps toward economic liberalization that ended up encouraging private economic activity. In August, he allowed greater foreign economic activity for state-owned firms, including investment abroad. In October, he legalized a type of producer cooperative, which was really just a disguised form of private enterprise. In November, he made a small expansion in the scope of permissible private economic activity. According to Gregory Grossman, these moves had three consequences, though the full impact would not come into play until 1987 and after. The foreign arrangements "turned into a cornucopia from which just-privatized capital gushed abroad by the billions of dollars." The co-ops "turned into a captive legal entity for asset- and profit-stripping activity in the state sector on a vast scale." The law on private activity "did more to shelter the expansion of illicit private ('shadow') activity than to promote lawful small-scale activity."[332] These moves would ominously augment the petty bourgeois layer of the second economy, and it would create sections of the state-owned sector and Party with a vested interest in private enterprise. Consciously or not, Gorbachev was augmenting a base for further capitalist-oriented policies.

The contradictory nature of Gorbachev's policies and the almost universal desire for reform among Party leaders explain the failure of a vocal left wing opposition to appear during Gorbachev's first two years. The course followed by Yegor Ligachev illustrated the slow development of a left wing opposition. Born in Siberia in 1920, Ligachev was raised in Novosibirsk, where his father worked in a factory. After becoming an aviation engineer in Moscow, Ligachev returned to Novosibirsk, where he worked in a plant building fighter planes used in World War II. After joining the Communist Party in 1944, he rose in the ranks, in 1959 becoming the head of the Novosibirsk district. In 1961 to 1965, he worked in the Central Committee offices in Moscow, and then at his own request he became the head of the Tomsk Province Party, a position he held for seventeen years. Ligachev, who always rejected the exaggerated idea that the Brezhnev years were a period of stagnation, recalled with pride his accomplishments in Tomsk during the Brezhnev years. Ligachev said, "I was building socialism. And there were millions like me." Historian Stephen F. Cohen said of Ligachev in these years: "Teetotaling, self-confident, hard-working, and a scandal-free family man, he modernized the province's industry and agriculture, developed new enterprises, preserved Tomsk's historic wooden buildings, patronized the arts, and minded the Party's monopolistic interests wherever necessary." In 1983, General Secretary Andropov brought Ligachev to Moscow, where like Gorbachev he became one of the reform-minded members of the Politburo.[333]

During the first stage of reform, Ligachev represented the most thoroughly grounded Leninist of any of the top leaders. As the person in charge of Party cadre, he also occupied the second most powerful position in the Party, second only to Gorbachev. Ligachev supported the general thrust of Gorbachev's reforms, which he thought were long overdue and which he believed would simply revive the course that Andropov had charted, a course to which Ligachev seemingly remained loyal. As an enthusiast of reform, Ligachev failed to see the rightward drift of Gorbachev's policies and even furthered some of them himself, moves he later regretted. For example, Ligachev helped select the editor of *Ogonyok*, who turned into one of the most anti-Party of all editors. Moreover, Ligachev later admitted that he "did not understand" the motives of the fast-paced reforms pushed by the media. Only after 1986, did he realize that ceding power over the media to Yakovlev "was clearly a big mistake."[334]

By the end of 1986, Gorbachev's reforms had become either Janus-faced, looking both left and right, or two-faced, looking left and marching right. Though some measures had failed, others showed promise. Though the ultimate direction and fate of his policies remained very much up in the air, Gorbachev maintained the support of the Politburo and the masses. Then in December from unexpected quarters a crisis arose, a sudden outburst of nationalist extremism in Kazahkstan that foreshadowed even more serious problems ahead. The crisis was clearly traceable to Gorbachev's weaknesses.

In ways that reflected his provincial Russian background, Gorbachev had repeatedly slighted the national interests of the Soviet republics on the periphery. Historian Helene D'Encausse said, "He paid scant attention to national sensitivities, and he blithely overlooked the rules for national representation that had been in effect since 1956." Whereas under Brezhnev, the Politburo contained three non-Russian members who were leaders of their republics, under Gorbachev, the PB had only one non-Russian republican leader, Scherbitsky of the Ukraine. Moreover, whereas under Brezhnev full members and deputies had represented the Muslim republics of Central Asia and from the Caucasus, Georgia, and the two Slavic states, the Ukraine and Byelorussia, under Gorbachev, "all the Muslim republics and the Caucasus disappeared from the Politburo." On top of that, other than Shevardnadze, no one in the leadership even had significant experience in the border republics. According to D'Encausse, the result was that the periphery felt "ignored and even scorned."[335]

Naturally, the problems in Kazakhstan did not begin with Gorbachev. The grievances of the Kazakhs had deep roots. Over the years, internal migration had reduced the Kazakhs to a minority (40 percent) in their own republic. Policies to develop local leaders and promote bilingualism had fallen short of their goals. Russian remained the language of public life. Consequently, some Kazakhs felt like outsiders in their own land. If such grievances provided the tinder, Gorbachev himself applied the torch. He simply refused or was unable to recognize the seriousness of the national question and was tone deaf to national sensitivities. At the Twenty-seventh Congress earlier in the year, he had said nothing about ethnic differences and frustrations, but had simply mouthed what D'Encausse called "celebratory rhetoric." While *glasnost* was giving people the license to criticize, Gorbachev's highhandedness was giving them something to criticize. After having previously expelled half of the secretaries of the Kazakh Central Committee, in December 1986 Gorbachev replaced the General Secretary, Dinmukhamed Kunaev, a native Kazakh, with Gennadi Kolbin, a Russian with no experience in Kazakhstan. This was either a huge mistake or a calculated provocation of monstrous proportions. Ten thousand students and others took to the streets of Alma Ata chanting nationalist slogans--"Kazakhstan for the Kazakhs and only the Kazakhs!"-- and attacking public buildings and the Party headquarters. The army had to suppress the riot. According to D'Encausse, Gorbachev learned nothing from having provoked the worst ethnic uprising in the history of the Soviet Union, and his statements afterwards revealed "his constant discomfort with the national question, even an inability to grasp the facts."[336]

The shards of broken glass in the streets of Alma Ata reflected the problematic course reform was taking. When Gorbachev departed from Andropov's precedents, he began exhortations for revolutionary change without a well-thought-out plan. He began entertaining the ready-made ideas of a Party reformist tradition stretching back to Khrushchev and Bukharin, ideas that reflected the interests of much of the intelligentsia and the sector of entrepreneurs and Party bureaucrats profiting from the second economy. Subtly, with tacking and weaving, and traditional rhetorical cover, Gorbachev began jettisoning traditional Marxist-Leninist ideas. In politics and ideology, Gorbachev departed from traditional notions of criticism and self-criticism and the Party's control of the media for his own version of *glasnost*, a model of the press drawn from Western liberalism. In foreign affairs, he began sacrificing both the ideas of class conflict and international solidarity and the policies of equality and reciprocity for the idea of eternal human values and the policy of unilateral concessions. In economic reform, Gorbachev began entertaining the ideas of those who advocated moving from centralized planning toward enterprise autonomy and the market, from state ownership toward cooperative and private enterprise, from suppressing the second economy to unleashing it. Moreover, when confronted with setbacks or opposition, Gorbachev showed a disturbing tendency to plunge ahead, "to escape forward."[337] It was a dangerous and uncharted course. The riots in Alma-Ata showed that this course could have consequences of a frightening magnitude.

5. Turning Point, 1987-88

The erosion or disintegration of central authority was unanimously regarded as the primary reason for the crisis. Ellman and Kontorovich.[338]

At some point in 1987, I personally realized that a society based on violence and fear could not be reformed and that we faced a momentous historical task of dismantling an entire social and economic system with all its ideological, economic and political roots. Alexander Yakovlev.[339]

Comrades, we have every right to say that the nationality question has been solved in our country. Mikhail Gorbachev.[340]

The impact of a personality like him [Bukharin] cannot be freely acknowledged, either because of political constraints that are today stronger than those under Khrushchev, or because of the lack of political and historical training among the debaters who sometimes do not know much about such affinities. It is astonishing to discover how many ideas of Bukharin's anti-Stalinist program of 1928-29 were adopted by current reformers as their own and how much of their critique of past practices followed his strictures and prophecies even in their expression.... Quite obviously in the present situation the question is no longer how to industrialize a peasant country, but how to run an industrial giant. The environment of the 1960s and 1970s is very different from that of the 1920s. Naturally enough the current debates have ramifications beyond those put forward by those originally advocating NEP. However, actual arguments used in both periods coincide astonishingly. Moshe Lewin.[341]

In 1987 and 1988, the turning-point years of *perestroika*, the Gorbachev leadership of the CPSU abandoned the reform project of 1985-86. In the name of speeding up *perestroika* and overcoming "conservative resistance," Gorbachev and his advisers adopted a new direction at the January 1987 Central Committee Plenum and the Nineteenth Party Conference in June 1988. These new policies objectively undermined the foundations of Soviet socialism--the leadership of the Communist Party, state property, and economic planning--and shattered the unity of the USSR as a multinational federal state. The turning point was not a discrete moment but an eighteen-month interval from January 1987 through June 1988, when the "radical political reform" and "radical economic reform" policies transformed *perestroika* from a potentially constructive program into its opposite, a demolition project that destroyed the socialist USSR.

The new policies weakened and dismantled centralized planning in favor of the market, promoted private property, and abandoned international solidarity. Central to all was the weakening of the Party. In the words of a U.S. historian, Robert V. Daniels, Gorbachev unleashed "a sequence of events at the political center, inherently unpredictable, that eviscerated the authority and legitimacy" of the Communist Party. Under the slogans "democratization" and "decentralization," the process that Gorbachev set in motion in 1988-89 in the name of the Communist Party and its leaders quickly became irrevocable.[342]

How was this mutation possible? How could a CPSU general secretary embark on such a course? How could he get away with a course that, as early as 1988 led to economic decline and separatist fury? Archie Brown, a leading British analyst, observed, "Gorbachev could have been removed--and surely would have been--at a moment's notice by the CC [Central Committee] of the CPSU on the advice of the Politburo had he openly criticized either Communism or socialism."[343] Brown was right. The attack on socialism did not come openly, but surreptitiously under the guise of improving socialism.

When the world remembers the Soviet drama of 1985-91 the mind's eye sees the outward signs of disintegration visible in the 1989-91 endgame: ethnic strife, mass protest rallies, bread lines, and miners' strikes. The processes and events of the two preceding years 1987 and 1988 are, by comparison, less visible.

In this middle period the class and political content of *perestroika* changed. In essence, the Soviet leadership replaced a seventy-year-old policy of struggle against capitalism and imperialism with a policy of surrender. The revolutionary movement had long harbored a tendency that favored an accommodation with capitalism at home and abroad. Since the 1950s, this tendency had acquired a new social base in the second, or private, economy that had been developing within socialism. The cost of competing militarily with the West, a competition vastly intensified by Reagan, added to the appeal of those seeking an accommodation with capitalism. In the 1980s, the need to deal with the chronic problems of slowing economic growth, poor consumer goods quality, political stagnation, and the strain of the Cold War, provided an opportunity for this tendency to reassert itself.

Gorbachev did not invent his new direction from thin air. Similar policy ideas had existed for decades in Soviet society and in the CPSU, though they fell out of favor after Khrushchev. Robert Kaiser of the *Washington Post* noted the history: "Gorbachev's brand of reformism caught much of the Western world by surprise, but he is actually part of a reform tradition almost as old as the party itself. Nikolai Bukharin, one of Lenin's closest comrades, was godfather to this group."[344] In effect, in 1987-88 Gorbachev took off one ideological coat and put on another, though he briefly had an arm in the sleeve of each. Since the Khrushchev's ouster in 1964, Soviet dissidents and a section of the intellectuals kept alive this political trend's main planks: cultural liberalism; a smaller, more relaxed ideological role for the CPSU; bourgeois liberal notions of democracy; emulation and appeasement of the West; and an antipathy to class struggle. This trend's analysis of nationalism, Russian and non-Russian, remained faulty or non-existent. Its economic ideology, even when frowned upon in the Kremlin, thrived in corners of Soviet academia that maintained a sneaking regard for Western bourgeois doctrines. As an economic ideology, it stressed the advantages of market relations, not the plan; decentralization, not centralism; evolutionary methods, never coercion. It had a high estimate of "the natural advantages of the system," a phrase much used early in the Gorbachev era. It stressed a "socialism of the productive forces,"[345] which downplayed the need for struggle to perfect the relations of production, that is, ending class divisions. Accordingly, this wing of the CPSU stressed output and growth, but underestimated the need to keep all market relations and private property within strict bounds.

In 1987-88 the new course took three forms. First, Party reform became Party liquidation, and the exclusion of the Party from power. Second, under the banner of *glasnost*, the Soviet media became increasingly anti-Communist. Third, Gorbachev embraced private entrepreneurial activity.

In 1985 and 1986 the Soviet Communist press had demanded an end to Party abuses. The press railed against corruption, cronyism, patronage, nepotism, bureaucratic departmentalism, protection of loyal toadies by higher-ups, insufficient cadre training, formalism, complacency, and ideological weakness. Responding to such criticism, the Twenty-seventh Congress launched a program of Party reform. The reforms included new Party rules to reinforce criticism and self-criticism, and a new approach to collective leadership emphasizing personal accountability. The Congress also called for close supervision of the performance of Party leaders.[346] Gorbachev never implemented the reforms.

Instead, in 1987-88 Gorbachev came to view the CPSU as the main obstacle to *perestroika*, and he decided to use "radical political reform," to weaken it. As part of the attack on the Party, Gorbachev initiated a "de-Stalinization" campaign. Twice, in early 1987 and 1988, Gorbachev and Yakovlev waged major campaigns to drive the media to revise Party history. Khrushchev had pioneered this practice against Party opponents in 1956 and in 1961.[347] Gorbachev gave his approval to economic exposés claiming Soviet statistics had been systematically falsified to understate economic failure, and that "Stalinist" stagnation was at the root of the crisis, which, Gorbachev alleged, was far worse than people realized. Gorbachev used denunciations of Stalin to weaken Ligachev and his allies. In February 1987, Gorbachev decided to relax even more the restraints on the media and to allow the media to air criticisms of Stalin. This represented an about-face from his warning six months earlier against "digging up the past."[348] An attack on Stalin helped Gorbachev create a coalition against honest socialist forces. As historian Stephen Kotkin said, his coalition joined together "those who denounced Stalin in the name of reforming socialism and those who denounced him in the name of repudiating socialism."[349] Stephen F. Cohen said that anti-Stalinism became the "ideology of Communist reform from above, as it was under Khrushchev."[350]

In 1987 anti-Communist control of the mass media began to have other consequences. For example, when the Politburo was debating a highly risky proposal by the Gorbachev team to slash the state orders by 50 percent and force enterprises to sell the rest of their production on the market, Yakovlev's appointments in the media whipped up a frenzy against the proposal's opponents with ominous warnings of "conservatism, deceleration, and a return to stagnation."[351] Because of such pressure, the Politburo opted for Gorbachev's ill-considered leap into the dark, and the economy went into a tailspin from which it never rebounded.

After 1987 no person outside of Gorbachev had more influence than Alexander Yakovlev on Soviet policies, particularly on those that undermined the CPSU and empowered anti-Party and pro-capitalist intellectuals. By his own admission Yakovlev was a social democrat. So were other key Gorbachev advisers. Georgi Shakhnazarov had referred to himself as a social democrat since the 1960s. Archie Brown, a British analyst, described Anatoly Chernyaev as "a longstanding liberal political thinker." Gorbachev introduced Chernyaev as my "alter ego" to Spanish Prime Minister Felipe Gonzalez, a Social Democrat.[352] According to D'Agostino, Chernyaev, Shakhnazarov, and Yakovlev did Gorbachev's writing.[353]

Under Yakovlev's tutelage, the political concepts of *perestroika* increasingly assumed a new meaning: "socialist pluralism," became "pluralism of opinion," and finally "political pluralism."[354] Gorbachev's phrase, "various forms of the realization of socialist property," soon lost "realization," then "socialist," to become simply "various forms of property." A "socialist rule-of-law state" became a "state based on the rule of law." Support for "socialist markets" evolved into "market socialism," then a "regulated market economy." As non-Russian republics succumbed to nationalist separatism, Yakovlev's media allies avoided the words "nationalism" and "separatism." Archie Brown, a Gorbachev sympathizer, discerned the pattern:

> What generally happened was that Gorbachev would introduce or endorse a concept that had previously been banished from Soviet political discourse, but within his first few years as General Secretary he would attach the adjective "socialist" to it. Reform-minded intellectuals would seize on the concepts and elaborate them; by 1988 the more radical among them were dropping the "socialist" qualifier.... What was striking about Gorbachev was not only that, having launched many ideas alien to Marxism-Leninism but with a "socialist" or other qualification, he would take them up two years later in their revised form with all reservations removed.[355]

By 1987, Yakovlev was consciously working toward anti-socialist goals. The doctrine of peaceful coexistence, originally a form of anti-capitalist struggle by every means except military, changed into "universal human values," a phrase that would eventually be used to justify an alliance with imperialism.[356] Socialist democracy became "democratization," interpreted as reducing the role of the Party. Socialism became "the socialist choice," not a stage of development but a mere aspiration for social justice. Security and cooperation between socialist and capitalist Europe became our "Our Common European Home," suggesting a far-reaching identity of interest going well beyond peace, mutually advantageous trade and other forms of cooperation.[357] The words changed slowly, turning slogans and doctrines inside out.[358] Ellman and Kontorovich said, "A veritable war on the official ideology was started…apparently before most of the radical policies were decided."[359] In early 1987, still outnumbered by pro-reform but non-revisionist Politburo opponents, Gorbachev and his allies boldly sought to use the *glasnost* media to fill the idea of *perestroika* with new "anti-Stalinist" content. Observing the same phenomenon, American journalist Robert Kaiser said, "Gorbachev, Yakovlev, Shevardnadze and their helpers were more resourceful and inventive than their conservative opponents. … By late 1986 and early 1987 he and his allies in the Party and in the intelligentsia were behaving a little like mischievous boys set loose in a china closet shattering taboos, while obviously relishing the sound of the breakage."[360]

The sheer frequency with which David Remnick, the *New York Times* chief correspondent in Moscow, cited Yakovlev in *Lenin's Tomb*, suggested constant contact. Having spent a decade in North America, Yakovlev understood the power of *The Times* to shape American perceptions. Ligachev repeatedly noted the coordination of Western and Soviet media.

Economic conditions were a big factor in shaping mass attitudes. In 1987, the burgeoning second economy began to shift all Soviet politics in the new anti-socialist direction. Anthony Jones and William Moskoff, writing of the "rebirth of entrepreneurship," noted that trade and consumer co-ops were a lawful and justifiable part of the economy over the whole Soviet era, accounting for about one-fourth of annual Soviet trade. Their character, however, changed radically in 1987.

The co-operatives that developed following the 1987 Law on Individual Labor Activity were quite different from either of these old co-operatives.... The idea of calling these new organizations co-operatives fooled few in the Soviet Union. It was recognized that this was private enterprise dressed up as socialist enterprise. Once the way had been cleared for legal non-state forms of economic activity, what came to be known as the alternative economy expanded rapidly.[361]

According to economist Victor Perlo, by the end of 1988 these crime-infested[362] fake co-ops employed a million hired workers. A year later they employed 5 million workers.[363] This unchecked and accelerating growth of the second economy imparted momentum to the drive to marketization, emboldened the anti-Communist opposition, and eroded the CPSU's confidence. Among other consequences, the second economy was serving, in Gregory Grossman's words, "as a living example of an alternative to the official centralized–planned-command system."[364] In short, the second economy was the material underpinning of the political collapse.

At the crucial January 1987 CC Plenum, under the slogan "democratization," the exclusion of the CPSU from political and economic power began. The leadership had postponed the plenum three times, a likely sign of widening differences at the top. At the January 1987 Plenum, Gorbachev broke with the assumptions of the preceding two years and "radiated immense willfulness and self-confidence."[365] At the plenum Gorbachev proposed political reforms, including multi-candidate elections for Party secretary posts from the district level to the Union Republic[366] and the appointment of non-Party persons to senior government posts. Gorbachev blamed "serious shortcomings in the functioning of socialist democracy" for putting a brake on his reforms.[367] Gorbachev also proposed secret ballot elections for enterprises and assemblies. Ligachev saw these changes as pivotal. After them, "the process of democratization became unmanageable," Ligachev said. "Society began to lose its stability; the idea that everything was permitted gained the upper hand."[368] Still, Gorbachev did not get all he wanted at the January 1987 Plenum, and, since the next Party Congress was not scheduled until 1990, he proposed a special Party Conference. Though the Central Committee initially rejected the idea, at the June 1987 Plenum, the Central Committee agreed to call a special Party Conference for June 1988.

John Dunlop of Princeton University attributed the democratization program to traditional considerations of Kremlin power politics: Gorbachev needed to isolate and remove Politburo competitors. Within weeks, Gorbachev gave a major speech referring to competitive elections of Party officials. Jerry Hough of Brookings suggested the Plenum signified the coming switch from Party to state rule. "He [Gorbachev] had already surely decided to change his base of power from the Party apparatus to a presidency."[369]

Actually, the political change in January 1987 represented something far more significant than a crude struggle for personal power, or a simple foreshadowing of new forms of governance. As defined by Gorbachev at this stage, democratization was tantamount to a shift from Marxism to social democratic notions of Party structure. Gorbachev was rejecting Lenin's doctrine of the leading role of the Party and democratic centralism as the principle of Party organization. Kotz and Weir, Gorbachev sympathizers, observed that, like social democrats elsewhere, "Gorbachev and his circle came to view democracy as an end in itself. They appeared to view it as an aim nearly equal in importance to their traditional goal of building socialism."[370]

Those seeking demolition of a Communist Party rarely call the move by its true name. At first, destruction of the CPSU assumed the form of a subtle, stealth attack, because, to most Soviet people, on the surface, the new policies appeared to be part of the effort to tackle long-standing, widely recognized problems of socialist construction. The constructive reform agenda of the CPSU leadership in 1985-1987 aimed to speed up economic growth, to slow the arms race, to raise Party standards, and to deepen socialist democracy. At first, the "democratization" drive of 1987 did not obviously conflict with such goals. Supporters claimed democratization would speed up and guarantee Party reform, make *perestroika* irreversible, and separate Party and state functions. Moreover, at no time did Gorbachev openly proclaim: "Let us now curb the CPSU's role, make the CC Secretariat non-functioning, substitute impotent commissions for the CC Secretariat, abandon check-up and control, and relieve the general secretary of responsibilities for implementing decisions. Let us deprive the local Party branches of advice from the center." Yet, this was precisely what occurred. Such left-sounding phrases as "ever more radical" reform and "truly revolutionary" *perestroika* cloaked the real pro-capitalist direction. In addition, the idea that a General Secretary of the CPSU would advocate doing away with his own Party seemed preposterous. Lastly, all this was occurring in a confusing context, where the Soviet media used a perplexing, upside down terminology in which genuine Communists who wanted to preserve the Party and socialism were called "conservatives," and those who worked for capitalist restoration were called "democrats," a terminology knowingly shared by the Western capitalist media.

In warfare, when an army surrenders one stronghold and retreats, its other positions are harder to defend. In politics, similarly, a retreat on one battleground often leads to retreats elsewhere. For example, Gorbachev's use of the media to weaken his Politburo opponents undermined collective leadership and deepened splits within the CPSU. Splits thwarted decisive and unified action on the economy and the national question. Similarly, the strident anti-Stalin campaigns and the rehabilitation of Bukharin and his economic ideas represented no balanced search for the truth about Party history. Successfully, these campaigns sought to throw the anti-revisionists on the defensive and to ready the doctrinal ground for ending CPSU management of the economy.

In March and April of 1988, a serious confrontation within the Party leadership occurred. Participants and commentators both offered widely differing accounts of what happened and its meaning. The variation in existing accounts makes it impossible to construct an exact and fully coherent chronology of events. Still, the basic outlines and significance are beyond dispute.

All commentators agree on these elements. First, the approach of the special Party Conference in June at which Gorbachev would seek approval of far-reaching political reforms increased the tensions in the top leadership and, no doubt, precipitated the crisis. Second, the affair began on March 13, 1988, when *Sovietskaya Rossiya* published a letter by Nina Andreyeva, a chemistry teacher at the Leningrad Soviet Technological Institute, entitled "I Cannot Renounce My Principles."[371] The letter sharply criticized some of the ideological consequences of *glasnost*. Third, when the Andreyeva crisis ended a month later, Gorbachev had routed and discredited his left wing opponents on the PB. Hence, the Nina Andreyeva crisis constituted the decisive turning point in the transformation of *perestroika* from an Andropov-inspired reform effort within the traditional context of Soviet socialism to an open attack on the major pillars of socialism--the Communist Party, socialized property, and central planning.

Gorbachev, his apologists, and many Western commentators, have propagated a one-sided interpretation of the events of March and April 1988. They characterized Andreyeva's letter as a "neo-Stalinist," anti-Semitic, Russian nationalist, anti-*perestroika* manifesto and asserted or implied that its publication resulted from a conspiracy headed by Ligachev intent on derailing *perestroika*.[372] Some even suggested the whole affair was a "micro-model for a coup d'etat."[373] These views, however, rested entirely on hearsay, rumors, and a tendentious reading of events. More plausibly, Gorbachev and Yakovlev deliberately used the occasion of this letter and Ligachev's support of it as a pretext to strike at Ligachev and throw their opponents into disarray before the upcoming Party conference. In any case, that was what happened.

Andreyeva's letter fell far short of a "rabidly anti-Semitic," "frontal attack" on *perestroika* from a "neo-Stalinist nationalist point of view."[374] Its title, which an American journalist called "provocative,"[375] actually came from a Gorbachev speech, and the letter closed with a quotation from Gorbachev on the importance of Marxist-Leninist principles. The letter contained no discussion of Gorbachev's economic, political or foreign policies. Instead, it confined its criticism to ideological matters, about which it warned of the ideological "confusion" and "one-sidedness" being sown by certain *glasnost* writers, confusion that was affecting her students. Andreyeva criticized the historical treatments of the playwright, M. Shatrov, and the novelist, A. Rybakov, for their distortions of history, particularly of Stalin's place in history. She also criticized two anti-socialist tendencies, the "neo-liberals" or "left-liberals" and "neo-Slavophiles" or Russian nationalists. She assailed the former for favoring a humanist socialism devoid of class partisanship, for favoring individualism over collectivism, for "modernistic quests in the field of culture, God-seeking, technocratic idols, the preaching of the 'democratic' charms of present-day capitalism and fawning over its achievements." She scored the neo-Slavophiles for romanticizing pre-revolutionary Russia and the peasantry, while ignoring the terrible oppression of the peasants and the revolutionary role of the working class.[376]

Belying the controversy that soon swirled around it, the letter exuded moderation, balance and reasonableness. The notion that Andreyeva simply spouted neo-Stalinism or in the words of journalist Robert Kaiser, "fiercely defended Stalin,"[377] represented a preposterous misreading. Andreyeva said she shared the "anger and indignation" of all Soviet people over the repression of the 1930s and 1940s, from which, she said, her own family had suffered. Moreover, she said the Party's 1956 resolution on the cult of personality and Gorbachev's speech on the 70th anniversary of the October Revolution remained "the scientific guidelines to this day."[378] The charge of anti-Semitism came from American journalists who saw a hidden meaning in her use of the word "cosmopolitan" to criticize "nationality-less 'internationalism.'"[379] She clearly aimed her criticism, however, at those who idealized the West, including "refuseniks" who would turn their backs on their country and socialism and emigrate to the West.[380] Even the Politburo's official rebuttal failed to charge Andreyeva with anti-Semitism. The notion that the letter represented Russian nationalism rested on nothing more than her crediting the nationalists with drawing attention to such problems as corruption, ecological decline, and alcoholism. But she also castigated the nationalists' romantic and distorted views of Russian history.

The idea that the letter represented an anti-*perestroika* manifesto crafted by the Ligachev camp lacked any foundation. Andreyeva and Ligachev denied any such thing. Historian Joseph Gibbs said interviews with the *Sovietskaya Rossiya's* staff could not verify Ligachev's involvement in the letter's publication.[381] Historian Stephen F. Cohen said that Ligachev was not an "intriguer" by nature and that the evidence of Ligachev's involvement in the Andreyeva letter was "highly inconclusive."[382] In his memoirs, Gorbachev gave only one reason for suspecting a conspiracy, that the letter "contained information known only to a relatively small circle,"[383] an unsupported claim, dubious on its face. Moreover, the letter's moderation, eccentricities and inaccuracies made it a highly unlikely candidate for a manifesto hatched at the highest levels.

The letter, for example, incorrectly attributed an Isaac Deutscher remark to Winston Churchill.[384] Moreover, for an allegedly anti-*perestroika* manifesto, the letter oddly called for backtracking on neither *glasnost* nor *perestroika*. Instead, Andreyeva merely argued for recognition in the ongoing debates that the "main and cardinal question" was "the leading role of the Party and the working class."[385] Nevertheless, Gorbachev and Yakovlev soon mounted a campaign transmogrifying this letter into a dangerous threat to the whole reform effort.

The day after the letter appeared, Ligachev held a meeting with certain heads of the mass media. Though one advocate of the conspiracy theory asserted that this was an "unscheduled"[386] meeting at which Ligachev ordered the reprinting of the letter, Ligachev himself said that the meeting had been scheduled a week before the publication of the letter, that the meeting dealt with many matters, that he mentioned the letter favorably in the context of a discussion of the media's treatment of history, and that he gave no instructions to reprint it.[387] Gorbachev, who first saw the letter while on a plane to Yugoslavia for an official four-day visit, initially told his chief of staff that it was "all right."[388]

After returning to Moscow, meeting with Yakovlev, and learning that Ligachev and some other members of the PB supported the letter and that the letter was being reprinted by the provincial press and was being circulated in Leningrad, Gorbachev's attitude changed. He ordered an investigation of the letter's origins, and he decided to make an issue of the letter and to use the letter as a pretext for a pre-emptive strike on his opponents in the Politburo. Gorbachev agreed with Yakovlev that he should strike back "from the highest level."[389] Soon, Gorbachev met with representatives of the mass media and denounced *Sovietskaya Rossiya*.[390] Then, according to Ligachev, rumors began to circulate about a "conspiracy" concocted by the "enemies of *perestroika*" who had timed the publication of the Andreyeva "manifesto" to appear when Gorbachev was out of the country.[391]

In March and April, the Politburo took up the Andreyeva letter on at least three occasions. One of these turned out to be an extraordinary session. For two days, six or seven hours a day, the Politburo took up one issue--the Nina Andreyeva letter. The PB had never before devoted itself to a newspaper article, let alone for two days. Ligachev said that a mood descended on the meeting totally different than the "democratic and free and easy" style that usually prevailed. "The mood was very tense and nervous, even oppressive." Yakovlev set the tone. He denounced the Andreyeva letter as a "manifesto of anti-*perestroika* forces." According to Ligachev, "Yakovlev acted like the master of the situation. Medvedev echoed Yakovlev. They wanted to impose on the entire Politburo their opinion that Andreyeva's letter was no ordinary statement: it was a recurrence of Stalinism, the chief threat to *perestroika*."

Though Yakovlev did not mention Ligachev by name, Ligachev said that Yakovlev implied that someone, presumably Ligachev, was behind this letter and was plotting a coup. According to Ligachev the meeting turned into a "witch hunt" reminiscent of the worst days of Stalin. Gorbachev came out "unequivocally on the side of Yakovlev." According to Ligachev, even PB members who had previously supported the letter "were forced to change their point of view." Moreover, "Gorbachev literally 'broke' those who, in his view, failed to condemn Nina Andreyeva's letter sufficiently."[392]

The witch-hunt continued for weeks. At one point, a Central Committee commission raided the offices of *Sovietskaya Rossiya* looking for evidence of a conspiracy.[393] On or about March 30, while Ligachev was on a three-day trip to the provinces, Gorbachev called another PB meeting at which he made a denunciation of the letter a loyalty test, allegedly saying, "I am asking all of you to declare yourselves." According to some accounts, Gorbachev threatened to resign "unless a clear choice" was made. Everyone present criticized the article and *Sovietskaya Rossiya*. The PB also passed a resolution condemning Valentin Chikin, the editor of *Sovietskaya Rossiya* and "warning" Ligachev. Finally, the PB voted unanimously to have Yakovlev draft an official rebuttal to the Andreyeva letter.[394] Thus, Gorbachev divided his opponents and threw them on the defensive, most of all Ligachev, whom Gorbachev had isolated and humiliated.

On April 5, *Pravda* carried the PB's rebuttal. Among other things, the rebuttal said, "For the first time the readers have been able to read in a highly concentrated form...the intolerance of the elementary idea of renewal, the brutal exposition of fixed positions that are in essence conservative and dogmatic." The rebuttal asserted that "by defending Stalin" those behind the letter were defending "the right to use power arbitrarily." The following day, *Sovietskaya Rossiya* was forced to print the rebuttal, and on April 15 the paper printed a retraction of the original letter and self-criticism. Newspapers began printing a flood of supposedly spontaneous letters from readers attacking the Andreyeva piece.[395] On April 8 in Tashkent, Gorbachev declared that "the destiny of our country and socialism are in question" and indicated that someone besides Ligachev should handle ideology.[396] At a PB meeting, on April 15 and 16, Gorbachev said that an investigation of the Andreyeva letter proved it "started inside here."[397] Yakovlev made a long speech attacking the letter that ended with "It's an anti-*perestroika* manifesto."[398] At the same meeting, Ryzhkov attacked Ligachev for stepping into areas "outside his competence."[399] According to Robert Kaiser, by the end of the meeting "Ligachev was isolated."[400] The meeting relieved Ligachev of some of his duties and transferred ideological responsibilities to Yakovlev.

In the end, Gorbachev and Yakovlev had turned Andreyeva's letter, one of scores that appeared critical of *perestroika*, into a pretext to ambush their leading PB opponent, Yegor Ligachev, and intimidate anti-revisionist opponents generally. In the

147

ensuing assault they stripped Ligachev of his allies and his authority, and turned the control of ideology and the media over to Yakovlev, the most extreme revisionist in the leadership. The rough handling of *Sovietskaya Rossiya* and the rest of the media sent a clear message, in the words of historian Gibbs: "the only acceptable use of *glasnost* was in promoting restructuring as Gorbachev directed it."[401] In the afterglow, Yakovlev told a friend, "We have crossed the Rubicon,"[402] and Gorbachev mused that the Andreyeva letter may have been "a good thing." With Ligachev dispatched and the media chastened, "an avalanche of anti-Stalinism" ensued. Chernyaev recalled thinking at the time, "if there had been no Nina Andreyeva, we would have had to invent her."[403]

The Gorbachev victory in the Nina Andreyeva affair signified the triumph of his brand of revisionism. Gorbachev's victory over Ligachev in this confrontation prepared the way for his domination of the Nineteenth Party Conference in June 1988. Meanwhile, Yakovlev and Medvedev assumed Ligachev's responsibility for ideology, and in September 1988, Ligachev was demoted to agriculture. Gorbachev eventually removed all the Politburo leaders who supported the Andreyeva letter, except Anatoly Lukyanov, Gorbachev's friend from student days.

If the January 1987 CC Plenum was a tremor, the June 1988 Nineteenth Party Conference was an earthquake. The ten theses distributed a month in advance of the Party Conference resembled the existing Soviet leadership consensus. When Gorbachev opened the conference, however, he went well beyond anything in the theses. He proposed the creation of a Congress of People's Deputies, a new supreme body of state power. The people would elect fifteen hundred deputies to five-year terms, with 750 reserved for the Party and related organizations. These deputies would elect from their number a small Supreme Soviet in two houses, a permanent body accountable to the Congress. The Congress would elect an executive president, the post that Gorbachev envisioned for himself. The proposal, introduced in the final minutes in a surprise resolution by Gorbachev in the chair, amounted to the overthrow of the Central Committee. According to one commentator, "As they sang the *Internationale* many delegates began to wonder what they had done."[404]

The Nineteenth Party Conference's decisions departed from past political practice in astonishing ways. Whereas the Party exercised the leading role in Soviet society and government, at a stroke the Nineteenth Party Conference reversed the roles by declaring that the state, rather than the Party, should lead. The Nineteenth Party Conference thus dramatically shrunk the role of the CPSU and turned it into a parliamentary party. It legalized non-Communist parties. As the CPSU faded in importance, the newly created executive presidency gave Gorbachev a platform from which to rule. Other steps soon followed. In September 1988, Gorbachev outlined a plan to replace the CC Secretariat with commissions, depriving Party leaders of an operating staff. This move weakened his opponents on the CC and, above all, weakened the allies of Ligachev for whom the CC Secretariat served as a political base. Each weakening and marginalizing of the CPSU had far-reaching consequences. Turning back became progressively more difficult. By April 1989, while chairing a Politburo meeting, Ligachev discerned a "strangely weak"[405] governing party.

At some point, Gorbachev's commitment to Party liquidation--indeed to dismantling the central government[406]-- must have become fully conscious. One intriguing clue about the timing of Gorbachev's conversion to revisionism occurred in his response to a Yakovlev memo in 1985 calling for splitting the CPSU into two parties, a Socialist Party and a People's Democratic Party, an echo of Khrushchev's decision to divide the CPSU along urban and rural lines.[407] According to Yakovlev, Gorbachev simply replied, "Too soon!" After this incident Yakovlev ascended in the hierarchy. If Yakovlev's account is correct, Gorbachev had in mind far-reaching political changes from the beginning of his tenure.[408]

Other evidence for the nature and timing of his political conversion varied. Gorbachev's own *Memoirs*, conflated early and later attitudes into a mess of contradictions. Fondness, pity, and disdain for the CPSU simultaneously filled the pages. Still, if he is to be believed, from the early days Gorbachev saw the CPSU as the main obstacle, and the Party apparatus as his main enemy, not as an instrument to carry the struggle for reform forward. He had to outmaneuver the Party, not struggle within it. He always appealed to intellectuals and the public over the Party's head. Everywhere, his *Memoirs* contain such sentiments as "Party structures are applying the brakes."[409]

Nevertheless, Gorbachev's final views stood out clearly. According to Anatoly Chernyaev, Gorbachev had only contempt for the CPSU. When Chernyaev, one of his most loyal aides, pleaded with Gorbachev to leave the Party, Gorbachev replied: "You know Tolya, do you think I don't see? I see and I read your memo. [Georgy] Arbatov, [Nikolai] Shmelev ... also say the same, they try to persuade me to abandon the general secretary post. But remember: that mangy dog can't be let off the leash. If I do that, the whole enormous thing will be against me."[410] The organization that had made him what he was he viewed as a mangy dog.

Outsiders viewed changes in 1987-88 through a glass darkly, but even insiders had trouble seeing things clearly. Possibly Gorbachev himself lacked an awareness of the full implications of what he was doing. At this time he wanted something like Western European social democracy without capitalist restoration. He told those critics who accused him of "social democratizing" the Party that the distinction between social reformism and Marxism-Leninism no longer had validity.[411] In capitalist society, of course, left-center coalitions are routine and make perfect sense. In a socialist society, they represent backsliding. In any case, he was pursuing a mirage, for social democracy's fundamental loyalty, in the last analysis, is to capitalism.[412]

The Gorbachev regime became a "transmission belt"[413] for ideas that repudiated the theoretical foundations of Marxism-Leninism. Gorbachev's speeches transmitted such ideas as "new thinking," "universal human values," bourgeois notions of democracy, and "market socialism" to the Party and the media. Then, the *glasnost* media expanded on the new ideas, setting the stage for new Gorbachev speeches embracing further shifts in an anti-socialist direction.

In essence, Gorbachev's new thinking amounted to substituting surrender to capitalism for the struggle against it. Substituting surrender for struggle has a psychological as well as a political dimension. To stop struggling produces relief. Certain recurrent phrases in the *perestroika* years evinced the opportunist psychology of the Gorbachev circle and its readiness to yield to rewards and pressure. Gorbachev knew that his concessions won him adulation in the West. Gorbachev once exclaimed, "We cannot go on living this way!" but, by any reasonable measure, no unbearable crisis existed. Similarly, *perestroika* promised to produce "a normal country." In a world where socialism must struggle to survive against a dominant capitalism which tries to strangle socialism, normality could only mean accommodating to capitalism. The CPSU leaders in Gorbachev's camp abandoned the notion of socialism as a system that working people consciously build, a desertion they would eventually regard with smug complacency. The lengths to which Gorbachev went to please the U.S. stunned American diplomats. No statesman surrenders a long-held bargaining position unless he gets something equivalent or better in return. Yet, Gorbachev did so in February 1987, when he accepted the "zero option," an utterly asymmetric deal to remove existing Soviet missiles in exchange for a U.S. decision not to build such missiles in the future. The move made sense only if Gorbachev aimed not to win the struggle, but to call it off.

Personal experience and qualities helped Gorbachev to assume a destructive role. Far more than earlier Soviet leaders, except Lenin, Gorbachev had traveled widely. As "Eurocommunism" was peaking, he visited Belgium and Holland in 1972, France in 1966, 1975, 1976, and 1978, and Germany in 1975.[414] He visited Canada in 1983. Spanish Prime Minister Felipe Gonzalez, a Social Democrat, beguiled Gorbachev. Gorbachev admired the West German "social market economy," comparing USSR economic performance not with its own backward Czarist past or with the contemporary Third World but with Germany, France, and Britain. From his student days through the 1990s Gorbachev maintained a friendship with Czech "Prague Spring" dissident, Zdenek Mlynar. He thought of himself as a "Sixties" man. His weaknesses as a personality also contributed to his weakness as a political leader. Even friendly analysts observed shallowness. William Odom, a U.S. observer, stated Gorbachev had no firm convictions.[415]

Gorbachev's revisionist policies could have taken hold only if organizational conditions were ripe. The corrosive effects of the policies of Khrushchev and Brezhnev had a cumulative impact on the caliber of the Soviet leadership. As Ligachev confessed, only a ruling party with an inadequate level of theoretical development and political skill among its leaders could have allowed such a fiasco.[416] Only a party with a weak tradition of collective leadership could have countenanced a party leader who repudiated basic party theory and policies. In 1964 Brezhnev and Suslov had ousted Khrushchev from office for lesser sins than Gorbachev's.

Moreover, Party theory had suffered before Gorbachev and helped prepare the way for him. The theoretical weaknesses included a rosy view of the national question, over-optimistic estimates both of socialism's strength and imperialism's weakness, and a Communist Party program with an overly upbeat assessment of the stage of socialist construction achieved. Yuri Andropov made a start toward correcting these organizational and theoretical shortcomings, but his life ended before he could finish the task.

Because of the slowing of the USSR's pace of economic growth, new burdens imposed by Reagan's dramatic escalation of the arms race, and a buildup of domestic problems, the Soviet Union needed a period of reform, rejuvenation, and renewal. Under these circumstances, some kind of retreat may have been needed. Lenin knew how to retreat if necessary, in difficult moments such as in 1918, with the Brest-Litovsk Treaty, or in 1921, with NEP. Later Soviet leaders did so, too: Stalin, in 1939, with the Nazi-USSR pact; Khrushchev in 1962, in the Cuban missile crisis. For Leninists, however, a retreat was a particular phase of struggle, when an unfavorable balance of forces required a backward step. Retreats were acknowledged as such, and a retreat was never the abandonment of struggle. Gorbachev's retreats in foreign policy assumed an entirely different character. His foreign policy rested on the notion that the Soviet Union's problems required an adaptation to the capitalist world.[417] Gorbachev portrayed his retreats as tremendous advances for mankind.

Gorbachev's failure to achieve anything at the Reykjavik Summit set the stage for the 180-degree turn in 1987-88. Soviet peace diplomacy then assumed a different character. What started as Soviet concessions in return for a better Soviet image became concessions in return for nothing at all. The USSR began to make concessions unilaterally without regard to the consequences. In the immediate aftermath of Reykjavik, the Soviet position on the Intermediate Nuclear Force (INF) issue repeated Andropov's in 1983. That is, the Soviet negotiators would not allow one more missile than what was already in the British and French arsenals. Early in 1987, however, Gorbachev changed. D'Agostino wrote that "instead of continuing to seek U.S. acceptance of the linkage between an agreement on missiles in Europe and the American SDI program," Gorbachev made a "sharp break" with the past and accepted essentially the Reagan formula to eliminate all INF missiles in Europe.[418]

In 1987-88 the Communist Party of Italy (CPI), began to influence Soviet thinkers and writers on foreign policy.[419] For years, in West European Communist politics the Italian Party had spearheaded thinking conciliatory to capitalism. It had, for example, defended Czech leader Alexander Dubcek and had condemned the Warsaw Pact intervention in Czechoslovakia in 1968. The CPI urged the Soviets to take a benign view of NATO as a "defensive and geographically limited alliance."[420] The CPI also hailed Gorbachev's universal human values slogan as vindication of the ideas of its leaders Enrico Berlinguer and Achille Ochetto. On intermediate range weapons, the Italians had obtained the idea of supporting the zero option from the German Social Democrats, and had pressed this on the Soviets.

In mid-1988, after weakening the CPSU, Gorbachev made nuclear weapons the centerpiece of his revisions in foreign policy.[421] To make way for unilateral Soviet nuclear cuts, Gorbachev needed to undermine the Brezhnev-era arms doctrine, the idea that the Soviet achievement of nuclear parity with the U.S. formed the basis of détente. The leap to revisionist positions on arms policy, as with so much else, came at the June 1988 Nineteenth Party Conference, where Gorbachev drew a distinction between political and military means to protect USSR security. Gorbachev actually blamed the nuclear arms race on the Soviet leadership and the idea of strategic parity. Gorbachev said, "As a result [of the idea of parity] we let ourselves be drawn into an arms race which was bound to affect the socioeconomic development of the country and its international position." In November 1988, the Politburo authorized drastic arms cuts. In December, Gorbachev announced the cuts at the UN in New York.[422] Increasingly, Soviet foreign policy consisted of unilateral disarmament without regard for the military, political, and economic consequences.

In November 1987, the keynote speech by Gorbachev on the seventieth anniversary of the Bolshevik Revolution, "October and *Perestroika*: the Revolution Continues," like a freeze frame in a video, captured the fierce rivalry in the CPSU leadership over Soviet foreign policy. Most Western commentators stressed the speech's attempt to straddle warring views of Party history, but the speech's new formulations on foreign policy had far more significance. The speech tried to bridge more than one chasm: with representatives of both Communist and social democratic parties in Moscow, Gorbachev sought to foster a reconciliation of the Communist and social democratic left. After noting that diplomats had accomplished little to rid the world of intermediate and long-range nuclear weapons, Gorbachev "examined the theoretical aspects of the prospects for advancement toward a durable peace." Certainly, he declared, imperialism was warlike and had militarism and neocolonialism as essential characteristics. What, then, was the basis for optimism that the Soviet peace offensive could succeed? New phrases entered his answer. Gorbachev proclaimed: "Contradictions can be modified," and "we are facing a historic choice based on our largely interconnected and integral world."[423] He stated, "The class struggle and other manifestations of social contradictions will influence the objective processes favoring peace." This approach revised the traditional Soviet view that the class struggle was itself an objective process favoring peace, that peace was the result of a struggle to impose peaceful relations on a reluctant and bellicose imperialism. Instead, Gorbachev was proposing "a joint quest for a new economic order which takes into account the interests of all on an equal basis." In the final analysis, the speech represented Gorbachev's opportunism straining against orthodox Marxist-Leninist formulations. He was seeking to retain the vocabulary of orthodoxy while evading its implications. The speech was less a call for a Soviet peace

155

struggle than a call for Soviet reconciliation and integration with imperialism.

Nowhere were unilateral Soviet foreign policy concessions more apparent than in Afghanistan. Since 1979 the Afghan revolutionary government and its Soviet allies had been pitted against the U.S., Pakistan, and China. At first Gorbachev favored intensifying the war,[424] a noble struggle against barbarism and reaction, not entirely unlike the fight for a democratic Spanish Republic in 1936-39. In early 1987, the new Afghan Communist leader, Najibullah, having taken over from Karmal in May 1986 with the blessing--and some believe, the connivance--of the Gorbachev leadership,[425] called for "national reconciliation," implying openness to negotiation, coalition, and eventual Soviet withdrawal. The uncompromising Karmal had always referred to the mujahadin counterrevolutionary opposition as "bandits." A more critical tone about the war had entered Gorbachev's public comments as early as 1986. In 1987 Gorbachev, Yakovlev and Shevardnadze began to use the *glasnost* media to build up Soviet domestic support for withdrawal. In 1987 Artyom Borovik, the correspondent of *Ogonyok*, a revisionist media stronghold, filed reports from Afghanistan critical of the Soviet war effort. His battlefield reports graphically described the casualties. At the December 1987 Washington Summit, Gorbachev announced that the Soviets would withdraw from Afghanistan. In February 1988 he proposed a timetable for the withdrawal of Soviet troops by early 1989. In 1988, letters critical of the war "spontaneously" began to pour into the *glasnost* press from mothers of soldiers. In mid-1988, *Ogonyok* published the first article in which a top Soviet military man criticized the war.

To the end, Najibullah, anti-revisionists in the CPSU leadership and military, and such Soviet allies as Cuba and Angola opposed an unconditional Soviet withdrawal from Afghanistan. Despite Western claims of a Soviet "Vietnam quagmire," and rising domestic opposition to the war--much of the latter orchestrated from above--Soviet casualties were lower than at the start of the intervention. According to an American scholar on the Afghan conflict, "The outcome of this war was ultimately determined at home in Moscow."[426] The withdrawal occurred with no agreement on Soviet demands for an end to U.S. military aid to the mujahadin, and no American guarantees for the safety of Afghan Communist leaders or for a non-aligned Afghanistan. On February 15, 1989 the last Soviet troops left, with nothing to show for their years of sacrifice.[427] The Afghans were left to the mercy of murderous warlords first, and then to the Islamic fundamentalists of the Taliban, as all of the economic, political, and educational progress of the erstwhile revolutionary regime was destroyed.

Gorbachev's betrayals of other liberation movements and socialist states came in the final three years of *perestroika*. Until December 1988, the USSR still largely supported the African National Congress (ANC) and other African freedom movements. In late 1988, however, came the first sign of a change in Soviet policy. The advancing liberation movements in Southwest Africa, aided by Cuba and the USSR, had compelled an election in Namibia whose fairness would be guaranteed by UN troops. Without consulting the liberation movement, the Southwest African People's Organization (SWAPO), or its ally Cuba, Shevardnadze suddenly agreed to an American proposal to cut down the presence of UN troops in Namibia.[428]

In 1987-88, other foreign policy concessions followed in rapid succession. In May 1988, Reagan visited Moscow. In June 1988, the Nineteenth Party Conference discarded the doctrine of nuclear parity. In September-October 1988, the next CC Plenum affirmed the priority of universal human values over class struggle. The Plenum, thus, "de-ideologized" Soviet foreign policy. This Plenum also retired Gromyko and demoted Ligachev. In December 1988 at the UN in New York, Gorbachev announced a cut of 500,000 in Soviet troops, including the removal of six tank divisions from Eastern Europe. In 1989 counterrevolution swept Eastern Europe.

Gorbachev abandoned the so-called "Brezhnev Doctrine," which held that the Soviet Union and other Eastern European states had a right and a duty to defend socialism in any member state of the Warsaw Pact. This doctrine was consistent with Lenin's classic writings that considerations of the class struggle take precedence over considerations of national sovereignty.[429] The doctrine expressed a form of class solidarity extended to interstate relations, the solidarity of one socialist state with another. According to David Lane, "In 1989 it was made clear that the USSR would not intervene in the affairs of other states, even if members of the same alliance."[430] In Eastern Europe where Communist governments had always been less deeply rooted than in the USSR, Gorbachev's policy of troop cutbacks and non-interference spelled disaster. In all Eastern European societies, the Communist governments rapidly lost self-confidence, and opposition elements took heart. Gorbachev gave up the Brezhnev Doctrine unilaterally. The fate of the German Democratic Republic (GDR) revealed the catastrophe of yielding something in return for nothing. Instead of a negotiated coming together of two German states with different social systems on the basis of mutual interest and equal rights, the end of the GDR became a humiliating forced annexation and capitalist restoration.

In early 1987 Gorbachev began to push for radical economic reform. Parallel with his political reform program, the radical measures that Gorbachev proposed abandoned earlier incremental efforts and experiments.[431] The leadership's plans and programs were not the only spurs to radical economic change. Three other forces drove economic developments in a pro-capitalist direction: the *glasnost* media, the weakening of the CPSU, including its withdrawal from economic management, and the unbridled growth of the second economy. In 1987-88, *perestroika* unleashed new economic forces and processes. Ostensibly, the Law on State Enterprise passed in 1987 at the July CC Plenum neither rejected centralized planning nor endorsed a transition to a full-blooded market economy. Its proponents claimed the law would make planning less rigid and would allow autonomy for the enterprises and experimentation with market mechanisms. It also provided for the election of plant managers, an ill-conceived idea that swiftly led to unacceptable wage increases to workers by managers whose eyes were on the ballot box. After its inflationary implications were understood, this feature of the law was repealed. Ellman and Kontorovich noted that the wording of the Law on State Enterprises bore little resemblance to a conventional economic statute for a planned economy. "It is hard to imagine similar wording, which does not oblige anyone to do anything, in the statutes of another country."[432] To a large degree the statute served as a political rallying cry signaling the direction of change.

The *glasnost* media pushed the Soviet leadership to implement new economic policies in the riskiest possible way. The media influenced the public policy debate and public sentiment about economic change enormously. The *glasnost* media, subservient to Yakovlev and Gorbachev until 1988, made sure every economic blunder or failure, even when due to Gorbachev's policies, strengthened the case for more enterprise autonomy and more marketization, never the case for reinvigorating the central plan. The public debate moved only in an anti-socialist direction. In time, "it became politically feasible to demand the complete liquidation" of the planning institutions.[433]

Media pressure drove what Ligachev called the "fateful error"[434] of December 1987--the drastic reduction of the state purchase of industrial output, a mad leap from a planned to an unplanned economy. Against the better judgment of Prime Minister Ryzhkov and Ligachev, Yakovlev and Gorbachev pushed to shrink the state orders--the guaranteed government purchase of Soviet industrial output at fixed prices--from 100 percent to a mere 50 percent of the whole of industry. Reducing state orders to such a degree meant that, in one leap, half of Soviet industry would gain autonomy to buy and sell its output in a new wholesale market--trade between enterprises--with prices set by fluctuations in supply and demand. Ligachev and Ryzhkov argued for a cautious experimental plan in which the state would purchase 90 percent of industrial output, leaving only 10 percent of industry to face the uncertainties of supply and demand. The Ligachev-Ryzhkov plan would have gently pushed enterprises to experiment with autonomy and free prices. The Gorbachev plan proved utterly reckless. It plunged the economy into chaos. In 1988, consumer shortages proliferated and, for the first time since World War II, inflation appeared.

The removal of the Party from economic management undermined the economy.[435] The sectoral ministries in Moscow were powerful tools of central planning. Through their large central offices in Moscow, the ministries linked enterprises to the highest planning bodies and the CC Secretariat of the CPSU. They oversaw the performance of enterprises, enforced plan discipline and maintained regional and sectoral industry links and balances. *Perestroika* reduced the ministries' powers again and again. In 1986, in 1987, and in 1988 these reductions destroyed the main coordinating mechanisms of the planned economy. The dismantling did not take the form of slashing the staff of the ministries. Rather, *perestroika* redefined the ministries' relationship to enterprises. New directions forbade the ministries from issuing commands and gave them the new role of developing "enterprise autonomy."[436] Rendering the ministries powerless was foolish enough, but the way that Gorbachev and his advisers implemented this policy achieved the maximum loss of public confidence. According to Ellman and Kontorovich, Gorbachev's team was "constantly discrediting itself and its policy by repeatedly making erroneous and halfhearted decisions, then quickly reversing and publicly condemning them."[437]

The major blow to the planned economy occurred at the Nineteenth Party Conference, which abandoned gradualism and issued a directive compelling the separation of the Party, the Soviet organs, and economic management. This directive played the major role in the Party's withdrawal from the economy, both on an organizational level and ideological level. New blows rained down on the planning system shortly after the Nineteenth Party Conference. In the fall of 1988 Gorbachev abolished 1,064 departments and 465 sectors in the Central Committees of Union Republics and regional and district Party committees. He slashed the number of departments by 44 percent. Ideologically, the Party's withdrawal from economic management undermined the willingness of leaders of state economic entities to obey directives from a single center in Moscow. Centrifugal forces began to gain the upper hand in the economy.

Gorbachev also tried to harness the second economy. A U.S. academic, S. Frederick Starr, noted that this decision represented a basic change in course. In effect Gorbachev rolled out a welcome mat for nascent capitalist forces in Soviet "civil society." "Gorbachev faced a momentous choice," Starr asserted. Either he could have improved the economy through tightened "controls" and better planning, or he could have sought to win to his side "the new economic and social forces that had brought themselves to life through autonomous action and intellectual contact with Russia's long suppressed tradition of liberal reform." He rejected the first and chose the second. He tried "to co-opt the second economy (and tax its profits) with his new law allowing private--nominally co-operative--businesses." He blessed the voluntary associations ("the informals") by claiming they had a legitimate place in Soviet society. "Gorbachev's genius," Starr declared, "is not to have created the elements of *perestroika* but to have taken them from the society around him."[438] British analyst Anne White confirmed Starr's opinion. The "informals" denoted "any kind of activity not directly organized by the Party." Many were non-political cultural entities, especially among the young, and many dated back to the Khrushchev Thaw. The oft-cited number, 30,000 informals in existence by February 1988, included both pressure groups and non-pressure groups, and over time, especially in the *perestroika* era, the former became ever more significant.[439]

Thus, the laws on Co-operatives and the law on Leases passed in 1988 contributed to the rapid expansion of the capitalist elements in the USSR. While slyly quoting Lenin --out of context--on the acceptability of co-operatives under socialism as a form of socialist property,[440] the law actually allowed private property in the guise of a co-op. Soon the remaining state enterprises developed economic relationships with privately owned co-ops, which were less regulated and less taxed than the state sector. The leasing of industrial property to co-ops became a way of privatizing assets while maintaining the fiction of public ownership.

The restoration of capitalism and the triumph of separatism were distinct processes. The USSR could have fractured with the pieces remaining socialist. The USSR could have restored capitalism without breaking up. In actuality, the two occurred together, and shared a similar lineage. The pro-market and pro-private enterprise trend also had a dubious analysis of nationalism, Russian and non-Russian. The differences between this trend and Lenin were fundamental, systematic and long-standing.[441] Lenin and those who followed in his footsteps saw the two sides of nationalism, progressive and reactionary. More importantly, from 1917 to 1991, they stressed the need to struggle with nationalism, if possible, to replace nationalism with internationalism, or at least to strengthen nationalism's democratic and progressive manifestations and to weaken its reactionary side. Those in the Party who leaned the most in the direction of blind markets, private enterprise, and liberalism, also consistently failed to come to grips with nationalism.

Nationalism had a special hold on the peasantry, and on the vast sections of the Soviet working class within a generation of the countryside. Even after collectivization, the attitudes of country folk toward land, property ownership, and the homeland made them susceptible to nationalist rhetoric. By and large, urban workers uprooted from the countryside long ago were more class-conscious. They found nationalism less attractive. Nationalism also had a hold on a section of the literary intelligentsia that identified with the Soviet peasantry and pre-1917 Russian history.

The Party trend with which Gorbachev identified had as its social base the large social classes and class fragments most inclined to nationalism: the peasantry, and sections of the working class with social ties to the countryside. Accordingly, this CPSU trend did not struggle with nationalism, ideologically and politically. It accommodated, ignored, or underestimated nationalism, Russian and non-Russian. It also overestimated the USSR's progress in the struggle against national inequality. Its premature claims of success influenced many, though by no means all, observers of Soviet life.[442]

Examples of the Gorbachev team's incomprehension of nationalism and the national question abound. In his 1987 Revolution Day speech Gorbachev declared that the Soviet Union had solved the national question. Well into the *perestroika* era, Gorbachev's top adviser Yakovlev defended his 1972 broadside against Russian nationalism. That article, "Against Anti-Historicism" assailed the inclusionary policies of Brezhnev and Suslov toward Russian nationalism, policies they hoped would limit the damage done to the Soviet state's legitimacy by Khrushchev's "de-Stalinization" campaigns, which the young Yakovlev had supported and an older Yakovlev revived under Gorbachev.[443] In 1972, Yakovlev had worried that an alliance of Russian nationalists (who shared some ideas with Marxism-Leninism, for example, a disdain for the capitalist West) and anti-Khrushchevites in the CPSU would threaten key policies of the Khrushchev era such as emulation of the West. In 1985-91 Yakovlev remained worried about such an alliance. To oppose Russian nationalism, therefore, was consistent with his defense of the policies of Khrushchev and Gorbachev.

Gorbachev proved utterly inept at handling the national question. When nationalist ferment arose in the Baltics, he first ignored it. Then, he used economic repression against Lithuania, and later changed course to a weak and hopeless re-negotiation of the Union Treaty that, by degrees, caved in to ever more extreme nationalist and separatist demands.

As the possibility of state fragmentation grew--in July 1988 mass demonstrations in the Baltic states protested their annexation to the Soviet Union[444]--the key allies of Gorbachev in the Politburo acted like ostriches. Nationalists increasingly dominated the "informal" *perestroika* groups that formed in outlying republics. Such nationalists increasingly spoke of separation from Russia and increasingly raised their cause even within the republican Communist Parties. In September 1988 when Yakovlev came back from a trip to the Baltics and reported to the Politburo: "There is no problem; *perestroika* is developing normally," Ligachev reacted with fury because he correctly saw a situation about to spin out of control. Yakovlev, however, counseled doing nothing, and he prevailed. Within several months the Lithuanian CP had split, Party organizations ceased to function, and emboldened separatists were on the verge of power.[445]

By contrast, orthodox Marxist-Leninists favored the self-determination of nations, including the right of secession, a right they hoped would never need to be exercised, as well as the development of national languages and culture, guarantees of minority representation in political leadership, and "affirmative-action-style" socioeconomic development in the case of the non-Russian regions. Even some bourgeois Sovietologists favorably compare Soviet nationality policy and U.S. affirmative action. For example, a recent American study that credited the Soviet Union with elevating previously oppressed nationalities, stressed how much its policies broke the mold of historical instances in which a large, more advanced nation embraced smaller, less advanced ones, by calling the USSR "the world's first Affirmative Action Empire." The author of the study, Terry Martin, said, the Soviet Union was the first state to respond to rising nationalism "by systematically promoting national consciousness of its ethnic minorities and establishing for them many of the characteristic institutional forms of the nation state."[446]

Gorbachev ignored national inequality, or utterly overstated progress against it. On his six-year watch he underestimated and misunderstood the depth of the national sentiment of specific peoples almost everywhere, including the way his other reform policies fanned national sentiment. Eleven months after the Alma Ata riots of December 1986, Gorbachev boasted the Soviet Union had solved the national question.

In the case of the conflict between Azerbaijan and Armenia, Gorbachev, when not ignoring problems or claiming to have solved them, indulged in cynical manipulation of national strife to improve his position in the Politburo, a blatant example of sacrificing principle for short-term gain. In April 1987, Gorbachev encouraged a rebellion of the Armenians in the Azeri province of Nagorno-Karabahk because doing so created an embarrassment for Gaidar Aliev, an Azeri Politburo member and Gorbachev opponent. Aliev came under fire from many quarters, including Ligachev, and his career went into eclipse in mid-1987. By the fall, he was off the Politburo.

Encouraging the Armenian claims in Karabakh formed part of a pattern of Gorbachev behavior. The pattern was to cheer "national fronts for *perestroika*" against local officials, usually the Party first secretaries who had put obstacles in Gorbachev's path. In April 1988, activists in the Baltic Republics began forming national fronts to support *perestroika*[447] and to affirm their nationalist aspirations. These fronts rapidly took on a separatist and pro-capitalist character. Yet, for Gorbachev, ethnic clashes had certain advantages. Each disturbance handed Gorbachev, if he did anything at all, an opportunity to oust local Party leaders if they happened to be his opponents. Each time the Gorbachev Politburo sided with the fronts or did nothing, it encouraged more extreme expressions of nationalism. In the words of Anthony D'Agostino,[448] Gorbachev played "sorcerer's apprentice," promoting nationalist resentments for his own purposes until they spun out of control.

As *perestroika* failed in one sphere, the damage rippled in all directions. Starting in 1988, economic hardship and separatism reinforced each other. As consumer shortages worsened in 1988, the tendency for various republics to hoard production and to go it alone increased. The USSR planned economy had developed as a single grid with a precise division of labor and specialization among republics. For example, one industrial complex in the Baltic region supplied paper cups for the whole USSR. As the economic authority of the center in Moscow grew feeble, barter between republics replaced planning, and economic disruption grew. The economic disorder and uncertainty fueled separatist fires, as each union republic sought to protect its economic interests as best it could.

Several of Gorbachev's moves strengthened outlying localities against the center. The CC Plenum of January 1987 launched a public attack on the nomenklatura system, the practice of selecting state and republican officials from a list developed by the CC Secretariat in Moscow. Beginning in 1987, Gorbachev and other Party leaders denounced this appointment system and refused to defend local officials from attacks in their regions and districts. Consequently, local officials became more preoccupied with accommodating local views rather than the views of Moscow leaders. When local and all-Union interests conflicted, survival required local leaders to favor local interests. Gorbachev's foreign policy also encouraged local interests, particularly in the Baltic states. Ellman and Kontorovich said that Gorbachev's policy of ending the Cold War and seeking close co-operation with the West "made him open to pressure from the West to recognize the rights of the Baltic states, especially Lithuania, to self-determination."[449]

As the 1987-1988 period closed out, Gorbachev and his circle had all but routed Ligachev and their other opponents. The rout transformed the nature of *perestroika*. The growing disarray in the Party, its removal from the economy, led to economic difficulties that became obvious in 1988. This took the form of inflation, shortages, budget deficits and disintegration of key economic institutions of the planned economy. In 1988, for the first time in forty years, prices began rising throughout the economy. A year later, inflation galloped at a yearly rate of 20 percent. As consumer goods vanished from shelves, hoarding proliferated. Gorbachev's edicts crippled the formerly powerful industrial ministries in Moscow.[450] In 1988, Soviet economist T. Koriagana calculated illicitly obtained personal wealth at 200 to 240 billion rubles, perhaps representing 20 to 25 percent of all personal wealth in the Soviet Union.[451] Economic crisis, in turn, strengthened reactionary nationalist separatism. Gorbachev's encouragement of "popular fronts" and "national fronts"--motivated by a desire to put pressure on his Party opponents in the union republics--handed power to separatists. A year later, in 1989, economic decline-- caused by the failure of *perestroika*, not by a long-term growth slowdown- -set in motion mass hostility to Gorbachev and the CPSU, and growing support for Boris Yeltsin's anti-Communist populism. In 1987 and 1988, Gorbachev made the turn. The unraveling had begun.

6. Crisis and Collapse, 1989-91

During 1989 the worst fears of those who had foreseen the potential of the changes wrought at the Nineteenth Party Conference were realized. The working out of those political reforms created a political situation, which the party and its leadership could no longer control. From the end of March 1989, the party leadership was reactive, trying to keep up with changes, which were occurring faster than it could control and propelled by political forces for the most part outside of that leadership and of the party as a whole. Graeme Gill[452]

The shadow economy has pervaded all economic sectors. Stanislav Menshikov[453]

In 1991, the masses supported demands for freedom and democracy, opposed the privileges and power so long monopolized by the Communist Party bureaucracy, and hoped for an improvement in their material conditions. The mass rallies for Yeltsin featured banners such as "Down with Gorbachev" and "Down with the CPSU," but I never saw a banner saying "Long Live Capitalism" or "All Power to the Bourgeoisie." Roy Medvedev[454]

In 1989-91, the final three years of *perestroika*, after having triumphed over his opponents, Gorbachev remade the Soviet Union in five crucial ways. First, he ended the leading role and monopoly position of the CPSU, changing it to a parliamentary party. Secondly, he undermined central planning and public ownership. He pushed the CPSU out of economic management while searching for a transition to a market economy. He began privatizing state-owned enterprises and encouraged the burgeoning second economy. Third, he surrendered to the United States on a range of foreign policy issues and eventually sought an outright alliance with imperialism. Fourth, he allowed the *glasnost* media to remake Soviet ideology and culture. Fifth, always baffled by the national question, he tried repression against Baltic separatists and then flip-flopped to negotiations in an ultimately fruitless search for a new basis for the union of republics.

Gorbachev was mindful of Khrushchev's overthrow by the Party in 1964, and he was bent on making his reforms irreversible by a "momentous break"[455] with Leninism itself. This took the form of rendering the CPSU powerless, turning it into a kind of advisory, strategic planning department for Soviet society and the parliamentary voice of the Soviet working class. He also wanted a multiparty system and a pluralist media and culture. To make the Soviet economy more flexible and dynamic, he demanded a large role for market forces, private ownership, and private initiative. He desired the continuation of the all-Union federal state. He wished to see less conflict with the West. Only his last wish came true.

Perestroika became "catastroika"[456] in 1989. What actually happened was three years of mounting chaos from one end of the USSR to the other, ending in the collapse of Soviet socialism. In 1989 counterrevolution shook Eastern Europe and a year later Germany re-united on NATO's terms. At the same time Gorbachev's worst enemy, Boris Yeltsin, whose career seemed dead and buried when Gorbachev publicly booted him out of the leadership in 1987, made a Lazarus-like political comeback. Reborn as a leader of the "democrats," he captured control of the all-important Russian Republic. By early 1990, dual power existed in the USSR, with Yeltsin controlling Russia and Gorbachev the Soviet Union.[457] In 1989-91, the economy went from bad to worse: production declined, shortages multiplied, store shelves emptied, paychecks sometimes failed to materialize, and popular resentment grew.[458] The destruction of East European socialism adversely affected the Soviet economy. The steady withdrawal of the Party from the economy proved disastrous. By the summer of 1991 Western analysts spoke of a Soviet "depression."[459] Soviet citizens blamed *perestroika*. Unprecedented mine strikes rocked the regime twice, in 1989 and in 1991. The government sank into debt to Western banks. As one after another union republic declared its sovereignty and then seceded, the Soviet Union crumbled as a unitary state.

The media drove all politics rightward. Anatoly Chernyaev called *glasnost* the motor of *perestroika*. "Under the increasing pressure of *glasnost*," Chernyaev said, "the de-ideologization of *perestroika* began."[460] Actually, the process was re-ideologization: opening the floodgates to non-socialist and anti-socialist ideas. Gorbachev could not control the genie he had let out of the bottle. By 1989 the media were falling into the grip of the pro-Yeltsin "democrats." By 1991, a frantic USSR Prime Minister Nikolai Ryzhkov rued that the Soviet media were almost wholly in the "democrat" opposition's hands.[461]

171

In *perestroika*'s last years, economic forces on the dark side of Soviet society demanded legitimacy and power. The black market and the Russian mob multiplied like vermin. The private enterprise, bogus "co-ops" grew.[462] The ambitious and acquisitive backers of Boris Yeltsin lobbied for a drastic shift to radical marketization. If the market replaced the plan and if Yeltsin privatized the Russian economy, high officials, directors of enterprises, and managers could look forward to "unprecedented wealth."[463] The dominant sections of the Party and state leadership could easily see which way the wind was blowing. Corrupt elements of the leadership began embezzling state and Party property and transforming it into their own private property.

In the bewildering last years of *perestroika*, the Soviet people grew to hate Gorbachev and to treat him with scorn. Frantically racing to quell one crisis here while another broke out there, Gorbachev cut a pitiable figure. A magician who had run out of tricks, he had few friends other than the Western media and governments. In late 1991, even his false friends in the American White House abandoned him.

Gorbachev's degeneration from a Communist to a social democrat was stark. His illusions about where events were heading were laughable. In May 1990, he gave an interview to *Time* magazine that took the measure of his "internal political revolution."[464] Answering the questions, "What does it mean to be a Communist today?" and "What will it mean in years to come?" he replied:

> To be a Communist as I see it means not to be afraid of what is new, to reject obedience to any dogma, to think independently, to submit one's thoughts and actions to the test of morality and through political action, to help working people realize their hopes and aspirations and live up to their abilities. I believe that to be a Communist

today means first of all to be consistently democratic and to put universal human values above everything else. ...As we dismantle the Stalinist system, we are not retreating from socialism but are moving toward it.[465]

A simple cause underlay the seemingly complex pattern of these tumultuous years. The Gorbachev leadership replaced a policy of struggle with one of compromise and retreat. Gorbachev retreated before the pro–capitalist coalition led by Boris Yeltsin. He retreated before the media that berated his centrism and timidity. He retreated before nationalist separatism. He retreated before U.S. imperialism with its unquenchable thirst for one-sided concessions and for global dominion.

Gorbachev was incapable of analyzing why his regime was disintegrating. He could not see that liquidating the CPSU was leading straight to the Soviet Union's collapse. By weakening the CPSU, he relatively strengthened the Yeltsin camp, the separatists, the second economy, corrupt elements in the Party, the Russian mob and Western imperialism. Soviet analyst Jerry Hough, rejecting the Western description of Gorbachev as "a man riding a tiger he could not control," observed that Gorbachev never seriously tried to restrain the tiger. "Instead he continually urged it on. In the rare case when force was applied it seemed very effective.[466]

Gorbachev's analysis of his political predicament lacked realism in some respects, yet he could count votes and read polls. With approval ratings slumping into the single digits, he lacked the courage to push his market policies to their logical conclusion. He never mustered the temerity to impose economic "shock therapy." Boris Yeltsin did. The very expression merits deconstruction. Economic "shock therapy" derived from a discredited and sadistic therapy of applying electric shock to severely mentally ill patients, causing needless suffering without helping most and providing a cure for few. Economic shock therapy treated people living under socialism as if they were suffering from a mental illness. This "shock therapy" forced the vast majority to suffer a loss of jobs, housing, children's education, health care, pensions, and security from crime, while providing to a few a chance at wealth.

Gorbachev tried to manage his worsening political position by maneuvering, vacillating, improvising, and dissembling. As mass discontent rose in 1989-91, the Soviet people mocked his wordy speeches about "new turning points" and "decisive tests" and laughed bitterly at his attempt to portray catastrophes as advances. Gorbachev frantically sought to stabilize the USSR, to reassert control, without abandoning policies that were de-stabilizing every aspect of economics and politics. Having jettisoned the Party, Gorbachev tried to evade the consequences. To stabilize the political system, he sought to govern through new state institutions, especially an executive presidency and the Congress of People's Deputies. The "democrats," however, swiftly won key positions in the Congress. To stabilize the sinking economy, Gorbachev searched for a transition to a market economy. To stabilize his influence over a CPSU shattered by his policies, he clung to the post of General Secretary of the CPSU and placated his opponents by appointments to his inner circle. The latter tactic was evident in his temporary about-face of late 1990 and early 1991, when arch-revisionists Yakovlev and Shevardnadze left Gorbachev's side and he elevated Vladimir Kryuchkov and other Communists. To prevent the fragmentation of the Soviet Union, he first tried repression, and then sought to negotiate a Union Treaty.

No attempts at stabilization succeeded, save one. Gorbachev achieved stability, of a kind, in foreign relations by turning Soviet foreign policy upside down. In the final years of *perestroika*, Gorbachev abandoned socialist and Third World allies, while seeking political support and financial credits from the West.

By late 1991 the Soviet Union had evolved into a compliant junior partner of the U.S.

This chapter treats the key events of 1989-91--the overthrow of socialist governments in Eastern Europe, the Party's destruction, the rise of the "democrat" opposition, the deepening economic crisis, and the USSR's dismemberment. They were interacting processes. In the final analysis one process drove them all: the leadership's determination to end the dominant role of the CPSU which, even at this late date, remained a latent obstacle to Gorbachev's policies.

If Gorbachev himself lacked a realistic view of the consequences of his policies, some in his inner circle were not so naïve. According to William Odom, Gorbachev's adviser Alexander Yakovlev knew all along where things were heading.

> In June 1994 I [Odom] put that same question ('Did he understand from the beginning that Gorbachev's reforms might require the collapse of the Soviet Union and the Soviet system?') to Yakovlev during a dinner chat. He replied that he did realize that they were destroying the old regime, adding with a certain glee 'and we did it before our opponents woke up in time to prevent it!'[467]

Similarly, Anatoly Chernyaev, Gorbachev's top foreign policy aide, described the mindset of the more realistic in the Gorbachev leadership as things fell apart. Without abandoning his revisionist prejudices and vocabulary, Chernyaev stated that at least some began to discern that the "third way" they were following was a mirage. On the eve of a Politburo meeting to discuss the draft Program of the CPSU's Twenty-eighth Congress, Chernyaev chose these words to characterize the predicament the core leaders thought they faced:

The crux of the matter was that the pendulum of opinion was swinging between two poles. One way was to hold on to Stalin's model of socialism only without the use of repression (a contradiction in terms). The other was to accept the precepts of a market society (in essence bourgeois democratic) that were already bursting forth. It seemed obvious that once we rejected the coercive model and its imposition on society by use of force and a state ideology, there would be no choice but to follow the second path. No one wanted to admit this. Indeed we hardly realized that this was how matters really stood.[468]

As the crises multiplied, some observers saw the signs of a U.S.–sponsored destabilization. They remembered the U.S.-campaign against Allende's Chile in 1970-1973, when Nixon and Kissinger "made the Chilean economy scream." Destabilization was a familiar imperialist policy for undoing Communist, left, nationalist, and other independent governments in weak Third World countries. The USSR, however, was too strong for external de-stabilization. The U.S. war buildup could strain the USSR, but not crush it.[469] After the Soviet collapse, Reagan Administration officials exaggerated their role in the Soviet disintegration.[470] The Bush Administration tried to impose a unified Western policy in support of Gorbachev. It believed Gorbachev was a reliable client who would deliver the whole Soviet Union to capitalism on a platter. At first, until it was clear Gorbachev was a spent force, the U.S. and NATO did not favor Yeltsin, who had only Russia to offer. The U.S. also feared the risk posed by ethnic clashes and military disintegration to the vast network of Soviet nuclear weapons and nuclear reactors. In 1991, Bush also wanted Gorbachev's support for the Persian Gulf War.

Toward the end, as Gorbachev's position sank into hopelessness, he seemed to have trouble distinguishing between wishes and facts. Some of his aides saw pathological irrationality at work. The lavish praise heaped on him during his foreign trips in 1990 and 1991 deluded him. Chernyaev said Gorbachev's thinking became "increasingly filled with circular and unrealistic logic" about his real political situation at home. "The narcotic of lionization by foreign leaders and journalists was warping his thinking in an increasingly visible way."[471]

Nothing was more irrational than the General Secretary's pursuit of a new Union Treaty, whose provisions he ostensibly opposed. Gorbachev bridled at each new draft of the Union Treaty that, at Yeltsin's insistence, gave a smaller and smaller role to the all-Union state. At the end of his tether and confused, he descended into self-deception and political self-destruction.[472] Jerry Hough remarked that history knows no other example of a government with full power over taxation stemming from its ownership of all property ruining itself by allowing local governmental units "under its control to take control of tax revenue. ...That is what happened from the summer of 1990 to the late summer of 1991."[473]

An illusion inspired the whole Gorbachev project--to turn the socialist USSR into a western European social democracy that, in his revisionist view, incorporated the best of socialism and the best of European capitalism.[474] He discovered, however, that projects founded on illusion fail. You cannot leap across a canyon in two steps. Some Marxists have said that Gorbachev was consciously pursuing outright capitalist restoration. Admittedly, the dismantling process looked much the same, but such a claim missed the ideological nature of Gorbachev's project: his non-class view of the world insisted the mirage was not a mirage, that there was a third way between the two systems and the two classes, that his version of "socialism," capitalism with a social safety net and class partnership policies, was socialism. Typically, this trend of political thought denigrated genuine socialism as "Communism" or "Stalinism." The fact that Gorbachev's project ended in capitalist restoration does not prove he was consciously seeking it. The crisis of 1989-91 steadily worsened because Gorbachev never gave up his pursuit of the third way and Party liquidation, the main causes of the crisis. In 1990 Alexander Yakovlev, the earliest, most conscious and most consistent promoter of enfeebling the Party, laid out one last plan for Gorbachev. Calling the Politburo and Central Committee "the main obstacles to *perestroika*," Yakovlev urged him to go further and faster in pushing the Party aside. "Convene the Congress of People's Deputies and establish presidential power." He advised undoing collectivization, public ownership, and the Union state under the disingenuous slogan: "Give land to the peasants, factories to the workers, and real independence to the republics." He counseled creation of a multiparty system with the CPSU relinquishing its monopoly of power, slashing the nomenklatura apparatus to the bone, and accepting large loans from the West. He pressed Gorbachev to "launch military reform, get rid of the generals, replace them with lieutenant colonels, start a pullout from Eastern Europe, liquidate the industrial ministries, grant freedom to entrepreneurs, get rid of [Prime Minister] Ryzhkov, and [Yuri] Maslyukov the head of Gosplan."[475] In the end, Gorbachev took most of Yakovlev's advice.

Two main processes dominated Soviet politics in 1989. One grabbed headlines; the other did not. The first was the swift collapse of the East European socialist states, a series of counterrevolutions that coincided with the bicentennial of the French Revolution. The second process was the implementation of Gorbachev's "radical political reform."[476] Gorbachev's revision of Soviet foreign policy triggered the Eastern European collapse, and the Eastern European collapse strengthened revisionism in the Soviet Union. In December 1988, Gorbachev gave a speech to the UN in New York announcing a Soviet policy of non-interference in the internal affairs of socialist states and military withdrawal from Eastern Europe. That shift in policy strengthened the internal opposition in Eastern Europe and emboldened the West. The domino-like fall of state after state in 1989 undermined the prestige and strength of socialism and adversely affected the USSR economy.

The cause of the collapse of the East European socialist states is beyond the scope of this account of the Soviet collapse. Suffice it to say the East European states were weaker than the USSR. First, the Eastern European socialist states were newer and less firmly rooted than Soviet socialism. Second, in much of Eastern Europe, socialist change stemmed less from homegrown revolutionary movements than from the wartime advance of the Red Army. Soviet occupation enabled small Communist Parties decimated by Nazi repression to build postwar antifascist government coalitions that evolved into socialist regimes. Thus, in Eastern Europe, outside circumstances made revolution comparatively easy and peaceful, but also less thoroughgoing. Third, national and religious sentiment worked against many of the regimes. Where such countries as Roman Catholic Poland viewed Russia as the historic oppressor, an extra problem in winning legitimacy burdened socialism. Where Russia was a historic friend and ally, as in Eastern Orthodox Bulgaria and Serbia, socialism walked an easier path. In the German Democratic Republic (GDR) the aspiration for national reunification clashed with the task of building a separate socialist state, but in Yugoslavia, socialism merged with the will for national independence. (This helps explain why in the 1990s NATO had to work so hard to stamp out the unity and socialist character of the remnants of the Yugoslav Federation.) Fourth, some states, bordering the West, notably the GDR, Czechoslovakia, and Hungary, felt the pressure of economic and ideological competition with richer capitalist neighbors that, unlike socialist states, drew wealth from the Third World and aid from the United States. Faced with such pressure, Poland and Hungary became heavily indebted to Western banks. In 1985 Hungary joined the International Monetary Fund (IMF). Fifth, the excessive repressions of the Stalin era created a reservoir of resentment in such countries as Czechoslovakia. The Czechoslovak Party suffered from strong revisionist currents that in 1968 became obvious. Finally, for decades, the West had pursued a policy of "differentiation," to sow disunity in Eastern European socialism by bestowing rewards on such states as Romania, willing to distance itself from the USSR.

The East European collapse intertwined with the Soviet story.[477] It was a humiliation, a warning, and a body blow to Communist political morale everywhere. The East European collapse emboldened separatists and proponents of capitalism in all parts of the USSR.

In 1989 the second major process, Soviet political reform, began in earnest. In June 1988, at the Nineteenth Party Conference, with a bit of last-minute parliamentary chicanery, Gorbachev rammed through "radical political reform."[478] Gorbachev and Yakovlev soon translated the conference resolution into organizational reality.

From June 1988 to March 1989, when the elections for the USSR Congress of People's Deputies took place, measures to weaken the Party came thick and fast. In July 1988, at the first CC Plenum after Nineteenth Party Conference, Gorbachev's forces called for the rank-and-file to break the power of the apparatus.[479] In September Gorbachev called for cuts in the local apparatus by 900,000.[480] Gorbachev sacked non-revisionist and anti-revisionist Politburo leaders. In the September CC Plenum decisions, he removed veteran Andrei Gromyko as a full PB member. Gromyko had slowed down Gorbachev's reforms. Yegor Ligachev, downgraded to head of agriculture from head of ideology, would now no longer run the CC Secretariat, his base.[481] Vadim Medvedev, a trusty ally of Yakovlev and Gorbachev, became a full PB member. Medvedev and Yakovlev took over Ligachev's responsibilities in ideology and foreign affairs.

Chernyaev described the caprice with which Gorbachev and his advisers cut the CPSU central apparatus. Gorbachev proposed cutting the apparatus in half. Chernyaev proposed two-thirds. They arbitrarily settled on a figure between one-half and two-thirds. Gorbachev then proposed eliminating the economic and governmental departments altogether. "We'll keep the socioeconomic one as a theoretical body," Gorbachev mused, "having stripped it of its management rights and functions."[482] This was impulsive downsizing for its own sake, without a plan, without a thought to consequences. Chernyaev frankly acknowledged the ubiquitous confusion and demoralization that resulted from what the Western media called a "mini coup d'etat." It wildly accelerated the weakening of central authority and power nationwide that had begun after the Nineteenth Party Conference. Local and regional Party organizations at all levels floundered helplessly, deprived of their previous economic and managerial function.[483]

In March 1989, the first public test of the new "radical political reform" occurred, the election for the Congress of People's Deputies. According to Ligachev, the elections brought a self-inflicted debacle on the CPSU.[484] Virtually no public discussion of the law on elections occurred. Moreover, the CC directed local and regional Party officials neither to interfere in the elections nor to mobilize their forces for candidates, calling such non-interference and non-mobilization "respect for democracy." Central Party offices let local branches fend for themselves. Some CPSU candidates soon quarreled publicly among themselves. Though his assignment was international work, Yakovlev played a big role in the elections. The same was true of his ally, Vadim Medvedev. Vitali Vorotnikov, a Politburo member, observed the election rules were one-sidedly skewed against anti-revisionist Communists.[485] Because the press had successfully attacked the principle of workplace elections, the March 1989 balloting led to results that over-represented intellectuals and under-represented workers and peasants.[486] Forced to compete with one arm tied behind its back, the Party suffered severely.

Although 87 percent of the delegates to the Congress of People's Deputies belonged to the Party, and many top officials won in their own right, many other Party leaders lost. Forty-four percent of the Party candidates who stood unopposed failed to gain the 50 percent of the vote required for election.[487] The defeated included the mayors of Moscow and Kiev, Party chiefs in Kiev, Minsk, Kishinev, Alma Ata, Frunze, the Latvian prime minister, the president and prime minister of Lithuania, thirty-eight regional and district Party first secretaries, and almost the whole Leningrad Party leadership. In the Baltics, only Party candidates backed by national fronts won. Boris Yeltsin, still a Party member though not Party-backed, won a resounding 89 percent of the vote.[488]

Princeton historian John Dunlop has called the convening of the newly elected First Congress of People's Deputies in May-June 1989 the event that "changed everything."[489] In a move without precedent, Gorbachev decided to televise the Congress. For thirteen days and nights, the proceedings transfixed two hundred million Soviet viewers. Obsessive TV viewing reduced economic output at the time by 20 percent.[490]

In the First Congress of People's Deputies, the intelligentsia loudly pushed an agenda markedly different from Gorbachev's. Andrei Sakharov demanded the abolition of the USSR Constitution's Article Six, the constitutional entrenchment of the CPSU's leading role. Yeltsin solemnly warned that a Gorbachev "dictatorship" loomed ahead. A Soviet athlete named Vlasov attacked the KGB's "history of crimes." A speaker named Karyakin demanded Lenin's removal from his mausoleum on Red Square. Delegates denounced the one-party system. Some speakers disputed the ideas of Karl Marx and Das Kapital. Congress set up commissions to review the 1939 Nazi-Soviet pact, and a massacre in Tbilisi. Political change accelerated from a "canter to a gallop."[491] After June 1989, more change occurred each month than had occurred from April 1985 to June 1989.

The proceedings of the Congress shook the self-confidence of the CPSU to its foundations. For millions, the Congress undermined the legitimacy of the Party, Soviet history, and the whole social order. It also emboldened socialism's opponents. It pushed back the boundaries of the politically thinkable. Managed reform was over. Gorbachev became "a surfboarder of events."[492]

In July 1989, the Soviet working class passed judgment on Gorbachev's *perestroika* and the First Congress of People's Deputies. In Kuzbas and Vorkuta in Russia, in Donbas in the Ukraine, and in Karaganda in Kazakhstan, a devastating mine strike erupted. Independent workers' organizations launched the stoppage. From 1986 onward, they had grown up in industrial areas, outside the official trade union structure, just as the "informals" grew up in Moscow.[493] The first mass labor unrest since the 1920s,[494] the strike caused the Gorbachev leadership to tremble. Yeltsin, sensing populist opportunity, promptly began to work to win over the miners to the "democrat" cause. The iconoclastic atmosphere at the June Congress had helped to goad the miners into action, but, mainly, severe economic hardships drove them to the picket line. The ill-considered cutback in the state orders hit coal mining particularly hard because mines had to buy supplies at market prices, but they could sell coal only at fixed government prices.[495] In 1989 miners chiefly demanded higher pay, although they also raised some political demands, for example, the ending of the central ministries' control, freedom to set coal prices, and the repeal of Article Six of the USSR Constitution. In a few places, miners directly challenged the CP. Moscow felt so threatened by a strike in such a vast and pivotal industry, employing 1 million workers of a total workforce of 160 million, that for ten days three major institutions--the Party high command, the Supreme Soviet, and the Council of Ministers--did little else than try to work out how to grant the miners' expensive demands.[496] Soon, Moscow shipped vast quantities of soap, fresh meat, canned milk, sugar and animal fat to mining areas.

Meanwhile, Yeltsin, on the eve of his election as president of the Russian Federation, gained considerable support among miners. In April 1991 a new strike, more like a general strike than a mine strike, broke out. It was a crippling two-month stoppage affecting many sectors of basic industry in an already weakened Soviet economy. This time the miners' demands reflected Yeltsin's program, including demand for the resignation of the Soviet government. In a sign of Yeltsin's rising authority, the strike ended only after Yeltsin transferred the mines from Soviet jurisdiction to Russian Federation jurisdiction. The new strike made Gorbachev even more accommodating than he had been to the surging strength of the Yeltsin camp.[497]

In 1989, diversity of opinion expressed in the Congress intensified the pressure on the Party to allow organized factions. The "democrat" argument was that multi-candidate elections within the Party were pointless unless candidates could differ on the issues. Already some Communist deputies to new legislative bodies publicly defied Party views. The Lithuanian CP, for example, differed with Gorbachev on Soviet unity. These developments raced ahead of CPSU internal discussions. The accomplished facts set the terms of debate over the handling of intra-Party differences.[498] After the Party decided to permit organized factions, it was but a short step to permitting other political parties. Not far behind that, lurked the far bolder notion of permitting parties that opposed socialism and the Union state. As late as November 1989, Gorbachev rejected the possibility of a multi-party system. As the Central Committee reconsidered Article Six of the Constitution, a half-million strong "democrat" rally in Moscow, addressed by Boris Yeltsin, demanded an end to Article Six. At the CC Plenum in March 1990, Gorbachev reversed himself and did away with Article Six, and opened the way to new, legal parties.[499]

A crisis of confidence struck the CPSU. In 1989, its 19 million membership stopped rising, and in 1990 the number of members fell by more than 250,000. Passivity and paralysis seized the ranks. Opinion polls revealed a decline of the Party's prestige, authority, and public support. By 1989 the CPSU was paying the price for its identification in the public eye with Gorbachev's policies that were sowing hardship and uncertainty in the general population. Neither Gorbachev nor any top leader had any clear plan for dealing with these problems or reversing the Party's fortunes.[500]

The CPSU had always had a diversity of ideas and ideological struggle, but following Lenin, it had avoided organized tendencies that would cripple the implementation of policy. Within the context of Leninism, contested elections inside and outside the CPSU were possible.[501] There was no problem with a multi-party socialist state, provided that the working class party had the leading role, and the other parties accepted working class state power and socialism, that is, they were not counterrevolutionary. Multiparty systems existed in the GDR, Poland, Vietnam, Czechoslovakia, Bulgaria, and North Korea.[502] No socialist state could brook the legalization of anti-Communist parties whose aim was to reverse the results of the revolution.

The next significant moment in the downward arc of the CPSU occurred at its Twenty-eighth Congress in mid-1990. In the lead-up to the Congress, the Party continued to unravel rapidly. The Party began losing the working class. Workers began "voting with their feet" and leaving. According to Graeme Gill, at the CPSU Moscow city conference only 7.2 percent of delegates were workers. "From the industrial oblast of Yaroslavl not one industrial worker was sent as a delegate to the national congress."[503] Angry at worsening conditions, workers wondered, "Why ...was economic reform begun with changes that hurt workers?"[504] In early 1990, the hemorrhage of Party membership accelerated. The Party grassroots loudly criticized the abandonment of Marxism-Leninism, something overlooked by those who attach great importance to the claim that few Soviet workers defended the system (a matter discussed more fully in Chapter 7 and the Epilogue). Graeme Gill wrote that in the lead-up to the Twenty-eighth Congress, "The reaffirmation of faith in Marxism-Leninism accompanied by the charge that the ideals of the party had been turned upside down was a common line of complaint against the party leadership at this time."[505]

In the first half of 1990, organized CPSU factions crystallized. The Democratic Platform dominated by white-collar workers and professionals favored turning the CPSU into a parliamentary social democratic party. The misnamed Marxist Platform favored a market economy. Internal surveys carried out by the Party in May 1990 suggested that a growing segment of the Party base believed that its leaders were corrupt and did not believe that the Soviet government could stop the economic decline. More than half of those polled no longer saw the Party as the country's leading political force.[506]

Convening in July 1990, the Twenty-eighth Congress of the CPSU represented the last pitched battle at a Party Congress over Gorbachev's policies. The Congress, however, did nothing to slow the General Secretary's revisionist march. The Congress marked another step for a Party rapidly losing both its mission and its working class base. The non-Communist media set the Party agenda. Debate occurred not over "whether the market economy?" but "what sort of market economy?" The Congress rendered the Politburo mostly ineffective. By acknowledging a new freedom of Party organizations in the union republics to review CPSU decisions and to work out their own Party programs, the Congress aided separatism. The Congress downgraded Marxism-Leninism as a source of ideological guidance and turned the Central Committee into a quasi-representative parliament, instead of the authoritative leadership body it had always been. The convention reduced the CC's powers in relation to the General Secretary. The whole CPSU Congress rather than the CC now elected Gorbachev, making an ouster between elections more difficult, if not impossible. The right to form "platforms," "seminars," "clubs" in CPSU was acknowledged, though not "factions." For opponents of Gorbachev, this was merely a semantic victory. Factions were already forming. The anti-revisionists also won a battle to keep the Party organization in the military and a meaningless verbal commitment to democratic centralism.

At the Twenty-eighth Congress Ligachev failed to get elected as Deputy General Secretary and withdrew from active, public CPSU work. Yeltsin ostentatiously left the CPSU, as did such noted "democrats" as Leningrad mayor Anatoly Sobchak, Moscow mayor Gavril Popov, and ex-Marxist historian Yuri Afanasyev. The Democratic Platform withdrew from the CPSU but not before staking a claim to CPSU assets. On balance, the political complexion of the CPSU shifted farther in an anti-socialist direction after the Twenty-eighth Congress not only because of Gorbachev's victories, but also because of the exodus of honest Communists. Anti-revisionists were giving up on the CPSU and devoting efforts to winning influence in the new Communist Party of the Russian Federation (CPRF). In 1989, Ligachev helped found the Soviet Peasant Union, and in 1990 the CPRF.[507] One reason Ligachev had stayed in the CPSU as long as he did was that he wanted to try one last attempt at reversing the direction of Party politics at the Twenty-eighth

Congress. Ligachev played by the rules long after Gorbachev and Yakovlev had stopped. As late as May 1990, Ligachev wrote a letter to Gorbachev in which he declared his loyalty to *perestroika*, while appealing to Gorbachev to circulate the letter through the Politburo and CC leadership and heed his call to convene a CC Plenum on the crisis in the Party and the country.[508] Gorbachev never circulated the letter.

After the Twenty-eighth Congress, from mid-1990 through August 1991, the Party "imploded."[509] The splintering into factions accelerated. Membership losses especially among workers mounted. Dues moneys, publication sales and other sources of Party income plummeted. Party finances worsened to near bankruptcy. Financial losses forced staff reductions that further weakened the organization's influence. In the new state bodies Communist deputies manifested open disunity. Meanwhile, "democrats" pressed for the elimination of CPSU members from all state and social institutions. After August 1991 and the failure of the "August coup," (discussed later) and the declaration of martial law by the Soviet government, the Party situation reached the nadir. Anti-CPSU hysteria in Soviet and world media exploded. A drive to outlaw the CPSU and confiscate its assets emerged and proved unstoppable. The CPSU's fate was sealed.

Paralleling the Party's dismemberment was the ruin of the military, as well as the Party's influence in the military. In 1989-91, Gorbachev went after the CPSU's influence in the Soviet military, which received intensive Marxist-Leninist ideological training compared to other sectors. Gorbachev and his associates viewed breaking the Party's grip on the military as part of breaking its grip on the whole political system. The first step in "de-partification" was to change Soviet military doctrine, dumping the idea that deterrence depended on U.S.-Soviet weapons parity and that the USSR should aid Warsaw Pact allies and other fraternal socialist states. Soviet unilateral disarmament eroded military morale and conditions. Military disintegration came from three other circumstances: force reductions ordered by Gorbachev, hostile media coverage of military conditions, and resistance to conscription. In 1989 and 1990, officers started to quit in large numbers. In 1989-91 the Soviet armed forces shrank from 5.3 million to just under 4 million men. The demobilized men often returned to homelands with no jobs and no housing awaiting them. Meanwhile, Gorbachev moved ahead with plans to abolish the the Military Political Administration, the organ through which the CPSU organized itself in the armed forces. Though Ligachev and his allies managed to prevent the Twenty-eighth Congress from doing that, the disintegration of Party influence inexorably moved ahead.

What explained the faint-heartedness of CPSU leaders who resisted Gorbachev, their underdeveloped political skill, their transparent illusions,[510] and the frequency with which they caved in and voted for policies they did not believe in? For a long time Gorbachev's opponents had the votes to remove him, but did not act. The Politburo even rejected Gorbachev's resignation.[511] Reflecting later on a stormy meeting, Gorbachev loyalist Chernyaev wrote furiously, "Did you think it [Gorbachev's resignation offer] was blackmail? A game?" Noting that Gorbachev's opponents were a big majority in the Politburo and Central Committee, Chernyaev taunted them after the fact: "The 'collapse' was only starting then; you could have "restored order"! But no! You had neither the guts nor any alternative concept."[512]

The revisionist side was better led than its opponents. Contingency, thus, played a role in the Soviet collapse. After the Nina Andreyeva clash in the Politburo, which ended in a debacle for Ligachev, the correlation of forces turned steadily against Gorbachev's opponents. The revisionists kept the initiative and chopped away at the Party base of their opponents. Ligachev avoided taking the offensive or vying for the leadership. Ligachev opposed Gorbachev's excesses, but according to Stephen F. Cohen, accepted some of Gorbachev's assumptions, for example, a belief in the advantages of partial marketization.[513] Until his demotion, Ligachev simply tried to compete with Yakovlev for Gorbachev's ear. He saw Yakovlev as the gray eminence of revisionism, giving Gorbachev foolhardy advice. Only after it was too late did Ligachev initiate a consistent struggle against Gorbachev, and by then he was outside the CPSU top leadership.

An organized and determined opposition might have ousted Gorbachev, as Khrushchev had been. As late as May 1990, 70 percent of the CC was against Gorbachev.[514] Why, then, did Ligachev lose his last battle against revisionism at the Twenty-eighth CPSU Congress? Why did no other major Communist emerge to lead the fight against Gorbachev inside the CPSU? Why had the CPSU leadership caliber declined so markedly since the 1960s? Why was the CPSU not able to overcome Gorbachev in 1987-91, though it had overcome Khrushchev in 1964?

The answer to these questions resided in the same place as the explanation of the collapse itself, in the economy and in politics. Politburo quarrels were not just clashes of ideas, where arguments were won on the merits. Underlying interests and forces determined the power of the opposing sides. Powerful political, ideological and economic forces were pulling the rug out from beneath Ligachev and his supporters. Most importantly, by the late 1980s, in contrast to the 1960s, the USSR's second economy was far bigger, its corrupting inroads into the social order deeper, and its penetration of top sections of the CPSU more flagrant and pronounced. Ligachev saw clearly that by encouraging the second economy and private enterprise with his economic reforms, Gorbachev was likewise furthering corruption in the Party. Ligachev said: "Suddenly in the space of a year or two came even more horrible and more absolutely corrupt forces that stifled the healthy start made in the Party in April 1985."[515]

There is evidence that from the highest Party levels down, Gorbachev encouraged corruption by example and toleration.[516] Valery Boldin, Gorbachev's one-time chief of staff, confessed that, throughout its history the CPSU had known inner struggle--against opportunists, deviations, splinter groups, Mensheviks, Trotskyites, and so on. He concluded however that, with Gorbachev, for the first time, the CPSU had a corruption problem, high and low, citing secretaries of district and regional Party committees, as well as members of the CC implicated in illegal schemes. According to Boldin, the Party has "never" had the same extent of corruption and greed "in high places." This weakened the Party's ability to defend itself. In Boldin's words, "The virus of dishonesty gravely impaired the Party's immune system and wrecked its stability." [517]

The growth of legal and illegal private enterprise and its entanglement with the Party sapped the efficacy and morale of honest Party functionaries at every level. They saw much of the upper Party and state bureaucracy purloining state assets with impunity. Meanwhile, the independent media run by anti-Communists were reshaping public perceptions, beliefs, and expectations. The Party was disappearing as the power center. Such trends altered the balance of forces in the CPSU. No such conditions existed in 1964.

At the same time a mobilization of the Party base and ordinary workers was extremely problematical because of the unprecedented political confusion accompanying a counterrevolution being led by a CPSU general secretary. Rank and file Communists were not inert, but they were accustomed to acting in response to Party initiative, not to initiating action against a Party leader. Moreover, rank and file workers were increasingly preoccupied with coping with inflation, shortages, and unemployment. By mid-1991 the economy was in a depression. Millions of workers defended their living standards through strikes, but the enfeebling of the CPSU made a fight within the Party difficult. Disorganization, disorientation, and disempowerment of the Party itself limited the possibility of grassroots resistance to the leadership. Notwithstanding these factors, in March 1991 Soviet workers voted by a huge majority to keep the USSR. Preoccupied with daily living, rank and file workers' protests typically did not go beyond economic struggles, and they were often either ill-led, or not led at all. Nevertheless, the opposition to the revisionists among the CPSU rank and file remained substantial and ended only with Twenty-eighth Congress in July 1990.

Another reason the anti-revisionist forces lost was likewise related to the second economy. In late Soviet society new private wealth acquired in the second economy flowed into the campaign coffers of emerging pro-capitalist politicians. Historian Stephen Handelman observed, "The *vory* [thieves] knew that Kremlin conservatives [i.e., orthodox Communists] were anxious to cut short the economic liberalization that had already produced such impressive black market profits." He added, "Gavril Popov who won election as Moscow mayor in the same campaign that took Yeltsin into the Moscow White House has admitted that reformers obtained support from *teneviki* (shadow businessmen often connnected to the underworld)." The influence of money in politics--with no precedent in Soviet history--strengthened anti-socialist elements and undermined the genuine Communists.[518]

Gorbachev's extraordinary media policies gave him, and later outright pro-capitalist forces, a crucial advantage previously enjoyed by authentic Communists. Yakovlev's appointees in the media set the terms and conditions of a political debate that went far beyond the mild liberalization of the Khrushchev era. After the 1989 birth of the Congress of People's Deputies, the anti-CPSU intelligentsia and its media allies went on an offensive against the active supporters of socialism. Thus, the favorable political and ideological circumstances around Gorbachev were far different than around Khrushchev twenty-five years before.

Individual and subjective factors played a real, but subordinate role. Leadership qualities did matter. If Ligachev and his supporters had possessed brilliant leadership qualities, and if the revisionists had not, matters might have turned out differently, regardless of objective conditions. In the battle Gorbachev, however, always held the favorable high ground, even when outnumbered. His main opponent--Ligachev--may not have been "the pathetic, principled Ligachev"[519] of one account, but Ligachev was definitely schooled in the Communist principles of democratic centralism, modesty, and loyalty, and those principles constrained his ability to mount an effective opposition. Even though Ligachev had wide respect and indisputable leadership qualities, for a long time he confined himself to attempts to moderate Gorbachev's policies and to counter pressure from the right with his arguments. With the same collective determination, organization, and planning that Khrushchev had used to arrest Beria, and that Brezhnev had used to oust Khrushchev, Ligachev probably could have turned the Nina Andreyeva affair to his advantage and could have unseated Gorbachev. Ligachev's failure to act except in his own defense, however, immobilized his allies, none of whom had Ligachev's prestige. Given this opening, Gorbachev and Yakovlev subjected Ligachev to withering criticism and sent Ligachev's allies in the leadership and the media scurrying for cover.

In 1989-91, the anti-Communist opposition rose as steeply as the CPSU declined. Many reform-minded CPSU leaders benignly entertained the idea of a multiparty system. The anti-Communists, however, still masked their pro-capitalist ambitions.[520] As they contemplated new political arrangements, Communist leaders attached astonishingly little importance to the question of state power, whether or not a new movement or party accepted the class character of the state and the Communist Party's leading role.

The "democrat" opposition that arose after 1985 had forerunners in the Khrushchev "Thaw" years, 1953 to 1964. Khrushchev had tolerated liberal intellectuals. After 1964, when Brezhnev became less tolerant, part of the intelligentsia created a dissident movement. The dissidents were the heirs of the Bukharin-Khrushchev tradition. The dissidents influenced Gorbachev. They also supplied key elements of the "democrat" program. As early as May 1970, foreshadowing the slogans and program of *perestroika*, an extraordinary open letter to Brezhnev and other Soviet leaders was signed by three prominent dissidents, physicists Andrei Sakharov and Valery Turchin, and writer Roy Medvedev. The letter put forward theses about the current state of the Soviet Union and advanced fifteen demands. The authors claimed to speak for the intelligentsia and "advanced section of the working class." The USSR's problems, it said, stemmed not from socialism, but from "the anti-democratic traditions and norms of public life established in the Stalin era." The main demand of the authors was "democratization," a word repeated many times. The letter also introduced the word "stagnation," a chief concept of the *perestroika* era. The authors also demanded the restoration of the rights of nationalities deported by Stalin, progress toward a more independent judiciary, public opinion research, wider dissemination of social science research, multi-candidate elections, industrial autonomy, more funds for primary and secondary education, amnesty for political prisoners, improvements in cadre and management training, and abolition of information on nationality in an individual's documents. The program wished to perfect socialism, but there was no criticism of the capitalist West.[521]

The self-styled "democrat" opposition went through many stages before it emerged in 1988-89 as legal, anti-socialist parties bidding for elective office and even state power.[522] First, in 1987 the so-called "informals" (informal organizations) emerged, some as humble as discussion clubs, neighborhood groups, and study circles. Gorbachev blessed the informals and invoked the ideas of Italian Communist theoretician Antonio Gramsci about the importance of "civil society," a favorite ideological construct of social democrats. Gorbachev and Yakovlev wished to foster non-Party social movements to support their policies and to bypass the "conservative bureaucracy" of the CPSU. The informals grew quickly, and they quickly changed in character. In non-Russian republics they became "national fronts" promoting separatism and in Russia "popular fronts" advocating the "democrat" line. Until mid-1988, a "democrat" meant a Gorbachev supporter against Ligachev. After mid-1988, a section of the intelligentsia criticized Gorbachev as not fully a "democrat." In May 1988 in Moscow, a dissident from the 1960s and 1970s formed the Democratic Union, the first anti-CPSU political party.

In May-June 1989, the Congress of People's Deputies gave a huge boost to the "democrats."[523] Soviet TV displayed Moscow intellectuals arguing for "democracy" in opposition to Gorbachev. In July 1989, some deputies formed the Interregional Group, (led by Andrei Sakharov and by Boris Yeltsin, still a CPSU member). This "democrat" parliamentary faction held 380 of the 2250 members of the Congress of People's Deputies. It called for a "transition from totalitarianism to democracy," and for "radical decentralization of state property," and "economic independence of republics and regions." This meant that an anti-Communist parliamentary opposition led by major popular figures was openly at work in Gorbachev's new state institutions.

In January 1990, Democratic Platform formed in the CPSU with delegates representing 55,000 Communists. It favored transforming the CPSU into a social democratic party at the upcoming Twenty-eighth Party Congress. Also in January

1990, Democratic Russia, a more ambitious project, formed. It favored "the ideas of Andrei Sakharov," who had died in December 1989. The "democrat" camp promptly canonized Sakharov as the patron saint of the "democrat" cause. Democratic Russia evolved out of the Interregional Group and had a Russian nationalist complexion. It called upon the Congress to enact a new RSFSR constitution, revoke Article Six of the Soviet Constitution, return churches to believers, place the KGB under parliamentary control, proclaim the Russian republic's sovereignty, and create a regulated market economy. Democratic Russia's demands went much further than any existing group toward open advocacy of capitalist restoration and USSR breakup. Democratic Russia would become the main base of Boris Yeltsin.

In March 1990 in the Russian Federation elections, the "democrats" won political control of Moscow and Leningrad by a large majority, a stunning result. By May 1990 the "democrats" claimed 25 percent of Russian Federation Congress. As in 1917, dual power existed in Russia, this time the "democrats" and the CPSU.

The "democrat" opposition found its Russian leader in Boris Yeltsin. Yeltsin's Party career had taken off in 1985 when he was brought to Moscow, ironically, on Ligachev's recommendation. An engineer by training, Yeltsin had been a construction manager in the Urals. He was ambitious, pragmatic, and alcoholic. At the Twenty-seventh CPSU Congress in 1986, Gorbachev brought him onto the Politburo as a candidate member.[524] Though a CPSU official, Yeltsin developed into a popular and erratic critic of the CPSU. At the Twenty-seventh Congress, Yeltsin battled with Ligachev over Party privileges. In 1987, Yeltsin's criticism of Gorbachev led to his ouster from the Politburo and dismissal as Moscow Party first secretary. Returning to his native Sverdlovsk, Yeltsin wandered in the political wilderness from late 1987 to early 1989. Gorbachev's creation of new state institutions made a comeback possible. In

March 1989, Sverdlovsk elected Yeltsin to the USSR Congress of People's Deputies. In March 1990, Russians elected Yeltsin to the RSFSR Congress of People's Deputies, and in May 1990 the Russian Supreme Soviet elected Yeltsin chair. In July 1990, Yeltsin left the CPSU at the Twenty-eighth Congress. In June 1991, he was elected president of the RSFSR, a new position created in April 1991 by a deal with Gorbachev in which Yeltsin pledged to support Gorbachev's Union Treaty.[525] With 57 percent of the vote, Yeltsin defeated five rivals and thereafter held a proven electoral mandate that Gorbachev lacked, an important advantage in the battle for supremacy. Sometime in 1989, Yeltsin's new trajectory had become clear. He planned to "play the Russia card" to achieve supreme power and capitalist restoration.

Why did Yeltsin succeed at becoming the leader of the counterrevolution? In the July 1989 miners' strike, Yeltsin forged an alliance with the most powerful and angry contingent of the working class. In 1989-90, he won support among intellectuals angry at Gorbachev's caution. He seized the banner of "radical" (overtly pro-capitalist) *perestroika*. He grew popular among non-Russian republican separatists whom he accommodated. He cultivated religious believers. He championed Russian sovereignty and the symbols of Russian nationalism. Above all, he favored a market economy far more decisively than Gorbachev and thereby won over the pro-capitalist elements in the proliferating second economy. Also important was the blossoming support Yeltsin won from Western business, Radio Liberty and other Western radio voices.

Yeltsin's willingness to sacrifice the USSR as a federal state if necessary to bring Russia to "radical reform"-- capitalist restoration--made him the leader favored by counterrevolutionary partisans at home and abroad. So long as Gorbachev controlled the all-Union institutions, his continual vacillations impeded full capitalist restoration. From August 1991 to December 1991, events developed in unforeseen and dramatic ways, and Yeltsin got his chance to seize power and dismember the USSR. Then, in January 1992, he started the economic shock therapy from which Gorbachev always shrank. A year and a half later, in October 1993, meeting legislative resistance to his policies, this leader of the "democrats" would order the artillery bombardment of the Russian parliament, killing and arresting hundred of legislators and citizens.[526]

Deepening economic confusion and crisis stemmed only partly from the madcap debates and wild zigzags that occurred under Gorbachev's plans for transition to a market economy. The overthrow of socialism in Eastern Europe also damaged the Soviet economy. Separatism disrupted economic links among Soviet republics and harmed production. Gorbachev's promotion of the second economy and his attack on the centrally planned state-owned sector also sharpened the crisis. Boris Kargarlitsky noted the enormous irony of a powerful campaign in support of privatization unleashed in 1990 by television, newspapers and magazines in most cases still controlled by the Communist Party. "Anyone who doubted the new wonder-working recipe was not allowed to be heard."[527] The Soviet media monopoly was now capitalist.

Columbia University Sovietologist, Marshall Goldman, concluded that the Soviet economic decline actually began before 1989: "By mid-1987 the damage had already been done. After two years or so of poor results, he [Gorbachev] had lost much of his credibility, at least on economic matters." Thereafter, the crisis grew more acute. By mid-1988 the deterioration began to feed on itself, and "important economic institutions were starting to disintegrate."[528]

A Soviet decision that pushed the ex-socialist states to re-direct trade into Western markets magnified the impact of the Eastern European political collapse. For decades the USSR had provided oil, gas, and raw materials on easy terms to Eastern

Europe in return for manufactured goods. According to Jerry Hough, the Soviet Union's abrupt decision to end the subsidy amounted to shock therapy for Eastern European states. Eastern Europe had to move toward Western markets as quickly as possible. By 1990 and 1991 the loss of Eastern European trade, however, was worsening Soviet economic and social problems. The sudden loss of Eastern European medicine imports, for example, was a major factor in the rapid decline in the Soviet health system.[529]

After what Ligachev dubbed the "fateful error,"[530] the drastic and hasty reduction in the state orders in 1987, shortages--meaning lines, rationing, empty shelves[531] and the resort to black markets--dominated the economic bad news in 1988 and 1989. Production for most consumer goods did not drop in 1988 and 1989, "but the increase in wages and the failure to control the food subsidies meant the population had progressively larger amounts of money at its disposal."[532] With too much money chasing too few goods, inflation began. In 1988 declining food production led to food shortages and price increases.[533] With the weakening of central economic authority, confidence in the stability of supply diminished. Private hoarding by consumers and, more important, public hoarding by republics and cities, spread dramatically, first with respect to food, then other consumer goods.[534] Empty food shelves, the most glaring and most resented shortage, drew sharp public anger and had widespread political, psychological, and economic results. A psychology of shortage and hoarding spread throughout the economy. Thus, even before production declined, lack of confidence in economic stability was creating shortages. Moreover, as the erosion of confidence spread and light industry could not get allotted inputs from its suppliers,[535] the output of consumer goods fell further, and shortages intensified. It was vicious circle.

More than any other factor, Party withdrawal from running the economy caused the worsening hardships from 1989 on. In 1990, production went down. "Economic production was down 2 percent in the first eight months of 1990 and inflation was rising rapidly."[536] Then the bottom really fell out. In early 1991 in *Der Stern*, the German mass circulation news magazine, Gorbachev appealed to the Germans for help: 500,000 tons of meat; 500,000 tons of vegetable oil; 100,000 tons of noodles. By then inflation had reached an annual rate of about 80 percent.[537] In mid-1991, analysts spoke of a Soviet "depression."[538] In July 1991, Gorbachev shocked the world by asking for Soviet membership in the International Monetary Fund. One superpower was going down on bended knee before the other.

In 1990-91 an immense rightward shift occurred in the economic policy debate. The Soviet leadership's focus on the economy had waned in 1988 and the first half of 1989. In that interval Gorbachev turned his attention to political reform. Economic debate became the center of politics again in late 1989. This time the whole character of the debate changed. The contrast between two books by Abel Aganbegyan, who was Gorbachev's chief economic braintruster in the early days of *perestroika*, *The Economic Challenge of Perestroika* (1988) and *Inside Perestroika* (1989),[539] reflected the change. Unlike the first, the second book favored an unregulated market.

Many factors caused the rightward shift of economic debate in USSR, but two stood out: the death-throes of the CPSU and the growth of the second economy. In the table below, two U.S. economists, Michael Alexeev and William Pyle, have estimated of the share of the second economy in the GDP of most Soviet republics midway through the Gorbachev era, and compared it to its size about three years into Yeltsin's rule. The comparison yields a rough indicator of the rate of growth of the second economy in 1989-91 and beyond. By the 1990s the conventional terminology becomes problematic. Scholars originally chose the label "second" economy to suggest the Soviet private economy's subordination to the centrally planned, state-owned "first" economy. By 1995, however, in at least three republics, the second economy, already swollen in the Gorbachev era, had become the "first economy," i.e., the dominant economic reality. In the biggest republic, Russia, the second economy output was close to half the Gross Domestic Product (GDP). In the Ukraine and the Caucasus, the second economy had truly become the first.[540]

Estimates of Unofficial Economies
Percentage Share of GDP

	1989	1995
Azerbaijan	32.8%	69.9%
Belarus	28.6	34.5
Estonia	22.1	21.9
Georgia	32.8	71.4
Kazakhstan	32.8	49.8
Latvia	22.1	40.9
Lithuania	22.1	30.6
Moldova	28.6	47.8
Russia	18.0	45.6
Ukraine	25.3	56.5
Uzbekistan	32.8	28.5

In 1989-91, over most of the country, embryonic Soviet capitalism was growing by leaps and bounds. The new co-ops permitted by law were private businesses. Top Soviet government ministers, including Prime Minister Nikolai Ryzhkov, ordered the formation of some co-ops. Roy Medvedev wrote that private businessmen as well as government enterprises and organizations formed "tens of thousands of co-ops" -- in trade, production, and construction. The co-operatives made it possible to "transform billions of rubles worth of non-liquid assets into cash." The ending of the previous government monopoly on foreign trade made it possible "to swing commercial deals on large scale through the co-operatives."[541]

Later, the new Russian business oligarchs claimed it had been easier to make a fortune under Gorbachev than Yeltsin. Gorbachev's economic officials turned the Communist youth organization Komsomol, 15 million strong, into a training ground for young entrepreneurs. Using Komsomol resources, youthful Soviet capitalists set up the country's first commercial banks and stock exchanges. Komsomol's aspiring millionaires also profited from such ventures as show business, video rentals, tourism, gambling, and international trade.[542]

Emerging into daylight with Gorbachev's blessing, the shadow economy contained a huge criminal component. According to Stephen Handelman, an authority on Russian organized crime, in the Gorbachev era, "60 percent of the co-operatives were run by former or active criminals."[543] By late 1991, after the legalization of much private enterprise, the black market still accounted for "15 percent of the Russian volume of goods and services."[544]

The more the CPSU and the plan died, the more the market became inevitable. In 1987, the decision to go for radical political reform entailed the assumption that the "command-administrative system"--the Party and the central government--was the chief problem. Such an assumption pushed the revisionists and their economists inescapably to the idea of an economy solely dependent on spontaneous market mechanisms, private ownership, and profits. With central ministries in Moscow unraveling and with a diminished Party to guide a transition, market advocates showed an interest in "shock therapy," a free market regime imposed, from above, all at once, with few or no safeguards.

Even Nikolai Ryzhkov, the prime minister and chief USSR economic official, opposed the blind leap to free market capitalism. Ryzhkov wrote that, unlike the Chinese reformers, Gorbachev was weakening the Party and the state when they would be most needed:

At first, I thought that Gorbachev simply did not understand the essence of the question, but further conversations and particularly Politburo sessions in which these problems were discussed showed he was consciously pursuing his line. The ultra-radicals demanded that the idea of the plan be totally rejected, asserting that the producers themselves would quickly understand everything and establish smooth, mutually profitable relations between each other, and nationwide tasks would be solved by themselves. Yakovlev, Medvedev and Shevardnadze insisted on this point of view, and Gorbachev supported them.[545]

Other factors hastened the turn to the market. Gorbachev's change of his political base from the Party to state institutions and his accession to the presidency in March 1990 gave him greater freedom of action. The July 1989 coal miners' strike, both reflecting and causing economic decline, panicked many leaders in Moscow, and made the unthinkable thinkable.

Ideologically, the distorted glorification of NEP prepared public opinion for the new pro-capitalist direction. Gorbachev sympathizers Anthony Jones and William Moskoff illustrated the revisionist use of NEP to make a case against central planning. They asserted that there are "parallels"--in reverse--to the industrialization debate between Bukharin and the CPSU majority led by Stalin in the USSR sixty years earlier. Then, the Soviets chose the plan, not the market, as the best way to catch up with the capitalist nations of the West. "But the contemporary debate has focused on whether, how, and at what speed the nation might find its way back to a market system."[546]

Not least of all, international pressure kept up. U.S. Secretary of State James Baker came to Moscow offering advice on price reform. The West began dangling loans.[547] There were accelerated contacts between Western and Soviet economists, joint conferences touting free market nostrums, seminars in Moscow featuring free market economists, and lucrative U.S. speaking tours for select Soviet economists. Through most of 1989, U.S. billionaire George Soros, whose wealth came from currency speculation, had a secret advisory team in Moscow with access to the highest circles, where they advocated the creation of an Open Sector, a kind of beachhead for capitalism until a full, countrywide restoration of capitalism occurred.

In 1990-91, Gorbachev found it difficult to steer a transition to a market economy because, with his own popularity slumping, he feared that shock therapy would make his opponents more popular. A circus parade of marketization proposals dominated the last two years of the Gorbachev era. This further discredited Gorbachev.[548] The Russian republican government under Yeltsin was moving faster than the USSR government toward "shock therapy," and its proposals pushed the more reluctant USSR authorities. In November 1989, Ryzhkov's economist, Leonid Abalkin, put forth a six-year plan involving privatization and price increases. In mid-February 1990, Abalkin and the head of Gosplan put forward a revised plan, to take effect in mid-1990 or January 1991, involving rapid steps to a market economy. Ryzhkov and the government officials and economists working for him resisted the Russian Republic's ideas for a lightning transition to a market economy. While Ryzhkov insisted on caution, Boris Yeltsin's power was on the rise. In July 1990, Gorbachev decided to dump Ryzhkov and make a deal on the economy with Yeltsin, recently elected head of the RSFSR Supreme Soviet. Together, Gorbachev and Yeltsin picked Stanislav Shatalin to prepare an "agreed upon conception of a program of transition to a market economy as a basis of the economic section of the Union Treaty."[549]

Shatalin's Five Hundred Day Plan was intimately bound up with the struggle between Gorbachev and Yeltsin over the Union Treaty. Calling for total privatization and monetary stabilization in the first one hundred days, the plan was a "laughable" departure from economic realism.[550] The plan involved major price increases for necessities. Crucially, the Five Hundred Day Plan gave all taxing powers to the republics, which would then decide how much to give back to the USSR and asserted the priority of republican laws over Soviet laws. The advocates of the Shatalin plan clearly wanted to abolish the USSR. Gorbachev rejected Shatalin's scheme. In November 1990, Gorbachev assigned his old adviser, Abel Aganbegyan, to work with Shatalin, Abalkin, and Petrakov, on another economic plan. This was vintage Gorbachev positioning himself as a centrist. The resulting presidential plan, like the Ryzhkov-Abalkin plan, involved price increases. Yeltsin's Russian Republic passed a law blocking price increases. That action put the demagogy of Yeltsin clearly on exhibit. He was willing to destroy the Soviet Union in order to race toward capitalism, but he would also damage Gorbachev by denouncing his acceptance of price increases, which were inevitable with the free market, of which Yeltsin was the staunchest advocate. This was trying to have one's cake and eat it too. By 1990, if not before, Yeltsin and his closest advisers understood that their drive to a full free-market economy meant the breakup of the Union state. Such an understanding was implicit in the Shatalin Five Hundred Day Plan. To restore capitalism in Russia, the USSR and Gorbachev had to go. Gorbachev's advisers also understood that point. When he rejected the Five Hundred Day plan, Gorbachev rejected a strong pro-capitalist orientation and the dissolution of the USSR, which would have meant the disappearance of his own position and power. His inner circle, however, Yakovlev, Shevardnadze, Medvedev, Shakhnazarov, and Chernyaev supported the Five Hundred Day Plan. Gorbachev then turned to opponents of the market to fill such key positions as minister for justice, director of TASS, and minister and first deputy minister of internal affairs. As a consequence, Yakovlev deserted Gorbachev. Soon after, Foreign Minister Shevardnadze resigned. In 1992 he returned to Georgia to lead his native republic. [551]

Gorbachev never implemented any comprehensive economic reform. No presidential plan ever became a reality. Yeltsin nullified all his plans. The continued economic deterioration in the Soviet Union stemmed mainly from the withdrawal of the Party from the economy, that is, the destruction of the centrally planned economy, as well as the disruption stemming from republics going their separate ways, and the impact of breaking economic links with Eastern Europe. After January 1992, with full power in Russia, Yeltsin and his economists imposed shock therapy with catastrophic results. By 1994, industrial production in post-Soviet Russia would fall to half of its already disastrous 1991 level.

The end of the Soviet Union as a multi-national federal state came in 1989-91. In these three years, Gorbachev stopped ignoring the national question. In September 1989, in an effort to deal with growing separatism, the CC held a Plenum on the national question, but things had unraveled too far to stop. Anatoly Chernyaev called the CC Plenum "stillborn, a platform that was outdated even before it was written."[552] On specific occasions in these years Gorbachev tried to repress the separatists. After February 1991, he switched strategies and tried to accommodate the separatists with a renegotiated Union Treaty.

Everything failed. Nationalist separatism triumphed in the outlying republics. Yeltsin took Russia out of the USSR to press ahead with his economic program. Years later Gorbachev admitted how late he came to appreciate the complexity of the national question.[553] From the Baku riots in December 1986 to

Yeltsin's removal of the Kremlin's red flag in December 1991, separatist feeling and national strife grew all over the USSR.

Eastern Europe's 1989 upheavals worsened national relations in the USSR. National feeling against the Soviet Union and Russians contributed to the downfall of many Communist governments in 1989. In turn, these upheavals encouraged separatists in the smaller republics in the USSR. In August 1989, a non-Communist government formed in Poland. In October 1989, the regime in Hungary collapsed. In November 1989, the Berlin Wall fell. In November 1989 in Czechoslovakia, a "velvet revolution" was victorious. In December 1989 in Rumania, anti-Ceaucescu elements forcibly overthrew and executed him and his wife.

The weakening of the CPSU in all areas of Soviet life weakened the one institution proven capable of holding a disparate people together. Ligachev remarked, "By April 1989, the Secretariat's sessions, at which we could and should have discussed such a question [Georgian nationalist secessionism], had long since ceased. ...I suddenly realized how strangely weak government authority in the country was becoming."[554]

Russia was the linchpin of the whole USSR, and Russian separatism posed the greatest threat of all. Jerry Hough said that, ultimately, Russia ended the USSR by seceding from it.[555] Lenin and Stalin had supported affirmative action, a Russian subsidy to bring the development of non-Russian peoples up to Russian levels. This policy enormously speeded up the economic and cultural progress of downtrodden peoples. Nevertheless, shortcomings remained. The Russians seemed blind to certain problems. For example, they ignored the threat to nationality and language involved when huge numbers of Russian workers emigrated to small republics, tipping the language and ethnic balance. In Estonia and Latvia, for example, this tipping created a festering sore. As elsewhere, when not skillfully handled, affirmative action caused a backlash. Some Russians resented the ongoing subsidy of outlying republics. Such resentment fueled Russian nationalism.

Russian nationalism grew for other reasons too. In the Brezhnev era, Soviet leaders had tolerated Russian nationalism. The dominant elements in the Brezhnev Politburo reasoned that Russian nationalism was a salutary counterweight to the Western influences penetrating Russian society because of detente.

Western influence on the national question in the USSR went far beyond the subtle, long-term effects of détente. Over the whole Soviet era--unobstructed in the final years--Western radio voices worked to aggravate national strife in the USSR. Radio Liberty, filled with rabid right-wing nationalists recruited from non-Russian Soviet republics, beamed a steady stream of broadcasts in non-Russian languages aimed at stirring separatist rage.[556]

Through the Interregional Group in the USSR Congress and the *glasnost* media, the dissident, Andrei Sakharov, popularized the concept of "sovereignization." This was the idea that Russia too was deprived of equality with other republics by the Stalin-era constitution and that a new constitution should give Russia its own republican institutions.[557] The "democrats" adopted Sakharov's sovereignization idea and, when elected chair of the Russian Supreme Soviet in 1990, Boris Yeltsin put it into effect.

Sakharov framed the sovereignization demand as a negation of the Stalin policy on nationalities. That appealed both to Yeltsin's "democrats" and to Gorbachev's reformers. In 1988 with Gorbachev's and Yakovlev's tacit support, Sakharov visited the disputed Nagorno-Karabakh enclave to make an on-the-spot analysis, surely a case of the blind leading the blind. In 1988-89, Sakharov aired his views in the media. His radical sovereignization view was:

All republics both union and autonomous, autonomous oblasts [regions] and national okrugs [territories] must be granted equal rights, with the preservation of the present territorial borders. They must all receive the maximum degree of independence. Their sovereignty must be minimally limited in such areas as defense, foreign policy, communications, and transportation. ...Russian autonomous regions such as Yakutiya, Chuvashiya, Bashkiriya, and Tatariya must receive the same rights as Ukraine and Estonia. There must be no distinction between republics and autonomous oblasts. All must be turned into republics and all must have the right to secede from the Union.[558]

What was the appeal of sovereignization? Sounding democratic, sovereignization departed from the traditional affirmative action policy. Sovereignization required no struggle against national inequality, certainly not on the part of the Russians, historically the dominant and privileged nation. Sakharov was explicit on this point, saying the Stalinist system "oppressed the large peoples as well as the small ones, particularly the Russian people, one of its main victims."[559] Sovereignization also required no struggle for multinational unity. The concept abandoned the Communist class-based approach to the national question, which affirmed the democratic right of nations to self determination, including the right of secession, and spelled out the conditions under which secession of a small nation from a larger state was justified as a last resort.[560] Sovereignization appealed to the separatists because it blessed their departure. It appealed to the pro-capitalist "democrats" because it was a classless and Party-less formula, and it was consistent with their "anti-Stalinism" program on other issues. Sakharov's doctrine dovetailed with Yeltsin's desire to pull Russia out of the USSR. The sovereignization notion placed Sakharov firmly in the Bukharin–Khrushchev tradition of blundering opportunism on the national question.

Unresolved national problems differed in various regions of the Soviet Union. Nationalism had strong appeal in the Baltic states, which had become part of the USSR in 1939 after twenty years of state independence. In the Transcaucasus, nationalism was fueled by a longstanding territorial dispute between Armenia and Azerbaijan. In the Islamic areas of Soviet Central Asia, nationalism was stimulated by resurgent Islamic fundamentalism in Afghanistan and elsewhere. The Tatars and Chechens, who had been uprooted by Stalin in the war years, nurtured unredressed grievances. Russia, the keystone of the USSR, had its own feelings of grievance too.

In 1989-1991, the epicenter of the nationalist earthquake shifted from region to region. In October 1988, the three Baltic states gave birth to national fronts that soon became channels of separatist feeling. Gorbachev's acquisition of emergency powers in early 1990 prompted Vytautas Landsbergis, head of the Sajudis nationalist movement in Lithuania, to proclaim independence on March 11, 1990. Historian Geoffrey Hosking said, "With these moves the Baltic republics became the focus of the struggle between those who wanted to preserve the Union and those who wished to emancipate themselves from it."[561]

Nationalism triumphed in the Lithuanian CP before it triumphed in Lithuania as a whole. During Gorbachev's three-day visit to Lithuania in January 1989, Algirdas-Mykolas Brazauskas, head of the Lithuanian CP, flatly told him that nationalist sentiment was so strong only an independent Lithuanian Communist Party could hold popular support. In elections on March 25, 1989, the Sajudis movement trounced the Lithuanian CP. In December 1989, the Lithuanian CP seceded from the CPSU.[562] By then, ethnic crises were breaking out simultaneously in far-flung regions. Gorbachev had his hands full. In January and February 1990, near Baku, Azerbaijan, Azeri pogroms against Armenians left twenty-six Armenians and six Azeris dead.

As a first response to the Lithuanian proclamation of national independence, Gorbachev imposed an economic blockade.[563] The USSR passed a Law on Secession in April 1990, spelling out the details of a legal separation process for republics and raising the political and economic cost of secession by allowing subnational units to secede from the seceding nation. The new Soviet law also provided for a five-year transition to independence for any seceding state, and made USSR approval of secession necessary. Events, however, overtook the law. On January 12-13, 1991, the Soviet Army shot at nationalist demonstrators in Vilnius, Lithuania, killing fourteen and wounding many more. A week later in Moscow, 100,000 marchers protested this repression. A short time later, new violence in Riga, Latvia, exacerbated the Baltic crisis. In late spring 1991, Gorbachev abandoned repression. Thereafter, he focused on re-negotiating the Union Treaty.[564]

In the struggle against Gorbachev's version of *perestroika*, both Ligachev and Yeltsin tried to harness Russian nationalist sentiment to their respective aims. A Communist-nationalist alliance was natural insofar as Russian nationalism resented the "Westernizing" aspects of Gorbachev's reforms, its slavish devotion to the Western capitalist market, its borrowed social democratic ideas, its sycophantic deference to the West as "the civilized world," and its downplaying of Russia's unique history. For many decades, a fault line in Russian politics had "Westernizers" on one side and "Slavophiles" on the other. That fault line persisted through the twentieth century and into the twenty-first.

Yeltsin first thought of himself as a Soviet, not a Russian patriot, but as his devotion to market reforms grew, he saw the potential benefits of playing the Russia card. In 1990 he said, "I soon understood that there would be no radical reforms at an all-Union level...and so I thought to myself: If the reforms cannot be carried out at that level, why not try in Russia?"[565]

As Yeltsin began appointing young pro-market whiz kids to top posts in Russia, they began to realize, in Hough's words, that "decentralization of power to the republic level would give them personal control over privatization."[566]

In 1989, many republics of the USSR had declared sovereignty, but this did not yet mean full and formal secession from the USSR. In the last twenty-one months of the USSR's existence, real declarations of independence came in waves. Lithuania declared independence on March 11, 1990, Latvia on May 4, 1990, and Georgia, on April 9, 1991. The second wave occurred in August 1991: Estonia declared independence on August 20, 1991, the Ukraine on August 24, Belarus and Moldova on August 27, Azerbaijan on August 30, Uzbekistan and Kyrgyzstan on August 31, Tajikistan on September 9, Armenia on September 23, Turkmenistan on October 27, and Kazahkstan on December 16. The Russian Federation never officially declared independence. The secession of other republics simply left it independent, willy-nilly.[567]

When given a chance to express a view, the overwhelming majority of the Soviet people wished to keep the Union. On March 17, 1991 in a non-binding referendum in all republics except the Baltics, Armenia, Georgia, and Moldava, 76.4 percent of the voters approved the preservation of the Union.[568] In Russia, 71.4 percent approved, in the Ukraine, 70.3 percent, in Belarus, 82.7 percent, and in Azerbaijan and in each of the Central Asian republics, over 90 percent.[569] These huge majorities mattered little to Yeltsin's "democrats."

The abandonment of multinational unity at home had a parallel in the abandonment of international solidarity abroad. Betrayal after betrayal of liberation movements and newer socialist states occurred in Gorbachev's last years. On the eve of Secretary of State James Baker's visit to Moscow in May

1989, Gorbachev told President George Bush of his decision to stop arms shipments to Nicaragua, even though the country remained terrorized by the attacks of U.S.-backed contras.[570] Beginning in 1986, Gorbachev's sympathy and solidarity with Cuba began to wane. In December 1988, he was thankful[571] when an earthquake in Soviet Armenia required him to cancel an oft-postponed trip to Havana. In April 1989, the visit finally occurred. Gorbachev told the Cuban National Assembly that he opposed "any theories or doctrines that justify the export of revolution."[572] In reality, the policy that Gorbachev was discarding was not the export of revolution but international solidarity in the defense of existing revolutions. Despite an outwardly warm public reception in Havana, the gulf widened between Cuba and the Gorbachev leadership. Not inclined to abandon principle, socialist Cuba did not budge. The next year Gorbachev cut off about $5 billion in yearly aid, including deliveries of oil and other necessities. Between 1990 and 1993, together, the collapse of the Council of Mutual Economic Assistance (CMEA), a tightening of the U.S. blockade, and the Soviet betrayal caused Cuba's GDP to plummet by 50 percent.

Meanwhile, Gorbachev's team boasted that their foreign policy based on "new thinking" was succeeding. This made sense if one measured success only in terms of increased "peacefulness" and "stability" of US-Soviet relations. Undeniably, unilateral Soviet disarmament lowered the odds of a U.S.-USSR thermonuclear exchange. Even so, the disintegration of the Soviet Union increased the odds of a disaster arising from the erosion of security over nuclear weapons and nuclear power plants.

Unilateral Soviet concessions and surrender did reduce other areas of Soviet conflict with the U.S. Of course, the Gorbachev men did not see their policy as surrender. Top foreign policy adviser Chernyaev believed that the betrayal of South Africa and Nicaragua was of little consequence compared with the consolidation of the U.S.-USSR relationship. Chernyaev also saw victory in each cherished moment when leaders of the West bestowed acclaim on Gorbachev. He faithfully noted when "Mikhail" established a first-name basis with "George"[Bush, the elder], "Margaret"[Thatcher], and "Helmut"[Schmidt]. Gorbachev and Chernyaev believed the new U.S.-USSR alliance marked a "most critical" change in world politics, "a new path toward civilization."[573] The gloss that Gorbachev applied to the abandonment of international solidarity was nowhere more frankly and succinctly stated than in Gorbachev's notes for his Revolution Day message for November 7, 1990:

> Re-iterate what perestroika has given to us... it brought freedom and emancipation...we opened up to the world ... having stood in opposition to the world, we denied ourselves the opportunity of participating in civilization's progress at its most critical turning point. We suffered terrible [losses], perhaps our greatest losses, thanks to this.[574]

The end of the USSR's "standing in opposition to the world" carried a high price for many. Eastern European socialism disappeared, replaced by new conservative governments cravenly seeking EU and/or NATO membership, leaving a still independent Yugoslavia alone to be hammered by NATO. By 1993-94 the abandoned but heroic Cubans were farming with wooden plows and oxen. In Africa, the continent most wronged by imperialism, the end of Soviet aid meant the extinction of thirty years of hope and struggle for independent development. Debt owed to Western banks soon throttled new states struggling since formal de-colonization in 1960, while AIDS and other diseases and collapsing social safety nets threatened to wipe out whole peoples. With "Don't displease the Americans" as the new be-all and end-all of Soviet foreign policy, the USSR even spurned such national liberation leaders as Nelson Mandela and Yasser Arafat. After the 1989 Soviet pullout from Afghanistan, the progressive Najibullah held power until 1992. He then sought refuge in the UN compound. In 1996 when the Taliban seized Kabul its first act was to break into the UN compound and shoot Najibullah, mutilate his body, and hang it for public viewing in the streets of Kabul.

As the Gulf War neared, James Baker, President Bush's deputy, asked the Soviets to join in a strike on the Iraqi army. Gorbachev replied: "I want to emphasize that we would like to be by your side in any situation."[575] Thus, step-by-step, his concept of an "integrated, interdependent world" and "universal human values" transformed Soviet foreign policy into an outright alliance with imperialism. Gorbachev's sycophancy reached remarkable depths. In a letter to President George H. W. Bush, Gorbachev even implied that the future direction of the Soviet Union depended on America:

> At the same time I get the impression that my friend, the president of the United States, hasn't come to a final answer on the main question: what kind of Soviet Union does the United States want to see? And until this question is answered we'll keep stumbling on one or another particular aspect of our relations.[576]

By August 1991, the deterioration of economic conditions and the unraveling of the Soviet Union had become so advanced and Gorbachev was so lacking in a plan to deal with the crisis that a group of Soviet leaders took a radical step to gain control of events. They formed the State Committee for the State of Emergency (SCSE), known also by its Russian initials GKChP. The state officials who made up the SCSE had exhausted other options aimed at limiting Gorbachev's power and stopping the erosion of the Soviet state's authority. As far back as

1988, Ligachev had lost his struggle against Gorbachev in the Politburo. In September and December 1990, the group that comprised the SCSE had criticized Gorbachev. In April 1991, it tried to remove him in a CC vote. In June 1991, it tried to outwit him in parliament.[577] In August 1991, Yeltsin's attempt to re-draft the details of the Union Treaty in order to deny the All-Union institutions revenue-raising powers propelled these men to take matters in their own hands. The SCSE leaders were infuriated by what they believed was Gorbachev's capitulation to Yeltsin's re-draft of the treaty.[578] Moreover, Yeltsin had also just prohibited the CPSU in the army and had denied the USSR exchequer access to any revenues from the Russian oilfields.[579] Gorbachev had even agreed to abolish the USSR Congress of People's Deputies, his own creation. Though the members of the SCSE were ostensibly Gorbachev men, they sprang into action because Yeltsin was winning every struggle with Gorbachev.[580]

The formation of the SCSE initiated a strange sequence of events. On August 18, in the late afternoon, five high officials: first deputy chairman of the USSR Defense Council Oleg Baklanov, president of the Association of USSR State Industries Alexander Tizyakov, Politburo member Oleg Shenin, commanding general of the ground forces of the Soviet Army Valentin Varennikov, Gorbachev's chief of staff Valery Boldin, and chief of the presidential personal security guard Yuri Plekhanov confronted Gorbachev in his summer home at Foros on the Black Sea. They proposed that he turn over power to USSR Vice President Gennadii Yanaev who would proclaim martial law and--with state disintegration looming--introduce order. Baklanov said to Gorbachev: "Nothing is required of you. We will do all the dirty work for you." According to historian Jerry Hough, "Some of the group thought Gorbachev would agree, but he reacted hostilely and aggressively."[581]

The single most important SCSE leader was KGB chief Vladimir Kryuchkov. Besides the previously named, the

SCSE's members were: USSR Prime Minister Valentin Pavlov, USSR Defense Minister Dmitrii Yazov, USSR Minister of Internal Affairs Boris Pugo, and Chairman of the USSR Union of Peasants Vasilii Starodubtsev. Other key members were: chairman of the USSR Supreme Soviet Anatolii Lukyanov (a Gorbachev ally for years), two first deputy chairmen of the KGB Viktor Grushko and Genii Ageev, and KGB General Vyacheslav Generalov.

At six the next morning on August 19, 1991 the SCSE announced on Soviet television that it had temporarily assumed power because Gorbachev was ill and that Vice President Yanaev would exercise the powers of the president until he returned. The SCSE sent troops and tanks to Moscow, but in every other way the SCSE leaders acted very indecisively. Its statement, the "Appeal to the Soviet People," published by TASS on August 19, stressed patriotism and the restoration of order. It began, "There have emerged extremist forces which have adopted a course toward liquidation of the Soviet Union, the collapse of the state and the seizure of power at any price." The document denounced the economic reforms of "adventurers" that resulted in "a sharp drop in the living standards of the overwhelming majority of the population and the flowering of speculation and the shadow economy." It declared that the prestige of the USSR had been undermined. It vowed to "clean the streets of criminals," as well as end "the plundering of the people's wealth." Labor discipline and law and order would be reestablished. The "Appeal" promised to carry out "a countrywide discussion on a new Union Treaty."[582]

On the evening of August 19 the SCSE leaders held a press conference for foreign and Russian journalists. Observers claimed that they seemed nervous, inept, and indecisive. They certainly were indecisive. During the three days in question, SCSE allowed Western news agencies, from CNN to Radio Liberty, to broadcast freely their own interpretation of developments, and even to promote Yeltsin. Top military officers were allowed to telephone and visit politicians in the Russian White House, i.e., the Russian Republic's parliament building. Meanwhile, Yeltsin and the "democrat" leaders continued to speak to the world and Soviet media, worked to win over the military, and built barricades around the Russian parliament building. SCSE took no action against them all day on August 20. It amazed Western analysts that top military leaders did not participate in any SCSE-directed assault on the Russian parliament at night on August 19 or August 20.[583]

The pivotal moment of the August events came on the night of August 20-21. The SCSE developed and then abandoned a plan to storm the Russian parliament. Then, on August 21 SCSE leaders Kryuchkov, Yazov, Baklanov, Tizyakov, and Lukyanov flew to Foros to persuade Gorbachev to join them in counteracting Yeltsin and the Russian government. They sought to convince him that the SCSE's actions so far had shown how little effort would be needed to restore order. Gorbachev would not meet them.[584] At 2:30 a.m. on August 22nd Gorbachev returned to Moscow on the presidential plane along with the Russian Republic's Vice President Rutskoi (Yeltsin's ally, who had arrived in Foros on another plane), and Kryuchkov. Kryuchkov had agreed to join Gorbachev on the presidential plane, on the basis of a promise he would speak as an equal with Gorbachev.[585] On landing, however, Kryuchkov was arrested by Soviet authorities.[586] Back in Moscow, Gorbachev resumed formal power, though his real power was fast slipping into the hands of Yeltsin. At 9 a.m. on August 22 the Soviet Ministry of Defense decided to withdraw its troops from Moscow, and the bizarre drama came to an end.

The meaning of what happened in August 1991 remains somewhat cloudy, though recent accounts have done much to clarify early misunderstanding. What is now established is that the "coup leaders" thought Gorbachev was on their side, gave assurances of this to Yeltsin, and when Gorbachev pulled the rug from under them, essentially panicked, since they had absolutely no plan for a seizure of power. They were not prepared to arrest Yeltsin and his key supporters, suppress the "democrats," or seize anything. Without either a plan or the will, the entire effort collapsed.

In the confusion of those days, many democrats--no quotation marks this time--condemned the events of August 19-21, 1991, particularly the declaration of martial law. Western governments and media promoted an understanding of these events as an attempted coup. Perched on a tank outside the Russian parliament, bellowing with a bullhorn, Yeltsin was portrayed by the media as successfully rallying the masses against the unjust usurpers. The coup mythology served to blame the Soviet collapse on the "diehards" in the KGB and CPSU, instead of Gorbachev, and to bolster Boris Yeltsin's image as a hero of democracy.

The research of the last ten years by U.S. historians casts grave doubts on such a History Channel version of August 1991.[587] A coup is the unlawful, forcible overthrow of a constitutionally legitimate government, but the SCSE *did not* try to overthrow the USSR government. The SCSE *was* the government.

Western media characterized SCSE leaders as cowardly bunglers. Though many blunders occurred in August 1991, the SCSE leaders did not have any prior reputation as weaklings and fools. SCSE leaders had authorized deadly force and used force effectively on several previous occasions. Dunlop called them "serious...men with ruthless intentions"[588] In 1956, Kryuchkov, the foremost SCSE leader, had served in the Soviet Embassy in Hungary with Andropov putting down the counterrevolution.[589] Moreover, though the SCSE had essentially declared martial law, this was not a bolt out of the blue; Gorbachev had authorized planning for martial law several times in the year before the August events.[590]

John Dunlop, considered the leading U.S. expert on the "coup,"[591] asserted support for the SCSE was substantial.

Yeltsin's own team believed that 70 percent of all local officials in the Russian republic, Communist and non-Communist, did not support Yeltsin.[592] Two-thirds of regional Communist Party committees openly expressed support for SCSE, while one-third took a "wait and see" attitude.[593] In the outer republics only Moldava, Kyrgystan, and the Baltic states showed big opposition to the SCSE. Polls conducted in the weeks before August 19 by the USSR Academy of Social Science at the Party Central Committee, admittedly a source with an anti-Yeltsin bias, showed huge majorities in favor of the integrity of the USSR and the preservation of state controls over enterprises.[594]

Gorbachev's version--that he had no complicity in the August 1991 events--lacks credibility. Supreme Soviet Chairman Anatoly Lukyanov said that Gorbachev had agreed to the action program of the SCSE provided the Supreme Soviet sanctioned it. Historian Anthony D'Agostino concluded that Lukyanov's assertion "cannot be so easily dismissed." Similarly, William Odom said "Gorbachev's complicity cannot be entirely discounted."[595] John Dunlop found "too many flaws in Gorbachev's account to absolve him." Those who have studied the August events most exhaustively have affirmed the likelihood of Gorbachev's involvement the most strenuously. Amy Knight, a U.S. researcher and expert on the KGB associated with the Congressional Research Service and John Hopkins University, concluded that Gorbachev was trying to make the KGB his scapegoat. She said Gorbachev reasoned that, if the SCSE succeeded in assuming control and stopping the disintegration of the Soviet Union, he could feign getting well and take charge. If it did not succeed, he could come to Moscow and arrest everyone. In either case he would have clean hands.[596] Jerry Hough asserted "the possibility cannot be totally dismissed" that Gorbachev created the impression that he desired a coup."[597] According to Hough, the SCSE leaders "thought that Gorbachev would eventually legitimate what they had done and they did not want casualties that would complicate the process of reconciliation."[598] Moreover, Gorbachev had powerful motives for choreographing this odd, arm's length complicity. His democratic, peace-loving reputation among his Western allies would suffer if he were seen as the initiator of martial law.

After the August crisis, Gorbachev tried to provoke the military to intervene on his behalf against Yeltsin. Soviet Air Marshal Shaposhnikov said that in early November 1991 Gorbachev suggested to him that a military coup was "the best of all possible variants."[599] In December 1991, Gorbachev made an open but futile appeal to the military for support against Yeltsin.[600] Such behavior suggested that he was fully capable of complicity in the August events.

Far from being a coup, the SCSE was a declaration of emergency by the existing Soviet government, albeit one with only the implicit approval of the Soviet President. Why did Gorbachev lead the SCSE to believe that he favored a declaration of a state of emergency and then reverse himself? In the end, Gorbachev's opposition undermined the SCSE's state of emergency. The evidence suggests his fear of the impact on his relationships with the West made him turn against the SCSE.[601] By August 1991, only the West solidly supported Gorbachev. In the USSR his popular support was hovering near single digits. When governments in the West refused to recognize the SCSE, Gorbachev got cold feet and reversed himself.

Could the SCSE have succeeded in establishing its legitimacy and reversing the state's disintegration? In the short run, it almost did succeed in legitimating itself. William Odom, a military analyst, declared: "I am inclined to the view the outcome of the coup was a close call."[602] Could the SCSE have reversed the collapse? Were matters too hopeless by August 1991? The main leaders of SCSE were Communists who wanted to turn the clock of *perestroika* back to 1985-87.[603] Gorbachev's political beliefs by 1991 were fundamentally different from theirs. Even if he had joined the SCSE, soon they would have parted ways. No success against the collapse of socialism and the breakup of the Union state was imaginable unless Communists reasserted control of the runaway media, ousted Yeltsin and the "democrats," and reversed Gorbachev's economic policies. By August 1991, at least in some regions of the USSR, such actions would have required force and risked civil war--a course few had the stomach for. Stopping the secession of the Baltics, the one region where separatism arguably had majority support, would have required force. Such actions would have set ablaze separatist feelings for generations to come. That would likely have been too high a price to pay for anyone committed to the right of nations to self-determination. Had the SCSE acted decisively and had it called upon the army and the workers for support, a peaceful restoration of authority might have occurred. The SCSE might then have permitted the secession of the Baltics but renegotiated a new Union Treaty with the other republics that preserved the all-Union state. Also the SCSE might have launched an anti-crisis economic program that restored central planning and remedied the hardships of Soviet workers and consumers.

Counterfactual speculation aside, the August crisis enabled Boris Yeltsin to seize full power in Russia, eliminate the moribund CPSU and do away with the USSR. That was the real coup. Historian William Odom stated that the SCSE leaders "occupied the most powerful posts in the regime when the crisis began." When the August crisis was over, an official with no formal position in the central government had amassed enough power to begin the dissolution of the Soviet Union. "Yeltsin was the coup maker, a successful one."[604]

On November 6, 1991, Yeltsin banned the CPSU and CPRF from operating on Russian soil and ordered their dissolution. On December 25, 1991, Gorbachev resigned. On the same day control over USSR nuclear weapons passed from Gorbachev to Yeltsin. Yeltsin simply took over the Soviet army and security services, renaming them Russian state institutions, and retaining most of their personnel. On December 31, 1991 the USSR formally went out of existence. Nikolai Ryzhkov called the dissolution "the greatest tragedy of the 20th century."[605]

7. Conclusions and Implications

Do we mean to say that, had Gorbachev and his associates not come to power, the Soviet Union would have hobbled along, and might have continued to muddle through without overt instability? That is the only possible conclusion. Alexander Dallin[606]

What do these two men [Gorbachev and Khrushchev] have in common? In the first place, their personal qualities: vigor, a reforming disposition, and an intuitive sense of democracy. They were both born in villages, Gorbachev, moreover, in the Cossack region that had retained its yearning for the Russian tradition of communities of free men who had escaped serfdom. Furthermore, they both represented the social democratic trend in the party, out of which emerged such figures as Bukharin, Rykov, Rudzutak and Voznesensky. This social democratic trend never died despite the Stalinist massacres.... This initial social democratism, fortified by the expectations of the people and the demands of the economy, lived on. And it is precisely this that explains such apparently inexplicable phenomena as Khrushchev's accession to power after Stalin and Gorbachev's after Brezhnev. Fedor Burlatsky[607]

Two opposing tendencies existed in the CPSU--proletarian and petty bourgeois, democratic and bureaucratic. Two wings, corresponding to the two tendencies, then developed in the CPSU. In the course of the ensuing continual political struggle between them, a political line was shaped in practice. Without taking this into account, it is impossible to understand such contradictions in Soviet history as that between the mass creative enthusiasm and the repression of the 1930s and 1940s. Only by keeping these conditions in mind can one reach an objective assessment of such Party and state leaders as Stalin and Molotov, Khrushchev and Malenkov, Brezhnev and Kosygin. Communist Party of the Russian Federation, 1997.[608]

What caused the Soviet collapse? Our thesis is that the economic problems, external pressure, and political and ideological stagnation challenging the Soviet Union in the early 1980s, alone or together, did not produce the Soviet collapse. Instead, it was triggered by the specific reform policies of Gorbachev and his allies. In 1987 Gorbachev turned his back on the reform course initiated by Yuri Andropov, the path Gorbachev himself had followed for two years. He took up new policies that replicated in an extreme way the Khrushchev policies of 1953-64 and even further back, the ideas espoused by Bukharin in the 1920s. Gorbachev's about-face was made possible by the growth of the second economy that provided a social basis for anti-socialist consciousness. Gorbachev's revisionism routed its opponents and went on to discard essential tenets of Marxism-Leninism: class struggle, the leading role of the Party, international solidarity, and the primacy of collective ownership and planning. Soviet foreign policy retreats and the evisceration of the CPSU soon resulted. The latter process occurred with the Party's surrender of the mass media, the unraveling of central planning mechanisms and resulting economic decline, and the end of the Party's role in harmonizing the constituent nations of the USSR. Mass discontent enabled the Yeltsin anti-Communist "democrats" to capture control of the giant Russian Republic, and to begin to impose capitalism there. Separatists won out in the non-Russian republics. The USSR fell apart.

Several major American writers, including ones highly critical of Soviet socialism, have come to conclusions resembling, in part, the thesis advanced here. For example, Jerry Hough, a Brookings Institution scholar, wrote,

> The revolution was not caused by the State's poor economic performance, nationalist pressures from the Union republics, popular discontent over the lack of freedom or consumer goods, or the very effort to liberalize a dictatorial regime....the key to the outcome is to be found at the top of the political system or 'the state.' ...The problem was not the weakness of the state as such, but the weakness of the state of mind of those running the state.[609]

The Soviet collapse was not inevitable. No basis exists for the conclusion trumpeted in the corporate media that Soviet socialism was doomed from the start, that all socialist states are

227

doomed, that in the end Marx was wrong and human history ends with "liberal capitalism."[610]

Gorbachev's policies may not have been inevitable but they were no accident either. Powerful internal and external forces sustained the revisionism that came to power with Gorbachev. Those forces--the internal legal and illegal private enterprise and its associated corruption, the external aggressiveness and militarism of the United States, as well as a resurgent free market ideology--had grown stronger in the decades before 1985; soon Gorbachev would unleash the internal forces and accommodate the external ones. The Gorbachev program after 1986, above all its core commitment to reducing the influence of the CPSU, reflected Gorbachev's determination to learn from what he saw as Khrushchev's failure to deal decisively with his opponents in the Party.

Though Gorbachev's revisionism had a long gestation in CPSU politics and in Soviet society, the Soviet collapse was not foreordained. There were many points in the previous thirty-five years where developments could have headed in another direction. The strongest argument for this belief is that the CPSU had defeated the opportunism of Nikolai Bukharin in the late 1920s, when its class roots were also strong, when an immense peasant majority surrounded the working-class state. In the 1950s, the Soviet Union, no longer encircled and invaded, could have entered a less repressive post-Stalin era without making Khrushchev's many blunders of theory and policy. Such critics of the Khrushchev policies as Viacheslav Molotov offered an alternative political course. Those critics were defeated. In the politically stagnant second half of the Brezhnev era, the leaders might have carried on a better fight against growing negative trends, in particular the second economy and corruption. Yuri Andropov, had he lived to evaluate the results of his first reforms, might have sharpened his analysis and made the reform process deeper and broader. Even in the *perestroika* era, the problematic direction policies took after 1986 was not a certainty, either in the leadership as a whole, or in Gorbachev's own mind. That the tendency that Bukharin, Khrushchev and Gorbachev represented kept re-asserting itself and finally won, bears witness to its stubborn material roots, no longer in the peasant outlook so tenacious in the first revolutionary decades but in the spreading commercialism and crime of the second economy.

The entire history of Soviet socialism shows that the class struggle, the struggle to abolish classes, does not end with the seizure of state power and does not end after seventy years of building socialism, although in truth the USSR actually had far less than seven decades to build socialism, since it had to devote so much time to preparing for wars, fighting wars, and recovering from them. Indeed the whole idea that the class struggle is over in a world still dominated by capitalism and imperialism, or within the socialist state, *is itself* a manifestation of the class struggle at an ideological level. Succumbing to that idea is one of the gravest threats to building socialism.

At times, as in 1928-1929 when the Soviet state embarked on rapid collectivization and industrialization, the class struggle intensified. Even when class relations in the countryside were altered at great human cost by these events, an old class outlook stubbornly survived, and beginning in the 1950s with the renewed growth[611] of the second economy, it experienced a rebirth.

Gorbachev and his circle understood this. They consciously targeted certain social groups to support their political line. In 1989 an American writer listed these groups: "many of the most entrepreneurial city and village dwellers," "capable workers," peasants, managers, scientists, technicians, teachers, and artists, "idealistic junior officials" and "democratic minded members of the party's rank and file."[612] Most of the categories represented people at some distance from material production.

Building socialism is difficult. It remains difficult after a socialist revolution demonstrates that it can handle the basic tasks: seizing and holding state power, defending itself from imperialism, supporting anti-imperialist struggles abroad, industrializing and building up the working class, providing the basic necessities of life, including education and culture for all, developing science and technology, and lifting up oppressed nationalities and promoting national equality.

Is it possible for socialism to meet these challenges? One does not have to be a misty-eyed idealist to answer in the affirmative. Both the path outlined by Andropov and the path followed by the surviving socialist states--none of them flawless--prove if nothing else that the Gorbachev debacle was neither the inevitable outcome nor the only path for dealing with socialism's challenges.

In many ways the most disturbing aspect of the Soviet collapse was *not* that Gorbachev's opportunism arose within the Soviet Communist Party. What was disturbing was that the Communist Party proved unable to thwart Gorbachev's opportunism as it had thwarted that of his forerunners. Why was the CPSU less able to deal with Gorbachev in 1987 and 1988 than with Khrushchev in 1964, or Bukharin in 1929? In part, the Party lacked the vigilance and will to suppress the second economy and attendant Party and government corruption. The Party became too lax about its membership, opening its door too widely, particularly to non-workers. Democratic centralism had deteriorated. Ties between the Party and the working class through the trade unions, soviets and other mechanisms ossified. Criticism and self-criticism withered. Collective leadership weakened. Party unity and defending the leader's line evidently became the supreme virtues. Ideological development waned. The ideological mistakes of Khrushchev, and the divergence of ideology from reality in many areas persisted. In many respects ideology became complacent, formalized, and ritualistic. As a result, ideology repelled many of the best and brightest. Many top leaders were insufficiently alert to the meaning and danger of opportunism. In short, the Party itself needed reform.

Contrary to an idea widely propagated in the early 1990s by anti-Communists, the collapse of the Soviet Union showed most conclusively not that socialism based on a vanguard party, state and collective ownership of property and a central plan was doomed but that trying to improve an existing socialist society by following a social reformist Third Way was catastrophic. The "Third Way" led straight to Russian robber baron capitalism and submission to imperialism. The *perestroika* story 1985-91, far from bolstering the case for social reformism, further discredited it.

Our main task was a narrow one: to determine the causation of the Soviet collapse. We believe, however, that our thesis carries far-reaching implications for wider questions of Marxist theory and the future of socialism. We offer the following reflections--brief, in some cases polemical--in the hope they will stimulate further thinking, research and debate.

These wider questions bear on opportunism as a Marxist-Leninist political category, the relative strength of the two systems, the central plan versus the market, the theory of the revolutionary party, historical inevitability, socialism in one country, and certain persistent evasions about the history of twentieth century socialism.

The Soviet collapse does not diminish historical materialism. Historical materialism explains the concrete processes in the USSR in 1985-91. It shows the material roots of counterrevolution, without resort to a flawed "bureaucracy theory." The recent declaration by Marxist philosopher Domenico Losurdo, that "even now we lack a theory for conflict within a socialist society" is mistaken.[613] Major political conflict springs from class interests. The Soviet counterrevolution occurred because the policies of Gorbachev set in motion a process by which social groups with a material and ideological stake in private property and the free market eventually overpowered and displaced the formerly dominant socialist economic relations, that is, the planned, publicly owned, "first" economy.

In 1989-91 the Communist Party of the United States debated whether the Soviet collapse resulted from "human error" or "systemic" weaknesses. The former viewpoint blamed bad leaders, while the latter blamed deep-seated problems of the Soviet system. Both insights contained truth, but not in equal measure. Those who stressed human error had a better, though not a conclusive argument. Gorbachev's blundering, vacillating, and ultimately pro-capitalist leadership provided the decisive cause of the collapse. Yet the proponents of "systemic" were right to seek a deep-seated cause. Many of them, however, mistakenly located it in democratic deficiencies rather than material interests. Supported by facts unknown in 1991, our explanatory framework transcends the way these earlier disputants placed the question.

The stakes for the present and the future are huge in the Soviet collapse--both its consequences and its interpretation--for democratic struggles, for the possibility of building socialism, for the Communist movement, and for the future of humanity. The end of Soviet socialism meant a setback for the remaining socialist countries, for the oppressed of the underdeveloped world, and for the working class everywhere. Soviet working people suffered the cruelest consequences, as Stephen F. Cohen wrote several years ago in The Nation,

> Nearly a decade later Russia is affected by the worst economic depression in modern history, corruption so extensive that capital flight exceeds all foreign loans and investment, and a demographic catastrophe unprecedented in peacetime. The result has been massive human tragedy. Among other calamities some 75 percent of Russians now live below or barely above the poverty line; 50-80 percent of school-age children are classified as having a physical or mental defect, and male life expectancy has

plunged to less than sixty years. And ominously a fully nuclearized country and its devices of mass destruction have, for the first time in history, been seriously destabilized, the Kursk submarine disaster in August being yet another example.[614]

If the century just ended is a guide to the present one, socialist revolutions will face many of the challenges similar to those faced in the Soviet Union. They will likely be victorious first in countries where class struggle and the national liberation struggle intersect. Where twentieth century socialism has so far survived, in China, Cuba, North Korea, and Vietnam, the overlay of class and national contradictions that led to revolution helps to sustain the commitment to socialism. If so, socialist states will come into being with support not only from the workers but also from peasants and other middle strata. Therefore the same or kindred political conditions and problems as those arising in the Soviet Union are likely to recur in new revolutions. Imperialism will continue to attack, its ideologues invoking "democracy" and the bogeyman of "Stalinism" at every step. Lenin said, "The Commune taught the European proletariat to pose concretely the tasks of socialist revolution."[615] The Soviet experience extended these tasks.

Our analysis implies that socialism's adherents must re-emphasize right opportunism as a crucial category for Marxist-Leninist political thought. It was so in the days when Marx and Engels criticized the Gotha Program, when Lenin castigated the Second International, and when the CPSU majority defeated Bukharin. Communists define right opportunism in essence as an unnecessary and unprincipled retreat under the pressure of a class adversary. In any struggle retreats are sometimes necessary, so the question of necessity always hinges on the actual balance of forces and a realistic assessment of conditions, on whether a retreat lays the groundwork for a later advance or whether it is just an easy way out. Communists call a theoretical justification of unnecessary retreat, revisionism. In the context of building socialism, right opportunism usually takes the form of an accommodation (rather than struggle) with capitalism, domestic and foreign. It also sometimes appears as an advocacy of "respecting realities" rather than struggling to change them, a one-sidedly evolutionary approach to building socialism, and a yielding to objective circumstances. It seeks a quick and easy route to socialism, by the path of least resistance. This habit of thought tends to overestimate the automatic, spontaneous nature of the process of creating the new system, and to overemphasize the buildup of productive forces as key to socialism's development while downplaying the need to perfect the relations of production, that is, the struggle to eliminate classes. Under Khrushchev, the explicit theoretical denial of opportunism in socialist construction began.[616] Unlike his two predecessors, the Soviet leader assumed no social basis for opportunism existed in developing socialism. This denial found expression in Khrushchev's notions that the working class state had become the "state of the whole people" and the Communist Party the "party of the whole people." Gorbachev's betrayal showed the folly of Khrushchev's optimism.

Ever since the Popular Front of the 1930s, Marxists in the capitalist world have been trying to find common ground with social reformists. While that policy of seeking unity in action with center forces, especially with masses of people influenced by social democracy, is altogether correct, it is not enough. As an ideology, social democracy remains an insidious and influential ideological competitor of revolutionary Marxism in the working class movement. There must be an unceasing ideological struggle against it, side by side with a tireless search for practical forms of left-center struggle against the right.

In the early 1990s the initial assessments of the Soviet collapse by Communist parties around the world tended to fall into two explanatory frameworks, though some were eclectic. The first group blamed the collapse on the shortcomings of Soviet democracy. The second group blamed the demise on opportunism. The first view sometimes echoed the very "anti-Stalinist" language of the Gorbachev leadership, a vocabulary shared by social democratic and liberal writers.

Democracy in the USSR could have been more advanced in 1985 than it actually was, but that is no reason to identify "lack of democracy" as the main cause of the end of the Soviet Union. Many observers have little understanding of the actual features of socialist democracy.[617] If the word "democracy" means the empowerment of working people, then the Soviet Union had democratic features that surpassed any capitalist society. The Soviet state had a greater percentage of workers involved in the Party and government than was the case with parties and governments in capitalist countries. The extent of income equality,[618] the extent of free education, health care and other social services, guarantees of employment, the early retirement age, the lack of inflation, the subsidies for housing, food, and other basics, and so forth, made it obvious that this was a society run in the interests of working people. The epic efforts to build socialist industry and agriculture and defend the country during World War II could not have occurred without active popular participation. Thirty-five million people were involved in the soviets.[619] Soviet trade unions had powers over such things as production goals, dismissals, and their own schools and vacation resorts that few, if any, trade unions in capitalist countries could claim. Unless there is enormous pressure from below, capitalist states never challenge corporate property. Advocates of the superiority of Western democracy ignore class exploitation, focus on process not substance, and give credit for capitalist democracy to capital, not its real defender and promoter, the modern working class. They compare capitalist democracy's achievements to its past, but, asymmetrically, compare socialist democracy's achievements to an imagined ideal.

Those who defend the notion that democratic shortcomings caused the collapse, that is, were its necessary and sufficient condition, cannot be right if the words "cause" and "collapse" retain their commonsense meanings. The betrayal of the Soviet Union consisted of the overthrow of socialism and the splintering of the Union state. This resulted directly from five concrete processes: Party liquidation, the media handover to anti-socialist forces, privatizing and marketizing the planned, publicly owned economy, unleashing separatism, and surrendering to U.S. imperialism. Amorphous, abstract shortcomings in socialist democracy did not "cause" these policies. The Gorbachev leadership of the CPSU initiated all of them as conscious political choices.

The "lack of democracy" theory survives in part because of the reluctance of some to carry out a concrete analysis. This reluctance involves implicit denial of the importance of the Soviet collapse, an implicit denial that it poses a major theoretical challenge to Marxism. This distancing is self-defeating and intellectually dishonest. Evading the subject leaves unchallenged the prevailing bourgeois explanations of the demise of the Soviet Union. This evasion leads to a self-righteous complacency that says: "The Soviet Union had deep problems of practice; it was bureaucratic and undemocratic. That was then. This is now. We won't be bureaucratic and undemocratic." This is about as far away from historical materialism as one can get.

After several major international conferences of Communist and workers parties, little unity of analysis has developed. One can still hear, "The Soviet comrades will deal with it." In contrast, Marx wrote *The Civil War in France* a few months after the fall of the Paris Commune. Lenin analyzed the August 1914 collapse of the Second International immediately.

Gus Hall, head of the CPUSA, expressed public skepticism about the direction of *perestroika* early on. Before 1987, though he had criticized socialist countries on occasion,[620] he sometimes implied that public criticism was inappropriate.[621] In winter 1987, however, in a *World Marxist Review* article generally positive about *perestroika*, the CPUSA leader cautioned that opportunism usually asserts itself in the guise of deeper appreciation for the "new."

> It is important to keep in mind that most errors, most of history's attempts to revise the science of Marxism-Leninism and most of the policies and acts of capitulation to the pressures of the exploiting class have been justified by arguments about the "new." Throughout the history of the working-class movement, the "something new" concepts have been used to bypass, cover up, or eliminate the concept of the class struggle.[622]

Hall went on to question "new thinking's" subordination of class to universal human values. In 1988 and 1989, while still supportive of *perestroika*, his criticisms grew more forceful and detailed. As Eastern Europe fell apart in late 1989, and as the USSR's crisis became terminal in 1990 and 1991, his public criticism of the policy of the Soviet leaders grew sharper still, though tempered by the hope that the saner heads would prevail.

Yet even Gus Hall, a dogged opponent of opportunism, did not see the conflicting approaches to socialist construction in the Soviet Union, or the material roots of the latter in the growing second economy. Until 1989 the CPUSA as well as other Communists underestimated the possibility of socialism ending and the Soviet Union fragmenting. This was probably due to the great ideological weight of the Soviet Communist Party in the world movement, and to the difficulty of understanding a complex society other than one's own. Nevertheless, in contrast, many social democratic writers did discern the two trends in

237

Soviet politics, and some bourgeois economists perceived the growth of the second economy.

A clear analysis of the Soviet Union was also undoubtedly hindered by the difficulty of sorting out legitimate criticism from the mass of generalized hostility directed the Soviet Union's way. The Chinese Communists did condemn "Khrushchev revisionism" in 1956-64. Their polemics, however, struck many as crude, dogmatic, and self-serving. The Chinese policy erratically veered from left to right, and included Mao's *de facto* anti-Soviet alliance with the U.S. For anyone with a shred of sympathy for the Soviet Union, the Chinese criticism increasingly lacked credibility. On the other end of the spectrum, the Eurocommunists merely echoed the hoary criticisms of the social democrats.

Among many friends of the Soviet Union an un-examined assumption grew that, after Stalin, the USSR was perfecting socialism. Khrushchev was better than Stalin. Gorbachev was better than Brezhnev. With the rare exceptions of Isaac Deutscher and Ken Cameron, few attempted to deal with the Stalin, Khrushchev, or Brezhnev periods in a critical but balanced way. Particularly in the case of Stalin, Soviet supporters gave up the effort of an overall assessment, perhaps because of its inherent difficulty, perhaps because such an effort could have no possible payoff, or perhaps because of an assumption that Soviet progress would make Stalin a historical anomaly of diminishing importance. The enemies of the Soviet Union readily filled this vacuum with shelves of books portraying Stalin as a monster or a madman. These caricatures in turn influenced the views of Communists whose only knowledge of the Stalin period was second hand.

The Soviet demise gave a new lease to the idea of "market socialism," or at least the idea that the jury is still out on the proper role of the market in the political economy of socialism. As in other times, literature on "market socialism" has come into vogue as socialists of all stripes search for answers to the economic disasters of 1985-91. Most of this literature is naively utopian, a lineal descendant of the petty bourgeois socialism of Pierre Joseph Proudhon demolished by Karl Marx. Most versions of "market socialism" contain contradictory theoretical constructs that evade the question of whether labor markets and labor exploitation will exist under market socialism. If so, how is "market socialism" socialism at all?[623]

During perestroika, market socialism served as a halfway house, briefly useful for justifying to the Soviet public the goal of "reforming" and "perfecting" socialism. As a slogan, it proved effective. By the end of his tenure, when economic "reform" had produced something almost indistinguishable from capitalist restoration, Gorbachev dropped the pretence of "socialism." He advanced the goal of establishing a "regulated market economy," something resembling Western Europe or Scandinavia.

Given the actual history of market socialism under Gorbachev, it would seem that the real lesson of the Soviet collapse leads in the opposite direction, to the conclusion that socialism requires central planning, public ownership, and restricted markets. The question ought not to be debated dogmatically by assembling quotations from classical texts. Rather, the most promising approach, as Marxist economist David Laibman has advised, involves studying the relevant practical experience of socialist construction since 1917.[624] The question of the market enters the discussion in three ways: the economic crises of the Gorbachev era; the long-term decline of the Soviet growth rate; and the role of markets in socialist and communist construction. A brief examination of each raises considerable doubts about the desirability of market socialism.

Economic discontent for millions of Soviet people in the Gorbachev era arose not from the central planning system but from its dismantling. In 1985, the economy, still centrally planned, delivered the highest living standards in Soviet history.[625] For decades the Soviet economy had grown faster than the U.S. economy, though by the 1980s, it was not closing the gap as fast as before, and the nature of the race was changing. As frontrunner, the U.S. had made important qualitative transitions to new industries. Nonetheless, growing at a respectable 3.2 percent a year in the early 1980s, the Soviet economy was--slowly--catching up with the U.S. economy in many ways.[626]

As for the long-term decline of Soviet growth rates, too many have uncritically accepted the notion that the market can impart dynamism to socialism, and that a wider use of markets could have accelerated Soviet growth rates. Even cautious proponents of markets within the context of a dominant central plan, have to explain the following awkward facts. In the final three and a half decades of the USSR's existence, the more market relations and other reforms were introduced--officially and legally in several reform waves (Khrushchev, Kosygin and Gorbachev), and quietly, steadily, and often illegally through the spreading second economy--the more the long-term economic growth rates came down. Even some bourgeois economists admit the downward impact of the second economy.[627] The fastest Soviet growth rates ever achieved came in 1929-53 when the Soviet leadership firmly upheld central planning and suppressed the market relations formerly tolerated in the NEP of 1921-29. It was easy to see why the economic reform that Khrushchev and Gorbachev advocated would lower growth rates. Less investment in heavy industry, more stress on consumer goods, more wage leveling,[628] all would tend to lower growth. Growth would also slacken due to decentralization that led to wasteful competition and disrupted the coordination between enterprises. Clearly from 1985 to 1991 "the magic of the market" was nowhere in evidence. The more commodity-money relations expanded, the more *perestroika* failed. In 1992 when Yeltsin fully imposed "shock therapy," the Soviet economy went into a catastrophic slump, from which it has not yet recovered. Since 1991, market relations remain associated with negative or low growth rates. Indeed, 20th century planned economies, as a rule, grew significantly faster than market economies.[629]

"The seizure of the means of production by society puts an end to commodity production, and therewith the domination of the product over the producer," wrote Engels.[630] Engels may have misjudged how quickly and automatically the latter would flow from the former, but clearly the founders of scientific socialism envisaged communism--the historical stage after socialism--as a society with no market. The forecast of a communist society where, in conditions of superabundance, free human beings would collectively organize production according to a plan and organize distribution according to need rather through the blind workings of an impersonal and cruel market has been central to the Marxist understanding of social emancipation. Marxists criticized commodity production for causing producers to lose control of their product. In the Marxist view, a great advantage of the planned economy in its socialist and communist stages was that the producers step by step regained control over the product of their own labor. In the end, under communism, conscious human beings, not blind, anarchic market forces, would fully determine the character and pace of economic development.

Until Khrushchev, the Soviet Union took the struggle to restrict the role of the market seriously. In the late 1940s and early 1950s, before the postwar recovery from Nazi invasion was complete, a theoretical discussion with big practical implications arose among Soviet leaders and economists. It was prompted by the positions of Gosplan chief, Nicolai Voznesensky, who argued for broader use of market relations, and by preparations for a long-overdue Soviet textbook on political economy. Stalin, summing up the various debates, took the position that the laws of socialist construction were objective, that the actions of people could not transform the economic laws of socialism, but human action could restrict the sphere of operation of those economic laws. He held that commodity production existed under socialism "for a certain period, without leading to capitalism, bearing in mind that in our country commodity production is not so boundless and all-embracing as it is under capitalist conditions, being confined within strict bounds." He opposed the selling of the machine tractor stations to the collective farms for various practical reasons and because it would expand the sphere of commodity production, a step backward from the already attained level of the industrialization of agriculture. In his view, commodity production in the USSR economy was confined to the sphere of personal consumption, and, pointing to the potential development of "product exchanges," he declared the rudiments of a non-commodity economy existed in 1952 and could be developed.[631]

The Soviet debate in 1952 was a fight over long-term socialist strategy. Stalin's view on commodity-money relations and the law of value under socialism signified this: If the nature of a commodity under socialism can be "transformed," in other words, if there can be "socialist commodities," then some in the CPSU leadership could logically argue for wholeheartedly expanding markets under socialism, which meant giving up the policy of keeping markets within strict bounds as socialism developed. Stalin rejected this path.

Then came Khrushchev. After 1953, a shift to pro-market political thinking occurred, and doctrinal shifts[632] in economic theory ratified them. An obvious conundrum arose, however. Those favoring expanded use of market relations in socialism discarded a major element of Marxist theory, namely that the admittedly distant historical stage after socialism, full communism, would have no market. The founders of Marxism forecast that full communism meant no market. How can

242

maximum use of the market in the socialist stage be followed immediately by its complete absence in the next stage? One example of the evasion of this problem is in a 1969 work *Categories and Laws of the Political Economy of Communism*, by A.M. Rumyantsev, an economist who had been close to Khrushchev. He buried in a long paragraph the notion that the use of "commodity-money relations" (markets) "accelerates the advance to full communism," and that in some unexplained way, socialism "grows over into full communism," while admitting "widespread theoretical discussion" of this "most complex problem" of the political economy of socialism in its "modern stage of development."[633] The pro-market turn in theory persisted long after Khrushchev. A late-Brezhnev-era textbook, *Political Economy: Socialism* (1977) stated in little more than one paragraph that commodity-money relations would "wither away" in the communist stage. How this withering would occur, the text leaves unexplained. Anders Aslund[634] noted that in the 1960s there were two main camps of Soviet economists, the "commoditeers," and the "non-commoditeers," in other words, those for or against the expanded use of "commodity-money relations," that is, markets. At least a decade before 1985, a number of Soviet research institutes and other corners of academia were occupied by social scientists who found Paul Samuelson more beguiling than Karl Marx.[635] One of these was Tatyana Zaslavskaya,[636] whose mentor was V. G. Venzher, the economist whose idea to sell the machine tractor stations to the collective farms was rejected by Stalin.[637] Zaslavskaya was an early influence on the Gorbachev pro-market reforms and his supporter almost to the end. There was remarkable continuity in the two competing streams of Soviet economic thought.

Yuri Andropov acknowledged that his path of economic reform still had unsolved problems of theory and practice. He complained, for example, of the lack of an adequate theory of how to speed up labor productivity growth and a clear method to set prices under central planning.[638] He considered his approach a better way forward than the Bukharinist ideology "which leans toward anarcho-syndicalism, the splitting of society into rival corporations independent of each other." American political scientist Michael Parenti vividly described the many unsolved problems of designing incentives for innovation in Soviet industry. Innovation sometimes threatened the careers of managers and often failed to reward them for taking risks. Pressure to fulfill the plan's production goals created disincentives for experimentation and even for the introduction of better technology, while sometimes creating incentives to cut quality. Well-run factories that met or exceeded the plan were sometimes punished with greater workloads, and so forth.[639] These were stubborn, difficult problems of planning and management to be sure, but hardly insoluble.

The Soviet counterrevolution has implications for the remaining socialist states. Since 1991, the four surviving socialist states,[640] China, Cuba, Vietnam, and North Korea, have been under imperialist pressure to make concessions to the market, to submit to capitalist world economic institutions (WTO, IMF, World Bank), and to create special zones for Western corporate investment within their borders, on penalty of being refused Western loans, access to Western markets, and technology transfers. All four countries have had to maneuver in conditions of economic warfare spearheaded by the U.S. To a large degree because there is a gun held to their heads, these states in varying degrees have made concessions to the market and private enterprise. This poses a real danger, for a key lesson of the Soviet collapse is that market relations must be held to a minimum.

Agriculture may be the great exception to the general rule that in the first stage of socialism, the socialist state works to restrict the market over time. Unlike the Soviet Union, which did not have the luxury of moving slowly toward socialist relations in the countryside, other socialist states, after rushing to collectivize agriculture, have pulled back. In China, after the reforms re-privatized agriculture in 1978, well before the end of the USSR, farm output vastly increased.[641] Later reforms in Chinese foreign trade and industry speeded up growth more moderately than in agriculture, and with harmful social, political and economic effects.[642] In socialist Cuba, agricultural reforms came about in quite different circumstances--the end of Soviet trade and subsidies in 1989-91. This required drastic measures to achieve the self-sufficiency of the island and adapt to the grave crisis. In one measure to increase output, workers at state farms became co-operative owners. Since the reform, output has increased substantially.[643] In today's Cuba too, some interpret the Special Period not as a forced, perilous, emergency backward step, but as a welcome, sound, long-term development course. To their credit the top Cuban economic and planning authorities, although willing to allow free debate, seem fully cognizant of the historic parallels.[644]

Not all the experimentation with the market is caused by post-Soviet dire necessity or heightened Western pressure. "Two revolutionary classes, two lines" is a general phenomenon. In China, the concessions to the market have been extreme and the future of socialism may be in doubt. According to a 1994 essay by the Harriman Institute's Rajan Menon,

> China's strategy of reform may well fail. It is hard to imagine that rampant capitalism, which is what is occurring however much the Chinese Communist Party may shy away from this term for ideological reasons, the increasing autonomy of the coastal regions, and the exposure of Chinese intellectuals to corrosive ideas from abroad can coexist indefinitely.[645]

In July 2001, the head of the Chinese Communist Party called for allowing capitalists into the CPC. Though a section of the national bourgeoisie participated in the Chinese Revolution and won a role in the governance of the early People's Republic of China, the new attitude towards a new class of capitalists was a wholly different matter. China is essentially pursuing "a gigantic and expanded NEP,"[646] and sooner or later the political and economic contradictions of the policy will force a choice, as it did in the USSR in 1928-29. Which side will win remains anyone's guess. The political outcome of this struggle in the ruling Communist Party of the most populous country on earth is certain to be one of the most momentous of the 21st century.

After 1991, capitalist restoration in the USSR meant a depression and the coming of an era of gangster capitalism. Nevertheless, capitalist restoration in Russia and the other parts of the former USSR remains unstable. Transnational finance is keeping post-Soviet Russia a hobbled, dependent resource-extraction zone, even at the risk of nuclear accident, ethnic warfare, and state disintegration. Scholars from many viewpoints have noted the American government does not seem overly apprehensive.[647] The contrast with the late 1940s, when a worried U.S. ruling class footed much of the bill for the Marshall Plan to stabilize West European capitalism, could not be plainer.

Erstwhile Gorbachev supporters debate what the post-Soviet system is, and what its prospects are. As in the classic horror film, Rosemary's Baby, the post-Soviet newborn is hideous, if it is a baby at all, and those who have seen it certainly deny that it is theirs! Some opine that the wretched little creature will not live long. Economist David Kotz[648] says post-Soviet Russian capitalism is not true capitalism at all, but a "non-capitalist predatory/extractive system" emerging from the previous "state socialist" system. Others, such as Roy Medvedev, say the capitalist revolution is "doomed" in Russia.[649]

Admittedly, the system in today's Russia is uniquely parasitic, deformed, and weak. The Eastern European socialist states have evidently made the transition back to capitalism, with plenty of problems,[650] but not with the extreme social evils seen in the former USSR. Just as socialism has proven reversible, so is neo-capitalism. If the contradictions of Russian capitalism remain acute, imperialism remains recklessly aloof, and the Russian left can unite around a realistic strategy, socialist restoration might re-emerge on the agenda. In spite of everything, in Russia political parties favoring socialism have more support than any other single party.

Many have anguished over the question: why was the Soviet socialist system so fragile? Without an understanding of the growth of forces opposing socialism from within, the system seemed stronger than it actually was, and its unforeseen fall was therefore all the more shocking and puzzling. A similar question, from another standpoint, is posed as a comparison: if U.S. capitalism survived a Herbert Hoover who in 1929 presided over an economic crash leading to 40 percent mass unemployment, and a decade–long depression, as well as the defeat of his long-ruling Republican Party, and yet U.S. capitalism recovered, grew and thrived after World War II, why could Soviet socialism not survive a Gorbachev?

The answer is: the subjective factor is vastly more important in socialism than in capitalism. This is both a strength and vulnerability. A qualitative difference between socialism and capitalism is captured in the saying "capitalism grows; socialism is built." At the risk of a tedious simile, the two systems are like a river raft and an airplane. With capitalism--the river raft--the pole man who steers the raft merely has to avoid shoals, rapids and waterfalls. Mostly, the flow of the current down river controls the pace and direction of the raft. It is a simple and mostly automatic system. Only loose supervision is required. Big blunders are usually not fatal.

An airplane--socialism--is a far superior mode of transportation. Its range, its freedom of direction and maneuver, and its speed far exceed that of the river raft. But the airplane requires conscious application of the laws of physics and aerodynamics, forethought, planning, science, training, ground crews, radar, and so on. It is a complex system requiring a massive social division of labor. Managing the system--its piloting, the subjective aspect of its steering--is far more crucial to the safe operation of this mode of transportation than is the case with the river raft. Big blunders in piloting a plane, though rare, are often fatal. There is a smaller margin for error. The fact that airplanes sometimes crash does not prove the superiority of the river raft. It is only an argument for better-engineered, better-piloted, safer airplanes.

The laws of socialist construction differ from the laws of capitalist development. Capitalism's laws operate blindly, without consciousness, like the law of gravity that sends the river raft down stream, no matter what the pole man is doing. But socialism's laws, while objective, require an airplane whose designers consciously master and use the laws governing such forces as gravity, thrust, lift and drag, and a pilot skillful in the technique and grounded in the underlying science.

Therefore a Gorbachev leadership could do far more damage to socialism than an even more blundering Hoover did to U.S. capitalism. As a Soviet scholar said, the economic laws of socialism "cease to be a spontaneously, anarchically operating force and are consciously applied by society in its self-interest." Ignoring the economic laws of socialism "leads to... the emergence of difficulties and disproportions and imbalance in the economy, and weakens coordination of the actions and comradely co-operation of social groups and bodies of workers."[651]

As opportunism developed within the Soviet Union, imperialism discovered a formula to promote its interests: from afar encourage those selfsame opportunist trends in the Communist leadership of the USSR. Czechoslovakian events in 1968, and the accumulation of problems in Yugoslavia suggested the formula, but would it work in the USSR where the new system's roots seemingly had sunk so deep? For a long time, the old system's main thinkers understood in principle how the new system could be destroyed. An architect of the Cold War, George Kennan, wrote prophetically in 1947:

> If...anything is ever to occur to disrupt the unity and efficacy of the Party as a political instrument, Soviet Russia might be changed overnight from one of the strongest to one of the weakest and most pitiable of national societies.[652]

It was a lesson that the enemies of socialism in the 21st century are still trying to apply in Cuba, China, Vietnam, and North Korea. They could not defeat Soviet socialism by intervening in its civil war, a Nazi invasion, the arms race, subversion, and economic warfare. They could not directly penetrate the leadership. From the outside, however, they did all in their power to encourage opportunist policies. In time, on their own, some Communist leaders drank the poisoned chalice of revisionism.

Can anything guarantee that opportunism never succeeds again? One safeguard might involve strictly limiting legal private enterprise and enforcing the law against illegal private enterprise and thus preventing associated corruption of the Party and the government. As for Party standards, it is hard to imagine higher ones than the ones that Lenin set. The lesson is probably not in the search for higher party standards or the invention of altogether new norms, but in the maintenance of those standards. Also, as Bahman Azad rightly observed, a policy of frank international Communist criticism might have helped expose the negative trends in Soviet socialism, and mobilized action against them.[653] By muting public criticism of the Soviet Union, the left committed a grave, if understandable, mistake.

In part, Gorbachev framed his program as completion of the "anti-Stalinist" agenda interrupted by Khrushchev's removal. By the end of his rule, Gorbachev was freely using traditional anti-Communist terms of abuse such as "Stalinism," "totalitarianism," and "command economy." Stigmatizing the past with borrowed invective paralyzed rational, honest debate about the past and present realities of the Soviet Union. In the future, supporters of socialism must come to terms with the Stalin era. In *Stalin: Man of Contradiction*, Kenneth Neill Cameron wrote,

> A few months ago I had lunch with a leading academic Marxist and faculty colleague. When I told him I had just finished a book on Stalin he said "Stalin! My God, every time I talk about socialism, some student brings up Stalin – and then, what can one say?" One can say quite a lot.[654]

Cameron's book was a start. At first even Gorbachev called for an all-sided view of the Stalin years. He said:

> To remain faithful to historical truth we must see both Stalin's incontestable contribution to the struggle for socialism and to the defense of its gains, and the gross political errors and abuses committed by him and those around him for which our people paid a heavy price and which had grave consequences for the life of our society.[655]

A balanced historical view of Stalin must include an assessment of not just the repression but the circumstances of it. As Hans Holz said, this means the recognition that "the despotic aspects of Soviet socialism"[656] occurred in the period of its encirclement. Historian Herbert Aptheker enumerated some of the aspects of this encirclement:

> ...the hostility, boycott, economic warfare, systematic sabotage, military assaults, creating and bolstering Mussolini, Hitler, and Franco, the tardiness and weakness of two-front assistance to the USSR and then after victory the rejection of any decent relationships between the triumphant but shattered Soviet Union and the victorious Western powers. When one writes "shattered" Soviet Union one has in mind the devastation of everything in its European territory, the loss of about 25 million dead and the serious wounding of some 40 million of its citizens.[657]

The gaps in knowledge of the Stalin era remain enormous. The fact that bourgeois historians cannot agree on whether Stalin's victims numbered 5, 20 or 100 million shows the abysmal state of historical understanding.[658] Using new information obtained since 1991, Michael Parenti has pointed out that post-Soviet scholars have made a promising start on an honest accounting.[659] Some historians are retreating from the wildly exaggerated claims of Cold War polemics.[660] Now that the Soviet archives are opened, the calumnies of rabidly anti-Soviet authors[661] will not be the last word on Soviet history.

The Soviet tragedy renders farcical the claim of one historian that "the 20th century will go down in history as the century of the greatest in world transformations--the socialist revolution."[662] Twentieth century history proved not so rectilinear. Yet historical materialism has an explanatory power great enough to survive the Soviet reversal. Anthony Coughlan wrote:

> People in the socialist tradition should above all be able to think historically. When did capitalism begin? Was it 15th century Venice? 16th century Geneva? 17th century Holland or 18th century England? If it took capitalism centuries to develop--and it is still in full spate in many parts of the world--is it not naïve to expect socialism to spring full-grown from the womb of history in our particular century? Moreover, as capitalism developed in a zigzag way, with periods of setback as well as advance, should not a historical perspective lead one to expect a long period of complex interaction between capitalism and socialism around the world before one gives way to the other?[663]

The Soviet experience demands a reconsideration of the idea of "socialism in one country." Socialism in one country involved a basic decision to try to hold on and build a new society, although many external and internal conditions militated against it. It was a calculated and reasonable risk, for a revolution in Soviet Russia had its advantages, namely, a huge territory, a large population, and geographical remoteness. Marx probably would have approved the gamble. He once wrote: "World history would be very easy to make if the struggle were taken up only on the condition of infallibly favorable chances."[664] In any case it is doubtful that the eventual demise of the USSR invalidated the attempt to build it in one country. Socialism develops country by country because capitalism develops unevenly. Simultaneous revolution in all remaining capitalist countries is impossible. As Lenin observed, "History has not been kind enough to give us socialist revolution everywhere." Uneven development meant that capitalism broke at its weakest link in 1917. Now, at the beginning of the 21st century, uneven development of the world economy is more extreme than ever. For example, the ratio of average incomes in the world's twenty richest countries compared to the world's twenty poorest has risen from twenty to one in 1960s to forty to one in the new century.[665] Since these are national aggregates, if anything this indicator understates the extreme inequality in the world. Thus the likelihood of revolutions in isolated countries remains, and revolutionaries in the 21st century will face a challenge similar to those in the last, having to build socialism alone or almost alone in the cauldron of imperialist pressures.

The breakup of the USSR as a socialist multinational federation underlines the importance of the national question. Marx himself underestimated the national question in one or more respects. Moreover, contrary to the expectations of some internationalists of old, and contrary to the claim of today's globalists, nationalism remains a growing phenomenon. Compared to 1945 when only about 40 flags flew outside the UN building, today more than 190 fly. Ethnic and national strife is likewise rising, often fomented by the transnational corporations (TNCs). As the TNCs, with their free trade and globalization ideology, assault national sovereignty and development, partisans of workers must be the best champions of the democratic right of nations to self-determination.

New forms of the national question are arising. Multinational federal states are under stress in many parts of the world, to mention a few: India, Britain, Canada, the Russian Federation, and Spain. The colonial legacy remains. Africa and the Mideast have ridiculous borders drawn by departing colonialists and bearing little or no relation to national or economic units. Many former socialist states, independent before 1989-91, are now prostrate semi-colonies. National feeling in those lands is on the rise. World domination by the USA as the sole global military power is accentuating the national question of all other states. Supra-national integration in the form of the European Union, NAFTA, and other schemes has become a main aim of transnational finance capital. The national question is producing unusual alignments where divergent political forces find themselves in common battle against the TNCs, although, of course, from different class positions and with different motives. For example, not long ago in the USA, the trade unions and Texas billionaire Ross Perot were at the same time opponents of NAFTA. In Britain, Communists and many conservatives, at loggerheads on almost everything else, oppose the EU.

Since the former Soviet and East European states had few or no native big capitalists of the traditional kind, restoring capitalism has meant putting them in hock to foreigners. Consequently, new national democratic demands have entered the programs of Communist Parties and other progressive parties in erstwhile socialist states. There is the possibility of organizing the defense of the nation-state and national independence as part of a campaign to reverse capitalist restoration.

We cannot leave this writing without sharing the impact of this study upon us. We came away with a renewed sense of awe at accomplishments of the seventy-year socialist experiment when, as Tom Paine said of an earlier revolution, workers "had it in their power to begin the world over again." We came away, also, with a deep sense of the great possibilities lost. The betrayal swept away an attempt at human liberation, which sustained the hopes of millions of working and oppressed people in the 20th century, a noble venture for which so many Soviet people made such staggering sacrifices and from which so many Soviets and non-Soviets reaped lasting benefits.

Nobody can undo the grim facts. Only the peoples in the former Soviet Union and the other former socialist states can decide whether and when socialism will return. It is unlikely the winners of 1991 will have the last word. In 1815 at the Congress of Vienna that restored Europe's kings to their thrones, the Austrian aristocrat Clemens von Metternich thought that he had done away with "liberty, equality and fraternity." A little more than a century later, more republican tricolors flew over European and world capitals than ever before. The contradictions that gave birth to 1917 are still growing and will give birth to new attempts at working class emancipation. Learning the lessons of the dismantling of the Soviet Union is the best way both to honor its memory and to ensure that such a calamity never happens again.

Epilogue–
A Critique of Explanations
of the Soviet Collapse

What needs explanation is that an international system of states collapsed in the absence of the most evident forms of threat: it was not defeated in war; it did not face overwhelming political challenges from below, Poland being the only partial exception. It was not, despite its manifold economic and social problems, unable to meet the basic economic demands of its citizenry. It did not therefore collapse, fail or break down in any absolute sense. What occurred rather was that the leadership of the most powerful state in the system decided to introduce a radically new set of policies within the USSR and within the system as a whole: it was not that the ruled could not go on being ruled in the old way so much as that the rulers could not go on ruling in the old way. Fred Halliday[666]

Explanations for the collapse of the Soviet Union abound. They reflect every ideological shade and emotional nuance. They range from the fanciful to the ponderous, from the gleeful to despairing. Many have contributed to our own understanding, which differs from all of them. These theories fall into six categories[667] according to the main cause:

1. Flaws of socialism
2. Popular opposition
3. External factors
4. Bureaucratic counter-revolution
5. Lack of democracy and over-centralization, and
6. The Gorbachev factor

In what follows, we shall explain our differences with these theories.

Proponents of the first theory believe that all socialist systems arc doomcd because they have a "genetic flaw." Socialism came about illegitimately in the Soviet Union. It was inherently unworkable because it went against human nature and the free market. Jack Matlock, a Columbia professor who served as ambassador to the Soviet Union from 1987 to 1991, said simply, "'Socialism,' as defined by Lenin, was doomed from the start because it was based on mistaken assumptions about human nature."[668] This theory with variations appears in the works of Martin Malia, Richard Pipes,[669] and Dmitri Volkogonov.[670]

In truth, in spite of its achievements, the Soviet system did have many flaws in 1985. Some were problems associated with centralized planning--insufficient quantity and quality of some consumer goods, decelerating productivity, lagging local initiative, the slow diffusion of computers and other technology, corruption and illegal private money-making. Some were problems associated with the political system. Some methods that were helpful for seizing and holding power proved problematic for wielding power in the long run. These included the overlap of Party and government functions that both kept political initiative at the top and reduced lower bodies to advisory and consultative functions, a problem that similarly affected mass organizations, like the trade unions. There was also the persistence of forms and levels of censorship above and beyond what was necessary in a mature socialist society and of privileges that separated the Party and government elite from the working population. Some problems were clearly related to the Cold War that absorbed resources to maintain a credible military strength and support allies abroad. Some problems had to do with the challenge of maintaining a revolutionary elan, high Party standards, and a relevant Marxist ideology and education in the face of the relentless march of time and inevitable temptations of bureaucracy. The main point, however, is that these problems did not produce a crisis let alone a collapse.

Moreover, the trouble with this theory is that it views Soviet history as unfolding toward an inevitable demise because of its departures from human nature, private property and the free market. Though these views gained ascendancy in the U.S. during the Reagan era, few historians subscribe to an historical determinism based on human nature. In addition, this theory is utterly incapable of explaining how Soviet socialism survived the collectivization of agriculture and the German invasion of World War II, only to fall apart under the seemingly far lesser challenges of the 1980s.

The second theory is that popular opposition brought down Soviet socialism. This category is a bit of a straw man, since no writer of note holds that popular opposition alone brought down Soviet socialism. Nevertheless, some writers have stressed such aspects of popular opposition as the disenchantment of intellectuals,[671] the protests of workers,[672] the rise of nationalists,[673] and the electoral successes of non-Communists. Certainly, the disaffection of intellectuals with the Soviet system was quite widespread. By the 1980s, for example, many prominent Soviet economists favored markets.[674] Reform schemes proposed by academics influenced some of Gorbachev's policies, and in this way intellectuals did contribute to the collapse.[675] Other aspects of popular unrest also played a role. The riots in Baku, the conflict between Azerbaijan and Armenia, the nationalist protests in the Baltics, the strikes by miners, and the formation of a liberal opposition bloc in the Congress of People's Deputies stood out as important moments in the unraveling of Soviet socialism. Still, the main defect of this theory is that popular discontent appeared toward the end rather than the beginning of the Gorbachev reforms. It resulted from Gorbachev's policies rather than caused them. As one wag said, *glasnost* gave Soviet citizens the license to criticize, and *perestroika* gave them something to criticize. In 1985, however, at the start of the reform process, popular unrest did not exist. While some Soviet people complained about the quality and quantity of goods and about official privileges and corruption, most Soviets expressed satisfaction with their lives and contentment with the system. Polls showed that the level of satisfaction of Soviet citizens was comparable to the satisfaction of Americans with their system.[676] Even in 1990-91, as their leaders moved toward private property, marketetization, and ethnic fragmentation, Soviet citizens by large majorities favored public ownership, price controls, and the maintenance of the Soviet Union.[677] In the final analysis, popular opposition acted as a dependent rather than an independent variable, a by-product of Gorbachev's policies rather than their cause.

According to the third theory, external factors rooted in the Cold War and global economy caused the Soviet collapse. The most extreme such view holds that the betrayal of Soviet socialism was due to the CIA's penetration of the Soviet leadership. Admittedly, this penetration reached further than most outsiders realized. According to one later report, "by 1985, the C.I.A. and F.B.I. had developed the most impressive inventory of spies against Russia in American history" and had "riddled" the K.G.B. and G.R.U. (military intelligence) with moles.[678] Still, unless future revelations show that Gorbachev or Yakovlev served as CIA agents, it stretches credibility to suppose that the CIA brought down Soviet socialism. Of course, more powerful external factors than the CIA were at work.

As many writers have suggested, external pressure generated by the world economy, technological changes, and the Carter and Reagan policies unquestionably figured in the Soviet difficulties. Andre Gunder Frank, for example, points out that the worldwide recession of 1979-82 encouraged Presidents Carter and Reagan to increase military spending and this compelled the Soviet Union to spend more. The recession also put a strain on socialist countries in Eastern Europe that had borrowed money from Western banks.[679] Manuel Castells and Emma Kiselova argue that the main strain on the Soviet Union came from having to adapt to the "information society."[680] Aside from these economic and technological factors, the main external strain on the Soviet system was that imposed by the intensification of the Cold War in the early 1980s.

Soviet society never enjoyed the luxury of internal development free of the threat of outside aggression. The cost of defending itself and aiding its allies escalated yearly and drained resources away from socially useful domestic investments. By 1980, Soviet aid to its allies cost $44 billion a year, and arms spending consumed 25 to 30 percent of the economy. This drain on the Soviet economy exceeded by a factor of two to three what Western experts at the time estimated.[681] The strain of the Cold War increased during the late Carter and early Reagan years. As both the conservative, Peter Schweizer, and the leftist, Sean Gervasi, have pointed out, Reagan opened up a second Cold War and initiated a multipronged strategy of destabilizing Soviet society. The strategy consisted of doubling military spending ("spending them into bankruptcy"), projecting the Strategic Defense Initiative ("Star Wars"), aiding anti-Communists in

Afghanistan, Poland and elsewhere, driving down the price of oil and gas on the world market (the Soviet's main source of hard currency), as well as engaging in various forms of economic and psychological warfare.[682]

Certainly, the external factors pressing on the Soviet regime challenged the Soviet system in varied and powerful ways and have a place in a full explanation of the Soviet collapse. Still, that is a far cry from saying, as Peter Schweizer does, that it is "not possible to understand the collapse of the Soviet Union separate from Ronald Reagan," who "won the cold war."[683] Frances Fitzgerald provides the most persuasive refutation of the decisiveness of Reagan's policies. Fitzgerald argues that no clear cause-and-effect relationship existed between the external factors and an internal crisis.[684] For example, Fitzgerald maintains that increases U.S. military spending under Reagan for Star Wars and other projects did not increase Soviet military spending.[685] Many Soviet insiders likewise rejected the idea that the arms race caused either Gorbachev's reforms or the collapse. A Soviet official in military intelligence said, "The notion that Gorbachev's *perestroika* was started as a result of Reagan's Star Wars was concocted in the West and is completely absurd."[686] A member of the Soviet Institute for the U.S.A. and Canada opined, "I am deeply convinced that neither SDI [the Strategic Defense Initiative, Star Wars] nor the arms race in general contributed to the collapse of the Soviet Union."[687] Authoritative opinion differs on the importance of the arms race. To a large extent the debate misses the crux of the matter. However great and in whatever form, the external pressure coming from the United States represented less of an external threat than earlier economic sanctions, sabotage, and foreign invasion. Moreover, the external pressure did not dictate the particular shape and direction of the Soviet response. In the end, Gorbachev's particular responses to the external pressures and internal problems provided the most proximate and decisive cause of the debacle.

A fourth theory is that the cause was a bureaucratic counter-revolution. This theory bears a striking similarity to Leon Trotsky's views of the Soviet Union in the 1930s. Trotsky argued that the Soviet system was "transitional," and that if a new socialist revolution did not overthrow the bureaucracy, then the bureaucracy itself could become the base for a capitalist restoration or could even transform itself into "a new possessing class."[688] The idea that the bureaucracy transformed itself into a new possessing class through a revolution from above is more or less the argument of David Kotz and Fred Weir,[689] Jerry F. Hough,[690] Steven L. Solnick,[691] and Bahman Azad (though Azad does not regard this new group as a class).[692] The accounts of Kotz and Weir and Azad deserve attention.

In *Revolution From Above*, Kotz and Weir illustrate matter-of-factly and convincingly the positive achievements of the USSR and the many democratic and humane features of Soviet life. They argue that the reform course launched by Gorbachev unleashed processes that created new coalitions of groups that favored replacing socialism with capitalism. Boris Yeltsin became the leader of the anti-socialist bloc. With the support of "the party-state elite," he was able to push aside two rival groups, the Gorbachev social reformists and the CPSU "Old Guard." The breakup of the USSR as a multinational federation occurred because of the specifics of the power struggle between the Yeltsin and Gorbachev forces. Yeltsin's anti-socialists held power in Russia while the Gorbachev social reformists held most of the Union institutions. The Yeltsin forces concluded they could maintain power and pursue capitalist restoration only by withdrawing Russia from the Soviet Union. Hence, the USSR fell apart.

The Kotz and Weir thesis has several strengths. It can explain why most of the top managers and capitalists in present-day Russia are former Soviet officials, often former CPSU members. As Yeltsin increasingly signaled his intention to go down the capitalist road, the party-state elite concluded that its power and privileges could be maintained and possibly improved by a shift to private ownership, with its members as the new owners. The swift collapse of the so-called coup in August 1991 may, in this way, be explained by the elite's shift of loyalties both to Yeltsin and capitalism. The absence of elite (as well as mass) support for either Gorbachev or the "coup" leaders is the chief reason why the "plot" fizzled and Gorbachev's fortunes sank between August and December 1991. It explains the rapid and relatively peaceful nature of the capitalist restoration as well as the great difficulties in making the new capitalism work.

The "bureaucratic revolution from above" thesis is, however, not completely convincing. An authoritative study[693] based on interviews with former members of the Party-state elite found "no evidence" for the "fashionable theory" that "the Soviet system was toppled by the Party and state officials in order to turn their power into private wealth." Indeed, such officials were "incapable of collective action to defend the system and incapable of consciously hastening its demise." The "top bureaucracy," if it can be said to have enough substance to be judged an authentic social group at all, clearly was too heterogeneous and scattered to act as a cohesive political force. Moreover, if the interests of the party-state elite were determining the pro-capitalist direction of events, how can one explain that both Gorbachev's *perestroika* and Yeltsin's free-market initiatives slashed the central bureaucracy by tens of thousands? Kotz and Weir posit an elite with wholly arbitrary boundaries of 100,000. If the elite was capable of conscious independent action in its own self-interest, why did it back Andropov's Marxism-Leninism in 1983, and Gorbachev's revisionism in 1987, and Yeltsin's free-market shock therapy in 1993? Were all three highly inconsistent ideologies in the bureaucracy's self-interest? The stealing of state assets by the bureaucratic elite was embryonic in 1987[694] as the dismantling of the CPSU began in earnest, and the stealing became fully developed only in 1990-1991, lending credence to the view that the developments elsewhere, not in the party-state elite, drove the collapse. The party-state elite was reacting to events, not initiating them. Some in the elite reacted opportunistically by seizing state assets to maintain their power and privileges, but they were not the protagonists of the process.

Several other aspects mar Revolution from Above. Kotz and Weir downplay the international situation; that is, the external imperialist pressure, as a contributing cause of the Soviet downfall. Also, they have illusions about the Gorbachev project. They call what was manifestly a counterrevolution a revolution, as if the distinction were trivial. They have no criticism of Gorbachev's concessions and retreats before the domestic pro-capitalists and foreign imperialists, including the abandonment of Cuba and Nicaragua, and the support of the Gulf War. In the final analysis, blaming the bureaucratic elite exonerates Gorbachev, whom Kotz and Weir wish to support.

On the surface, Bahman Azad also supports the thesis that the bureaucratic elite fostered a counter-revolution. In Azad's analysis, certain political developments in Soviet history prepared the way for the Gorbachev debacle, and these elements of his analysis remain compelling even if the ideas about a bureaucratic counter-revolution are stripped away. Azad offers a sympathetic and persuasive history of the accomplishments and limits of Soviet socialism--from War Communism, 1918-1921, to the New Economic Policy, 1921-1928, Rapid Industrialization, 1928-1945, World War II, and postwar rebuilding. Azad argues that the real problems began with Khrushchev. The "rapid consumption model" and wage leveling adopted by the 20th Congress in 1956 sapped incentives, created shortages, reduced economic growth, and fostered the black market and corruption. Khrushchev's idea that the Soviet Union had begun "the full scale building of a Communist society" adopted by the 21st Congress in 1959 was overly optimistic, sowed illusions, and led to further wage leveling and stagnation. The adoption by the 22nd Congress in 1961 of the idea that the Soviet state had become the "state of the entire people" and the CPSU "a Party of the entire people," signaled a weakening of the Party vis-à-vis the state and a growing predominance in the Party of intellectuals and bureaucrats. In short, Azad argues that the Soviet Union's problems and Gorbachev's policies were the aftershocks of the mistaken policies of the Khrushchev era.[695]

Azad treats the Gorbachev period as a footnote to Khrushchev's mistakes, a part of the "hiatus of 25 years in failing to implement much-needed changes."[696] Azad does not see that Gorbachev extended and amplified Khrushchev's policies and all of their weaknesses. In place of an analysis of the proximate policies and processes leading to the collapse, Azad simply telescopes the whole process: Andropov's reform program was hijacked by state bureaucrats under Gorbachev, who betrayed socialism and restored capitalism. In our view, the real problem was not the bureaucracy as such but the second economy that had corrupted sections of the Party and state, fostered a petit bourgeois mentality outside as well as inside the bureaucracy, and turned some bureaucrats along with the second economy entrepreneurs into a base for Gorbachev's opportunism.

The fifth theory argues that the Soviet Union collapsed because of a lack of democracy and an over-centralized administrative system. This view of the Soviet collapse has much in common with the theory of the flaws of socialism. The difference is that those who believe in the inherent flaw of socialism think all socialist systems are doomed, whereas the lack-of-democracy theorists believe that only Soviet-style socialism was so fated. For these theorists, the lack of democratic institutions and the over-centralization of the economy derived from Stalin, or Stalin and Lenin. This view is widely held by left social democrats and Euro-communists. Historian Stephen F. Cohen and the Soviet writer, Roy Medvedev, also reflect this view, and so do some contemporary Communist Parties.[697]

This explanation has a superficial attractiveness; it does not require any defense of Soviet socialism. To blame the Soviet collapse on a lack of democracy and over-centralization thus serves as a psychological or political distancing mechanism. It is a way of asserting that the socialist ideal remains pure and untarnished in spite of what happened in the Soviet Union. It says: "History does not matter. The actual experience of a socialist country does not count. The only thing that matters is what socialists or Communists say today. What happened in the Soviet Union was there and then; this is here and now. Those Soviet Communists messed up, but we are different and smarter. They were too bureaucratic, undemocratic, and over-centralized, but we either knew it all along or have learned it from their mistakes."

However much this view may serve those who want to get on to the next leaflet, demonstration, lecture, book promotion or media interview, it leaves a lot to be desired as an explanation. As soon as one tries to apply its lofty phrases to actual events, its explanatory power vanishes. This theory so lacks precision as to elude either proof or refutation. To say that the Soviet Union collapsed because of a lack of democracy and over-centralization can mean one of two things: Either the collapse occurred because the Soviet Union lacked the political and economic forms and practices familiar in Western social-democratically governed countries like Sweden (i.e., a liberal democracy and a mixed economy), or it occurred because the Soviet Union failed to develop a new kind of socialist democracy and mixed economy hitherto unknown anywhere in the world. Both ideas fail as historical explanations because they rest on idealist constructs that attempt to explain history by the degree to which it conforms or fails to conform to an ideal. Though Hegel would have found this thought congenial, modern historians, Marxist or not, believe that historical explanations must adhere to the actual details and contradictions of history, the internal logic of events. This precludes understanding history by measuring it against an outside standard.

Moreover, those who think that the Soviet Union collapsed because it failed to follow European social democracy have an additional problem. It is clear that after a certain point, Gorbachev shared the same ideals as these theorists and tried to move the Soviet Union toward a liberal democracy with a mixed economy. Yet, these moves led to a political and economic meltdown that has still not been overcome. This is an embarrassment that none of the lack-of-democracy theorists have been able to explain away.

Those who think the explanation resided in the failure of the Soviets to develop a new kind of socialist democracy with a new kind of mixed economy also face a problem. First, a concession to this viewpoint is in order. Even the strictest of historical materialists would grant that Marxist-Leninists have ideals and believe that socialism should develop toward their ideal of communism. This ideal is a very general one: a society governed by the principle of from each according to his abilities and to each according to his needs, a society of abundance where rationing will be unnecessary and where people will make their own history by replacing the exploitation of wage labor and the anarchy of private production and the market with the conscious control made possible by common ownership and planning; a society where classes, commodity production, and the state along with the divisions between mental and physical labor and town and country, will disappear. Thus, Marxist-Leninists have an ideal with which to guide and assess the development of socialism. Still, it is a quite different matter to suggest that the failure to approach an ideal will cause the collapse of a socialist society. This is what the lack-of-democracy theorists say, and this is why their idealism departs from a credible historical explanation.

More to the point, the lack of democracy theorists ignore the actual history of liberal democracy and socialist democracy. The meaning and evaluation of democracy have changed over time, and neither capitalism nor liberalism has an exclusive claim to it. Until the second half of the nineteenth century, democracy meant rule by the lower classes or the oppressed, and almost all major political thinkers from Aristotle to the founders of the United States opposed democracy. Above all, liberalism valued choice and competition--the choice and competition between parties in the political arena and between commodities in the market place. Democracy came to the United States and other liberal republics gradually and then not as rule by the lower classes as such, but as participation by the lower classes in elections, as the franchise was extended first to men without property and then to ex-slaves, women and youth.

Historically, socialism had a stronger claim to democracy than liberalism. Whereas liberalism only gradually claimed democracy as a value, socialism from the start embraced its classical meaning as rule by the lower classes. In the *Communist Manifesto* of 1848, Marx said that "the first step in the revolution by the working class, is to raise the proletariat to the position of ruling class, to win the battle of democracy."[698] Whereas liberal democracy venerated choice, socialist democracy valued equality, in the sense of the abolition of the capitalist class' superiority, domination and exploitation. Just as liberalism assimilated democratic forms, so socialism developed democratic mechanisms. Lenin had argued that workers would not spontaneously develop socialist ideas and revolutionary organizations and that consequently a vanguard party had to lead a socialist revolution. Rule by a vanguard party, however, did not mean the same thing as rule by the workers and peasants themselves. Over time socialism had to develop ways to increase the participation and control by the workers and peasants, including broadening membership in the Communist Party and developing soviets, trade unions, and other mass organizations.[699]

Though the process of developing democracy was far from over, the Soviet Union had developed a variety of political institutions and practices designed to provide popular participation. Every subsequent socialist country adopted and adapted the Soviet innovations. The Soviet practices included using newspapers as ombudsmen as well as news sources, vesting trade unions with power over workers' rights, production norms, and the disposition of social funds, and creating soviets, production committees, community assemblies, governing committees of living complexes, and other Party and government bodies. Though many of these populist institutions atrophied during the difficult years surrounding the Second World War, they revived in the 1950s and involved greater and greater numbers of working people. Even under Brezhnev, popular participation in government showed many signs of vitality. Writing in 1978, when the Soviet Union contained 260 million people, a group of Soviet writers gave the following figures on Soviet political activity: 16.5 million Communists, 121 million trade union members, nearly 38 million Young Communists, over 2 million Soviet deputies, 35 million people who work with the deputies in the Soviets of People's Deputies, 9.5 million members of People's Control bodies, and 5.5 million members of production conferences of industrial enterprises.[700] Of course, participation in a socialist soviet, just as participation in a bourgeois election, provided no conclusive proof of popular control, but it nonetheless represented, however imperfectly, the striving for a kind of socialist democracy.

If Soviet democracy was developing in some areas, however, it was experiencing problems in other areas. The special Party stores and privileges, however modest, as well as the growth of some wealthy beneficiaries of the second economy, mocked socialist equality. The primary authority of the Party had the effect of making the soviets advisory bodies at best or rubber stamps at worst. The second economy corrupted some in the Party and government. The point is that socialist democracy had both strengths and weaknesses. The complexity of the actual situation is generally not acknowledged by those who assert that a lack of democracy brought down Soviet socialism. Of course, that a society that was suffering neither invasion, economic crisis, nor popular discontent fell apart makes for an arresting paradox. To this paradox, now another must be added: it fell apart in spite of political organizations in which millions of people participated.[701]

The idea that centralization played a pivotal role in the collapse is just as problematic as that of the lack of democracy. The Soviet Union was the first country in history to try to organize its economy around state-owned enterprises (with some elements of non-state enterprises) and centralized state planning (with limited markets). Only a strong central government with a planned economy could achieve the goals of socialism: socializing property, protecting the revolution from enemies within and without, achieving rapid electrification and industrialization, elevating education, health care, and housing for all, and developing the most backward and oppressed areas of the country. There was no blueprint for this, and no guarantees that this would work. The entire history of the Soviet Union involved constant experimentation with various kinds planning mechanisms, different price, wage, and investment policies, and degrees of centralization and decentralization within the context of state property and central planning. To say the Soviets were continually confronting problems associated with central planning is manifestly true. They repeatedly strove to find the proper role for decentralized decision-making within the context of a centrally planned economy. To say, however, that the problem was simply centralization itself is like saying the problem with socialism is socialism. Such a position, by the way, is pretty much where Gorbachev ended up when he scuttled the central plan and opened the door to private enterprise. In other words, to say that centralization caused problems is a truism, but to say centralization itself is a problem amounts to a rejection of socialism.

The proponents of the lack-of-democracy theory believe they hold one trump card. If the Soviet Union had possessed a vital socialist democracy that really expressed the will and interests of the working class, and if the Communist Party really represented the vanguard of the working class, then the workers, including the Communists themselves, would have resisted the overthrow of the Communist Party, the evisceration of socialism, and the restoration of capitalism. Since, according to this view, neither the working class nor Communists did resist, something was lacking in Soviet democracy. The actual history of the Soviet collapse escapes this logical net. As we show in Chapter 6, working class resistance did occur. Why this resistance was not great enough to stop the dismantling of socialism is, of course, a great puzzle. In a sense, however, the lack of democracy theory actually understates the puzzle. The vast majority of people in an advanced industrial society submitted passively while a small minority turned the common wealth into their private gain, impoverished the rest of the population, and de-modernized a society for the first time in history.[702] The acquiescence of a people to policies that are demonstrably not in their own self-interest constitutes a deeply troubling phenomenon, well-known in capitalist countries, and much more common than we would like to suppose. That Soviet socialism did not manage to create citizens capable of transcending the kind of inertia, willful ignorance, and business-as-usual attitudes that immobilize most people most of the time may disappoint but should not surprise us. It is as much an indictment of liberal democracy as of socialist democracy.

Moreover, placing the responsibility for Soviet passivity solely on socialist political institutions contains another problem. Many of the traditional Soviet *political forms*--the newspapers, the soviets, and the Communist Party itself--were undermined by Gorbachev after 1985. Thus, while the majority

Soviet people remained opposed to privatization of property, the elimination of price controls, and the break-up of the Soviet Union, the traditional modes of expressing political views were evaporating. In addition, such new institutions as the Congress of People's Deputies proved entirely ineffective at enforcing such public sentiments. On top of this, every weakening of traditional institutions and re-establishing capitalism was spearheaded by Gorbachev and other Communist leaders with the befogging assurance that they were returning to Lenin and advancing to a better socialism. In other words, it is likely that part of the workers' passivity occurred because at the very time that Gorbachev and other Communist leaders were eroding the people's standard of living, economic security, and socialism itself, they were promising workers a better socialism and depriving them of the very institutions through which they had previously expressed their views.

The final theory is that the Soviet collapse was mainly due to Gorbachev. Quite naturally, almost all accounts give great weight to Gorbachev's role. Some accounts, however, go further than others in placing responsibility on him. According to British historian, Archie Brown, the key to the unraveling of Soviet society was "the Gorbachev factor," mainly Gorbachev's departure from Communist orthodoxy.[703] For Brown, this apostasy undermined the system in unforeseen ways, but Gorbachev nonetheless played the role of a heroic Westernizer, a modern-day Peter the Great. Others, who also see Gorbachev as the decisive factor, see him as more calculating than Brown does. Jerry Hough thinks that Gorbachev was a free marketeer.[704] Euvgeny Novikov and Patrick Bascio suggest that Gorbachev was a Gramscian Eurocommunist.[705] Anthony D'Agostino argues that Gorbachev was a Machiavellian, for whom ideas came second to getting and maintaining power.[706]

Though we agree with the common element of these views, that Gorbachev's ideological deviations played a key role, we nonetheless disagree with several other elements. It is not just that where Brown sees a positive, we see a negative. Rather, accounts that over-emphasize Gorbachev obscure the extent to which he was not alone but operated in a historical and social context. When he first departed from Andropov, Gorbachev represented ideas that nonetheless had precedent in the Communist movement, namely in the ideas of Bukharin and Khrushchev, and ideas that had appeal to some in Soviet society. Such ideas as the weakening of the central power of the Party and the government, the legitimizing of private property, and allowing more freedom for markets had potency in the 1980s because they palpably reflected the interests of the dynamic (if parasitic) sector attached to illegal, private enterprise. Thus, Gorbachev was both a legatee of a certain tradition and the product of his times and not just a lone "factor" making history.

Moreover, in some writers, a stress on Gorbachev leads to seeing in his actions a longstanding, preconceived plan. The weight of evidence, however, seems to point more toward a shallow leader who acted rashly, impulsively, and contradictorily. Though Gorbachev's policies eventually formed a pattern of capitulation to the petty bourgeois, liberal, and corrupt interests at home and imperialist pressure abroad, this was not evident at the start. Opportunism rather than a preconceived plan or aim provided the beacon that guided his steps.

In the end the story of the Soviet collapse was not the inevitable unfolding of a tragedy rooted in the impossibility of socialism. Nor was it a defeat brought about by popular opposition or foreign enemies. Nor was it due to Soviet socialism's failure to match up to some ideal of socialism that embodied liberal democracy and a mixed economy. Nor was it primarily the story of the conscious betrayal of one man. Rather, it was the story of a triumph of a certain tendency within the revolution itself. It was a tendency rooted at first in the peasant nature of the country and later in a second economy, a sector that flourished because of consumer demands unsatisfied by the first economy and because of the failure of authorities to appreciate the danger it represented and to enforce the law against it. It was a tendency that had manifested itself in Bukharin and Khrushchev before Gorbachev. It was a tendency that believed that prosperity, democracy, and its vision of socialism could come quickly and easily without sacrifice, without struggle, and without strong central authority. It believed in making concessions to imperialism, liberalism, private property and the market. Some adherents of this tendency believed they were true socialists, though they allied themselves with others whose true sympathies were with money-making and private property. Not until Gorbachev had this tendency in the revolution held full sway and been carried to its logical conclusion. Only with Gorbachev was the full folly of this course realized, when it led not to a new kind of socialism but to new kind of barbarism.

At the beginning of Homer's *Odyssey*, Zeus decries the way mortals blame the gods for their miseries, since "they themselves, with their own reckless ways, compound their pains beyond their proper share." It is a long way from the destruction of Troy to the collapse of the Soviet Union, but the temptation of men to blame gods, nature, or some other powerful, outside force remains. In the case of the Soviet Union, Fidel Castro decried this temptation in words more prosaic but no less apt than Homer's. "Socialism," Castro said, "did not die from natural causes: it was a suicide."[707] If our account has any lasting value, it will be in furthering a discussion of the "reckless ways" that wrecked the first socialist state.

Endnotes

Notes for Introduction

1. Anthony D'Agostino, Gorbachev's Revolution (New York: New York University Press, 1998), 9.
2. Alexander Dallin, "The Causes of the Collapse of the Soviet Union," Post-Soviet Affairs, Vol. 8, No. 4 (1992), 279.
3. Fidel Castro quoted by Andrew Murray, Flashpoint: World War III (London: Pluto Press, 1996), 38.
4. Victor and Ellen Perlo, Dynamic Stability: The Soviet Economy Today (Moscow: Progress Publishers, 1980), passim; USSR: 100 Questions and Answers (Moscow: Novosti, 1977), 60, 63; Albert Szymanski, Class Structure: A Critical Perspective (New York: Praeger, 1983), 590.
5. Perlo, 144; USSR: 100 Questions and Answers, 65-66, 71.
6. Szymanski, 586-592.
7. Karl Marx, "The Civil War in France" and Frederick Engels, "Introduction," in Karl Marx and Frederick Engels Selected Works in Two Volumes (Moscow: Foreign Languages Publishing House, 1962), 473-545.
8. Edward Boorstein, Allende's Chile (New York: International Publishers, 1977).
9. Edward Hallett Carr, What Is History? (New York: Vintage Books, 1967), 125-127.
10. Eric Hobsbawm, On History (New York: The New Press, 1997), 243-249.

11. Omar Noman, ed. <u>Poverty in Transition</u> (New York: United Nations Development Program, 1998), 6.

12. Stephen Cohen, <u>Failed Crusade</u> (New York and London: W. W. Norton, 2000), 40-42.

13. Marx and Engels, 485, 542.

Notes for Chapter 2

14. Dmitri Volkogonov, <u>Stalin: Triumph and Tragedy</u> (New York: Grove Weidenfeld, 1988), 80.

15. Albert Resis, ed., <u>Molotov Remembers: Inside Kremlin Politics</u> (Chicago: Ivan R. Dee, 1993), 360.

16. Resis, 408.

17. "Socialism in the Soviet Union: Lesson and Perspectives, From the Program of the Fourth Congress of the Communist Party of the Russian Federation 20 April 1997," <u>Nature, Society, and Thought</u> (May 2, 2000), 421.

18. <u>Lenin Collected Works</u>, ed. Yuri Sdobnikov, vol. 32 (Moscow: Progress Publishers, 1975), 165-240.

19. <u>Lenin Collected Works</u>, vol. 33, 63.

20. <u>Lenin Collected Works</u>, vol. 32, 218.

21. <u>Vladimir I. Lenin: A Political Biography</u> (New York: International Publishers, 1943), 242-259.

22. Barrington Moore, Jr., <u>Soviet Politics--The Dilemma of Power</u> (Cambridge: Harvard University Press, 1951), 98-102.

23. Moore, 102-108.

24. Anatoly Chernyaev, <u>My Six Years with Gorbachev</u> (University Park: Pennsylvania State University Press, 2000), 138-139.

25. Kenneth Cameron, <u>Stalin: Man of Contradiction</u> (Toronto: New Canada Publications, 1987), 30.

26. Moore, 108-113.

27. E. H. Carr, <u>Studies in Revolution</u> (New York: Grosset & Dunlap, 1964), 214-215.

28. Joseph Stalin, "The Right Deviation in the Communist Party of the Soviet Union," in Joseph Stalin, <u>Leninism: Selected Writings</u> (New York: International Publishers, 1942), 98-101.

29. George Katkov, The Trial of Bukharin (New York: Stein and Day, 1969), 55-60.

30. V. Y. Zevin, "Lenin on the National and Colonial Questions," in Lenin the Great Theoretician (Moscow: Progress Publishers, 1970), 307-308.

31. V. Zotov, Lenin's Doctrine of National Liberation Revolutions and the Modern World (Moscow: Progress Publishers, 1983), 15, 21.

32. Joseph Stalin, Marxism and the National and Colonial Question (New York: International Publishers, 1934).

33. Albert Nenarokov and Alexander Proskurin, How the Soviet Union Solved the Nationalities Question (Moscow: Novosti Press, 1983), 11.

34. Stephen Cohen, Bukharin and the Bolshevik Revolution (New York: Knopf, 1973), 35-38.

35. Stalin, 185, 177, 168-170.

36. Yitzhak M. Brudny, Reinventing Russia: Russian Nationalism and the Soviet State, 1953-1991 (Cambridge, Mass. and London: Harvard University Press, 1998), 42.

37. Bahman Azad, Heroic Struggle Bitter Defeat (New York: International Publishers, 2000), 92-95.

38. Leonard Shapiro, The Communist Party of the Soviet Union (New York: Vintage Books, 1971), 515.

39. Werner G. Hahn, Postwar Soviet Politics: The Fall of Zhdanov and the Defeat of Moderation, 1946-1953 (Ithaca and London: Cornell University Press, 1982), 12-13, 19-27.

40. Hahn, 32-33, 45-57, 182-184.

41. William Taubman, Khrushchev: The Man and His Era (New York and London: W. W. Norton, 2003), 250-255.

42. Roy A. Medvedev and Zhores Medvedev, Khrushchev: The Years in Power (New York: W. W. Norton, 1978), 67-71.

43. Medvedev and Medvedev, 71.

44. Taubman, 324.

45. Carl Linden, Khrushchev and the Soviet Leadership (Baltimore and London: Johns Hopkins University Press, 1990), 224.

46. Hahn, 47.

47. Roy Medvedev, Khrushchev (London and New York: Blackwell and Doubleday, 1982), 32.

48. Medvedev and Medvedev, 35, 58-60.

49. Maurice Dobb, Soviet Economic Development Since 1917 (New York: New World Paperbacks, 1965), 317, 332.

50. Joseph Stalin, Economic Problems of the U.S.S.R. (New York: International Publishers, 1952), 21-22.

51. Hans Heinz Holz, "The Downfall and Future of Socialism," Nature, Society, and Thought, 5, no. 3 (1992), passim.

52. Holz, 105.

53. Holz, 105.

54. Resis, 391.

55. Giuseppe Boffa, Inside the Khrushchev Era (New York: Marzani and Munsell, 1959), 108.

56. Boffa, 110.

57. Medvedev and Medvedev, 75.

58. Alexei Adzhubei quoted by Linden, 225.

59. Roger Pethybridge, A Key to Soviet Politics: The Crisis of the 'Anti-Party' Group (London: George Allen & Unwin, 1962), 93-98.

60. Resis, 345-347; Molotov and Malenkov quoted by Pethybridge, 98-99.

61. Pethybridge, 95, 103-109; Shapiro, 569.

62. Taubman, xix.

63. Cameron, 130.

64. Michael Parenti, Blackshirts & Reds (San Francisco: City Lights Books, 1997), 76-80.

65. "Secret Speech of Khrushchev Concerning the 'Cult of the Individual,'" in The Anti-Stalin Campaign and International Communism (New York: Columbia University Press, 1956), 2-89; Cameron, 121-137, 170.

66. Yegor Ligachev, Inside Gorbachev's Kremlin (New York, Pantheon, 1993), 284.

67. Cameron, 123.

68. Gerald Meyer, "The Virgin Lands Project, 1953-1963: Khrushchev's Panacea for the Soviet Union's Agricultural Crisis," (M.A. thesis, City College of the City University of New York, 1969).

69. Meyer, 35-37.

70. Stalin, 16-17.

71. Medvedev and Medvedev, 85-88.

72. Dobb, 372-377.

73. Alex Nove, An Economic History of the USSR (New York: Viking Penguin, 1984), 358.

74. Medvedev and Medvedev, 106-107.

75. Dobb, 321, 324.

76. Dobb, 329-330.

77. J. P. Nettl, The Soviet Achievement (Norwich, England: Harcourt, Brace & World, 1967), 236.

78. Brudny, 42-43.

79. Medvedev and Medvedev, 73, 148.

80. Medvedev and Medvedev, 43.

81. A Proposal Concerning the General Line of the International Communist Movement (Peking: Foreign Language Press, 1963), 5-36.

82. Joseph Stalin, For Peaceful Coexistence: Postwar Interviews (New York: International Publishers, 1951).

83. In contrast, the Chinese, who were the most vigorous critics of Soviet foreign policy for not being sufficiently anti-imperialist stood silently on the sidelines during this confrontation and afterwards spoke up only to criticize the Soviets. O.B. Borisov and B. T. Koloskov, Sino-Soviet Relations (Moscow: Progress Publishers, 1975), 173.

84. Taubman, 336-337, 450-451, 609-610; Kirby quoted by Taubman, 337.

85. Shapiro, 575.

86. Linden, 224.

87. Azad, 128-131.

88. George Breslauer, "Khrushchev Reconsidered," in Stephen F. Cohen et al., eds., The Soviet Union Since Stalin (Bloomington: Indiana University Press, 1980), 56, 59.

89. Medvedev and Medvedev, 151, 153.

90. John Gooding, Socialism in Russia: Lenin and his Legacy, 1890-1991 (New York: Palgrave, 2002), 187-209.

91. Dmitri Volkogonov, Autopsy for an Empire (New York, London, Toronto, Sydney, Singapore: The Free Press, 1998),

262, 264, 302, 320, 324; Peter Kenez, <u>A History of the Soviet Union from the Beginning to the End</u> (Cambridge, UK: Cambridge University Press, 1999), 215, 217; Roy Medvedev, "Brezhnev: a Political Sketch-Portrait," in <u>Leonid Brezhnev: The Period of Stagnation</u> (Moscow: Novosti Press, 1989), 6, 9.

92. <u>Pravda</u> quoted by Breslauer, 64.

93. Fedor Burlatsky, "Brezhnev and the End of the Thaw," in <u>Leonid Brezhnev: The Period of Stagnation</u>, 38.

94. Stephen F. Cohen and Katrina vanden Heuvel, <u>Voices of Glasnost</u> (New York: W. W. Norton, 1989), 20.

95. Victor and Ellen Perlo, <u>Dynamic Stability: The Soviet Economy Today</u> (Moscow: Progress Publishers, 1980), 331.

96. Abel Aganbegyan, <u>The Economic Challenge of</u> *Perestroika* (Bloomington and Indianapolis: Indiana University Press, 1988), 45, 52-53, 90.

97. Victor and Ellen Perlo, 275.

98. Victor Perlo, <u>Super Profits and Crises: Modern U.S. Capitalism</u> (New York: International Publishers, 1988), 491.

99. Aganbegyan, <u>The Economic Challenge of</u> *Perestroika*, 3, 23, 67, 71.

100. Leonid Brezhnev, <u>We Are Optimists: Report of the Central Committee of the Communist Party of the Soviet Union to the 26th Congress of the CPSU</u> (New York: International Publishers, 1981), 57.

101. Ligachev, 211-212, 219.

102. Brudny, 15-17.

103. Victor and Ellen Perlo, 284.

104. Moshe Lewin, <u>Political Undercurrents in Soviet Economic Debates</u> (Princeton, New Jersey: Princeton University Press, 1975), xiii.

105. Anders Aslund, <u>Gorbachev's Struggle for Economic Reform</u> (Ithaca, New York: Cornell University Press, 1989), ix, 4.

106. Perlo, 260-280.

107. Perlo, 260-280.

108. Perlo, 282, 284.

109. Zhores Medvedev, <u>Andropov</u> (New York and London: W. W. Norton, 1983), 17-54; Martin Ebon, <u>The Andropov File</u> (New York et al.: McGraw-Hill, 1983), 272-273.

110. Ebon, 17-22, 70-71, 86-92, 109.

111. Ebon, 64-74; Zhores Medvedev, 32-40; Herbert Aptheker, <u>The Truth About Hungary</u> (New York: Mainstream Publishers, 1957), 184-246.

112. Ebon, 64-74; Zhores Medvedev, 32-40.

113. Ebon, 70-71, 32, 24, 104; Zhores Medvedev, 32-40, 64-65.

114. Ebon, 22, 24, 27, 29, 65.

115. Quoted by Zhores Medvedev, 87.

116. Ligachev, 27.

117. Zhores Medvedev, 146; Ebon, 119.

118. Yuri Andropov, "The Better We Work, the Better We Will Live" (November 22, 1982) in Ebon, 239-249; Y. V. Andropov, <u>Sixtieth Anniversary of the Union of Soviet Socialist Republics</u>, (December 21, 1982), (Moscow: Novosti, 1983); Yuri Andropov, <u>Analysis of the Existing Situation and Landmarks for the Future</u>, (June 15, 1983), (Moscow: Novosti, 1983); Yuri Andropov, "Karl Marx's Teaching and Some of the Problems in the Building of Socialism in the USSR," (1983) in <u>A Reader on Social Sciences</u> (Moscow: Progress, 1985), 395-419.

119. Martin Ebon, <u>The Andropov File: The Life and Ideas of Yuri Andropov General Secretary of the Communist Party of the USSR</u> (New York, St. Louis, San Francisco, Toronto and Mexico: McGraw-Hill Book Company, 1983), 239-249.

120. Andropov, <u>Analysis</u>, 12.

121. Andropov, <u>Analysis</u>, 17.

122. Andropov in Ebon, 241.

123. Andropov in Ebon, 241.

124. Andropov in Ebon, 241.

125. Ebon, 136-137.

126. Zhores Medvedev, 134.

127. Medvedev, 131-133.

128. Andropov, "Karl Marx's Teaching," 407.

129. Ebon, 186.

130. Ebon, 173, 174, 193, 205, 208.

131. Andropov in Ebon, 246.

132. Ebon, 238.

133. Andrei Gromyko, Memoirs (New York, et al.: Doubleday, 1989), 247.

134. Anatoly Dobrynin, In Confidence (New York: Times Books/ Random House, 1995), 444.

135. Jonathan Harris, The Public Politics of Aleksandr Nikolaevich Yakovlev, 1983-1989, The Carl Beck Papers in Russian and East European Studies, No. 901 (Pittsburgh: University of Pittsburgh Center for Russian and East European Studies, 1990), 12.

136. Andropov quoted by Dobrynin, 512.

137. Ebon, 234.

138. Dobrynin, 478.

139. Ligachev, 148.

140. Ebon, 118.

141. Andropov, Analysis, 18.

142. Ligachev, 28.

143. Andropov, Analysis.

144. Ebon, 26.

145. Ebon, 152, 201, 166, 168, 199.

146. Ebon, 192, 203, 219, 230.

147. Andropov, "Karl Marx's Teaching," 400-401.

148. Andropov, Sixtieth Anniversary, 11-21.

149. Andropov, Sixtieth Anniversary, 18.

150. Andropov, Sixtieth Anniversary, 18-19.

151. Volkogonov, 332, 370, 387.

Notes for Chapter 3

152. Gregory Grossman, "Subverted Sovereignty: Historical Role of the Soviet Underground," in Stephen S. Cohen, et al., eds. The Tunnel at the End of the Light (Berkeley: University of California, 1988), 24-25.

153. Vladimir G. Treml and Michael Alexeev, "The Growth of the Second Economy in the Soviet Union and Its Impact on the System," in Robert W. Campbell, ed., The Postcommunist Economic Transformation (Boulder, San Francisco and Oxford: Westview Press, 1994), 222.

154. Quoted by Treml and Alexeev, 238.

155. Moshe Lewin, Political Undercurrents in Soviet Economic Debates, from Bukharin to the Modern Reformers (Princeton: Princeton University Press, 1975), 254.

156. Gregory Grossman, "The 'Second Economy' of the USSR," Problems of Communism (September-October, 1977), 25.

157. Maurice Dobb, Soviet Economic Development Since 1917 (New York: International Publishers, 1966).

158. According to Anders Aslund, Gorbachev's Struggle for Economic Reform (Ithaca, New York: Cornell University Press, 1989), 5, by the 1960s three of the four leading academic economic institutions were dominated by economists who favored "money commodity relations" or simply "market relations." Koriagina, who was the leading Soviet expert on the second economy, belonged to the Economic Research Institute, which until 1986 was headed by the anti-market economist, Tigran Khachaturov. Gregory Grossman, "Subverted Sovereignty: Historic Role of The Soviet Underground," in Stephen S. Cohen et al., eds., The Tunnel at the End of the Light (Berkeley: University of California, 1998), 36.

159. G. A. Kozlov, ed., Political Economy: Socialism (Moscow: Progress Publishers, 1977); L. Leontyev, Political Economy: A Condensed Course (New York: International, 1974); P. I. Nikitin, The Fundamentals of Political Economy (Moscow: Progress Publishers, 1983); G. S. Sarkisyants, ed., Soviet Economy: Results and Prospects (Moscow: Progress Publishers, 1977); and Yuri Popov, Essays in Political Economy (Moscow: Progress Publishers, 1985).

160. Joseph Stalin, "Economic Problems of Socialism in the USSR," in Bruce Franklin, The Essential Stalin (New York: Anchor Books, 1972), 445-481.

161. Victor Perlo, How the Soviet Economy Works (New York: International, 1961), 34.

162. Victor and Ellen Perlo, Dynamic Stability: The Soviet Economy Today (Moscow: Progress Publishers, 1980).

163. "List of Berkeley-Duke Occasional Papers in the Second Economy in the USSR with Abstracts and Notes," http://

econ.duke.edu/Papers/Treml.BDOP.html (date accessed August 6, 2010)..

164. Gregory Grossman, "The Second Economy in the USSR and Eastern Europe: A Bibliography," (Berkeley-Duke Occasional Papers on the Second Economy of the USSR, July 1990).

165. Grossman, "The 'Second Economy' of the USSR," 25-27.

166. Grossman, "The 'Second Economy' of the USSR," 26-27.

167. Grossman, "The 'Second Economy' of the USSR," 35.

168. Grossman, "The 'Second Economy' of the USSR," 29-30.

169. Grossman, "The 'Second Economy' of the USSR," 30.

170. Grossman, "The 'Second Economy' of the USSR," 31.

171. Konstantin Simis, <u>USSR: The Corrupt Society: The Secret World of Soviet Capitalism</u> (New York: Simon and Schuster, 1982), 145-147.

172. Vladimir G. Treml, "Purchase of Food from Private Sources in Soviet Urban Areas," (Berkeley-Duke Occasional Paper, September 1985).

173. Gregory Grossman, "A Tonsorial View of the Soviet Second Economy," (Berkeley-Duke Occasional Paper, December 1985).

174. Vladimir G. Treml, "Alcohol in the Soviet Underground Economy," (Berkeley-Duke Occasional Paper, December 1985).

175. Michael V. Alexeev, "The Underground Market for Gasoline in the USSR," (Berkeley-Duke Occasional Paper, (April 1987).

176. Michael V. Alexeev, "Expenditures on Privately Rented Housing and Imputed Rents in the USSR," (Berkeley-Duke Occasional Paper, November 1991).

177. Kimberly C. Neuhauser, "The Second Economy in Funeral Services," (Berkeley-Duke Occasional Paper, February 1992).

178. Clifford G. Gaddy, "The Size of the Prostitution Market in the USSR," (Berkeley-Duke Occasional Paper," November 1989) and Kimberly C. Neuhauser, "The Market for Illegal Drugs in the Soviet Union in the Late 1980s," (Berkeley-Duke Occasional Paper, November 1990).

286

179. Marina Kurkchiyan, "The Transformation of the Second Economy in the Informal Economy," in Alena V. Ledeneva and Marina Kurkchiyan, eds., <u>Economic Crime in Russia</u> (The Hague, London, and Boston: Kluwer Law International, 2000), 86-87.
180. Treml and Alexeev, 221,235.
181. Byung-Yeon Kim, "Informal Economy Activities of Soviet Households: Size and Dynamics," (PERSA Working Paper No. 26, University of Warwick, 29 January 2003), 9.
182. Tatiana Koriagina, "The Shadow Economy of the USSR," <u>Izd-vo Pravda</u> 3 (1990): 113 [in Russian].
183. Gregory Grossman, "Subverted Sovereignty: Historic Role of the Soviet Underground," in Stephen S. Cohen et al., <u>The Tunnel at the End of the Light</u> (Berkeley: University of California, 1998), 36.
184. Treml and Alexeev, 224-225, 239.
185. Gregory Grossman, "Sub-Rosa Privatization and Marketization in the USSR," <u>Annals, ASPSS</u> (January, 1990), 49.
186. Gregory Grossman, "Sub-Rosa Privatization," 49.
187. Byung-Yeon Kim, 6, 9.
188. Estimates developed by Gregory Grossman, in "The Second Economy: Boon or Bane for the Reform of the First Economy?" in <u>Economic Reforms in the Socialist World,</u> Stanislaw Gomulka et al., eds., (London: Macmillan, 1989), 94. According to Grossman, "Some idea of the magnitude of informal (or private) incomes in the USSR can be grasped from the findings of questionnaire survey of 1000 recent Soviet émigrés in the United States, conducted by Professor V. G. Treml and the present author [Gregory Grossman]. The data center on 1977 and refer only to urban areas. The figures presented refer only to families in which both husband and wife were present and at least one of them was officially employed at the time." In Grossman's view the second economy continued to grow after the late 1970s. The table suggests that by the late Brezhnev era,

the second economy was roughly about 30 percent of the largest republic, Russia, and about 40 percent of the other major Slavic republics, Ukraine and Belorussia. In other parts of the USSR for which data were available to him, the second economy was even larger, perhaps even equaling or outweighing the 'first' -- the planned, state-owned -- economy.

189. Simis, 153; Grossman, "Subverted Sovereignty," 39-40.

190. Kim, 12, 23.

191. Brezhnev quoted by David Pryce-Jones, The Strange Death of the Soviet Empire (New York: Henry Holt, 1995), 53.

192. Gregory Grossman, "Inflationary, Political, and Social Implications of the Current Economic Slowdown," in Hans-Hermann Hoehmann, Alex Nove, and Heinrich Vogel, Economics and Politics in the USSR (Boulder and London: Westview Press, 1986), 192.

193. Michael Alexeev, "The Russian Underground Economy in Transition," in Michael Walker, ed. The Underground Economy: Global Evidence of its Size and Impact (Vancouver, Canada: Fraser Institute, 1997), 259.

194. Treml and Alexeev, 225; Valery M. Rutgaizer, "The Shadow Economy in the USSR," (Berkeley-Duke Occasional Papers on the Second Economy in the USSR, No. 34, February 1992), 41.

195. Grossman, "Subverted Sovereignty," 31.

196. Rutgaizer, 6.

197. Grossman, "Subverted Sovereignty," 31.

198. Alexeev, 255-256.

199. Treml and Alexeev, 238.

200. Alexeev, 260.

201. Alexeev, 261.

202. Simis, 179.

203. Congress, Joint Economic Committee, Soviet Economy in a Time of Change, report entitled "Notes on the Illegal Private Economy and Corruption" by Gregory Grossman, 96th Cong., 1st sess., 1979, Committee Print, pp. 840-841.

204. Grossman, "Subverted Sovereignty," 32.

205. Pryce-Jones, 51-55, 377-83.

206. Simis, 47-48.
207. Grossman, "Subverted Sovereignty," quoting Andrei Grachev, 34.
208. Stephen Handelman, <u>Comrade Criminal: Russia's New Mafiya</u> (New Haven: Yale University Press, 1995), 56.
209. Kozlov quoted by John and Margrit Pittman, <u>Peaceful Coexistence: Its Theory and Practice in the Soviet Union</u> (New York: International Publishers, 1964), 69.
210. Alexeev, 261.
211. Alena V. Ledeneva, <u>Russia's Economy of Favours</u> (Cambridge: Cambridge University Press, 1998).
212. Gregory Grossman, "The Second Economy of the USSR," <u>Problems of Communism</u> Vol. XXVI, No. 5 (September-October, 1977): 25-40.
213. Georgy Shakhnazarov, <u>The Destiny of the World</u> (Moscow: Progress, 1978), 121-122.
214. S. Frederic Starr, "A Usable Past," in Alexander Dallin and Gail W. Lapidus, eds., <u>The Soviet System from Crisis to Collapse</u> (Boulder: Westview Press, 1995), 14-15.
215. Rutgaizer, 19-22.
216. Rutgaizer, 7, 10-13.
217. Rutgaizer, 7-10.
218. John Gooding, <u>Socialism in Russia: Lenin and his Legacy, 1890-1991</u> (New York: Palgrave, 2002), 208.
219. Victor Trushkov, "The Place of the Restoration of Capitalism in the Historic Process," <u>International Correspondence</u> (English language edition), 2(2000), 33-34.

Notes for Chapter 4
220. Mike Davidow, *Perestroika* (New York: International Publishers, 1993), 8.
221. Albert Resis, ed., <u>Molotov Remembers: Inside Kremlin Politics</u> (Chicago: Ivan R. Dee, 1993), 373.
222. Yegor Ligachev, <u>Inside Gorbachev's Kremlin</u> (New York: Pantheon Books, 1993), 44.
223. Oleg Kalugin, <u>The First Directorate</u> (New York: St. Martin's Press, 1994), 292-293.

224. Michael Ellman and Vladimir Kontorovich, The Destruction of the Soviet Economic System (Armonk, New York, and London: M.E. Sharpe, 1998), 12, 30, 31, 35, 38.
225. Yegor Ligachev, Inside Gorbachev's Kremlin (New York: Pantheon Books, 1993), 16.
226. Gennady Zyuganov, My Russia (Armonk, New York, and London: M. E. Sharpe, 1997), 54.
227. Abel Aganbegyan, The Economic Challenge of *Perestroika* (Bloomington and Indianapolis: Indiana University Press, 1988), 68.
228. Aganbegyan, 23.
229. Fred Halliday, "A Singular Collapse: The Soviet Union, Market Pressure and Inter-State Competition," Contention Magazine (1992), 324.
230. Peter Kenez, A History of the Soviet Union from the Beginning to the End (Cambridge: Cambridge University Press, 1999), 217.
231. Mikhail Gorbachev, Memoirs, (New York: Doubleday, 1995), 10-11.
232. Sean Gervasi, "A Full Court Press: The Destabilization of the Soviet Union," Covert Action, Fall 1990, 21-26.
233. Peter Schweizer, Victory: The Reagan Administration's Secret Strategy That Hastened the Collapse of the Soviet Union (New York: Atlantic Monthly Press, 1994), xviii-xix.
234. Schweizer, 76, 86-87, 88-89, 150, 153, 188, 193-194, 215.
235. Schweizer, 93-94, 140-141, 154, 195, 242-243.
236. Schweizer, 72, 109, 125-126, 139, 188.
237. Arch Puddington, Broadcasting Freedom: The Cold War Triumph of Radio Free Europe and Radio Liberty (Lexington, Kentucky: University Press of Kentucky, 2000), 223, 288; Gene Sosin, Sparks of Liberty: An Insider's Memoir of Radio Liberty (University Park, Pennsylvania: Pennsylvania State University Press, 1999), 196, 198, 203, 205.
238. Gervasi, 22, fn. 15.
239. Frances Fitzgerald, Way Out There in the Blue: Reagan, Star Wars, and the End of the Cold War (New York, et al.: Simon & Schuster, 2000,) 19, 148-149.

240. Fitzgerald, 148.

241. Schweitzer, 197.

242. Euvgeny Novikov and Patrick Bascio, Gorbachev and the Collapse of the Soviet Communist Party (New York: Peter Lang, 1994), 31.

243. T. H. Rigby, The Changing Soviet System: Mono-organizational Socialism from Its Origins to Gorbachev's Restructuring (Aldershot, England and Brookfield, Vermont: Canberra University College), 211.

244. Rigby, 211.

245. Helene Carrere D'Encausse, The End of the Soviet Empire (New York: Basic Books, 1994), 12-13.

246. Anthony D'Agostino, Gorbachev's Revolution (New York: New York University Press, 1998), 52-67.

247. D'Agostino, 76.

248. Vladimir Yegorov, Out of a Dead End Into the Unknown: Notes on Gorbachev's Perestroika (Chicago, Berlin, London, Tokyo, and Moscow: Edition q, inc., 1993), 33.

249. John B. Dunlop, The Rise of Russia and the Fall of the Soviet Empire (Princeton: Princeton University Press, 1993), 11-12.

250. Anatoly Dobrynin, In Confidence (New York: Times Books/ Random House, 1995), 513, 518-540.

251. Our Course Remains Unchanged: Peace and Progress (Moscow: Novisti Press, 1985), passim and Mikhail Gorbachev, "On the Convening of the 27th CPSU Congress," April 23, 1985) in For the Forthcoming XXVIIth CPSU Congress (Moscow: Novosti, 1985), passim.

252. Our Course Remains Unchanged, 14-15.

253. David Kotz and Fred Weir, Revolution from Above The Demise of the Soviet System (London and New York: Routledge 1997), 78, 82.

254. Kotz and Weir, 78.

255. Anders Aslund, Gorbachev's Struggle for Economic Reform (Ithaca, New York: Cornell University Press, 1989), 70-71.

256. Novikov and Bascio, 35.

257. Aslund, 81-82.

258. Gorbachev, <u>For the Forthcoming XXVIIth CPSU Congress</u>, 23-24.

259. The untranslated memoirs of Vladimir Kryuchov, head of Soviet foreign intelligence, referred to by Jerry Hough, <u>Democratization and Revolution in the USSR, 1985-91</u> (Washington, D.C.: Brookings, 1997), 193.

260. Fitzgerald, 286, 302.

261. Fitzgerald, 307.

262. D'Agostino, 86-87; Gill, 19-24; Novikov and Bascio, 35.

263. Gorbachev, <u>Political Report</u>, 106.

264. Gorbachev, <u>Political Report</u>, 115.

265. Dmitri Volkogonov, <u>Autopsy for an Empire</u> (New York, London, Toronto, Sydney, and Singapore: The Free Press, 1998), 443.

266. Volkogonov, 450.

267. Joseph Gibbs, <u>Gorbachev's</u> *Glasnost* (College Station: Texas A & M University Press, 1999), 27.

268. Davidow, 8.

269. Gus Hall, <u>The Power of Ideology</u> (New York: New Outlook, 1989), 22.

270. Raissa Gorbachev, <u>I Hope</u> (New York: Harper Collins, 1991), 136.

271. Aslund, 26-27.

272. Ellman and Kontorovich, 14.

273. Aslund, 25.

274. Novikov and Bascio, 42.

275. Dunlop, 6-7.

276. Ellman and Kontorovich, 10, 178.

277. Aslund, 35.

278. Kotz and Weir, 75-78.

279. Aganbegyan, 32-33.

280. Aganbegyan, 190-191.

281. Kotz and Weir, 78, 82.

282. Volkogonov, 464-465.

283. Ellman and Kontorovich, 22.

284. Aslund, 37-47, 55.

285. Aslund, 48-54.

286. Aslund, 88-100.

287. Aslund, 108.
288. Mikhail Gorbachev, <u>Political Report of the CPSU Central Committee to the 27th Party Congress</u> (Moscow: Novosti, 1986), 4-5, 26, 29, 40-46, 49, 86.
289. Neil Robinson, <u>Ideology and the Collapse of the Soviet System</u> (Aldershot, England and Brookfield, Vermont: Edward Elgar Publishing Company, 1995), 107-111.
290. Gibbs, 23, 28-29, 33.
291. Gorbachev, <u>Memoirs</u>, 210.
292. Gorbachev, <u>Political Report</u>, 111.
293. Gibbs, 37.
294. John and Carol Garrard, <u>Inside the Soviet Writers' Union</u> (New York: Free Press, 1990), 205.
295. Gibbs, 5-6, 8.
296. Alexander Yakovlev, <u>The Fate of Marxism</u> (New Haven and London: Yale Unversity Press, 1993), x.
297. Jonathan Harris, <u>The Public Politics of Aleksandr Nikolaevich Yakovlev, 1983-1989</u> (Pittsburgh: University of Pittsburgh Center for Russian and East European Studies, 1990), 8.
298. Yitzhak Brudny, <u>Reinventing Russia: Russian Nationalism and the Soviet State, 1953-1991</u> (Cambridge, Mass. and London: Harvard University Press, 1998), 94-100.
299. Robert Kaiser, <u>Why Gorbachev Happened</u> (New York, London, et al.: Simon & Schuster, 1991), 111.
300. Garrard, 198-199; Brudny, 197; Harris, 20.
301. Garrard, 202, 207.
302. Gibbs, 39; Brudny, 197-198.
303. Garrard, 201.
304. Garrard, 199.
305. Roy Medvedev and Giulietto Chiesa, <u>Time of Change: An Insider's View of Russia's Transformation</u> (New York: Pantheon, 1989), 27-28.
306. Medvedev and Chiesa, 29-32.
307. Medvedev and Chiesa, 32.
308. Gibbs, 44.
309. Garrard, 202; Medvedev and Chiesa, 32.
310. Medvedev and Chiesa, 35.
311. Davidow, 21-22.

312. Graeme Gill, The Collapse of a Single-party System (Cambridge: Cambridge University Press, 1994), 28-29.

313. For the Forthcoming XXIIth CPSU Congress, 24-25.

314. Political Report of the CPSU Central Committee to the 27th Party Congress, 86.

315. Mikhail Gorbachev, *Perestroika*: New Thinking for Our Country and the World (New York et al.: Harper & Row, 1987), 144-147.

316. Fitzgerald, 323.

317. "Blueprint for the Year 1986: Statement by Mikhail Gorbachev General Secretary of the CPSU Central Committee," Pravda (January, 16, 1986) reprinted in Reprints from the Soviet Press (February 15, 1986), 5-20.

318. Fitzgerald, 364-365.

319. The Truth About Afghanistan: Documents, Facts, Eyewitness Reports (Moscow: Novosti, 1981); Phillip Bonosky, Afghanistan--Washington's Secret War (New York: International Publishers, 2001).

320. Brzezinski quoted by Pankaj Mishen, "The Making of Afghanistan," The New York Review of Books (November 15, 2001), 20.

321. Sarah Mendelson, Changing Course: Ideas, Politics, & the Soviet Withdrawal from Afghanistan (Princeton, New Jersey: Princeton University Press, 1998), 69.

322. Mendelson, 60-61, 73-76.

323. The untranslated memoirs of Vladimir Kryuchkov, head of Soviet foreign intelligence, referred to by Jerry Hough, Democratization and Revolution in the USSR, 1985-91 (Washington, D.C.: Brookings, 1997), 193.

324. Fitzgerald, 323.

325. Mikhail Gorbachev, Political Report of the CPSU Central Committee to the 27th Party Congress (Moscow: Novosti, 1986), 86.

326. Mendelson, 112.

327. Mendelson, 112.

328. Mendelson, 112-113.

329. Vladimir Shubin, ANC: A View from Moscow (Bellville, South Africa: Mayibuye Books, 1999), 340.

330. Gorbachev, <u>Political Report of the CPSU Central Committee to the 27<u>th</u> Congress</u>, 41-57.

331. Gorbachev, <u>Political Report of the CPSU Central Committee to the 27<u>th</u> Congress</u>, 41-57.

332. Gregory Grossman, "Subverted Sovereignty: Historic Role of the Soviet Underground," in Stephen S. Cohen et al., eds. <u>The Tunnel at the End of the Light</u> (Berkeley: University of California, 1998), 28.

333. Stephen Cohen, "Introduction," to Yegor Ligachev, <u>Inside Gorbachev's Kremlin</u>, (New York: Pantheon Books, 1993), viii-xix.

334. Ligachev, 96, 100, <u>passim</u>.

335. D'Encausse, 10-12.

336. D'Encausse, 4, 9, 23-27, 31-33, 40-41.

337. D'Agostino, 174.

Notes for Chapter 5

338. Michael Ellman and Vladimir Kontorovich, <u>The Destruction of the Soviet Economic System</u> (Armonk, New York, and London: M.E. Sharpe, 1998), 309.

339. Alexander Yakovlev, <u>The Fate of Marxism in Russia</u> (New Haven and London: Yale University Press, 1993), 227.

340. Mikhail Gorbachev, <u>October and <i>Perestroika</i>: the Revolution Continues</u>(Moscow: Novosti Press Agency, 1987), 47.

341. Moshe Lewin, <u>Political Undercurrents in Soviet Economic Debates: from Bukharin to the Modern Reformers</u> (Princeton: Princeton University Press, 1975), xiii, xvii.

342. Robert V. Daniels, "Soviet Society and American Soviet Studies: a Study in Success?" in Michael Cox, <u>Rethinking The Soviet Collapse,</u> (London and New York: Cassell, 1999), 121.

343. Archie Brown, <u>The Gorbachev Factor</u> (Oxford and New York: Oxford University Press, 1997), 15.

344. Robert G. Kaiser, <u>Why Gorbachev Happened</u> (New York: Simon & Schuster, 1991), 15.

345. Delia Luisa Lopez Garcia, "Economic Crisis, Adjustment, and Democracy in Cuba," in Jose Bell Lara, ed., <u>Cuba in the 1990s</u> (Havana: Editorial Jose Marti, 1999), 25.

346. Graeme Gill, The Collapse of a Single-party System (Cambridge: Cambridge University Press, 1994), 19-29.

347. Stephen F. Cohen and Katrina van den Heuvel, Voices of Glasnost (New York: Norton, 1989), 17.

348. Marshall I. Goldman, What Went Wrong With Perestroika? (New York: Norton, 1991), 102.

349. Stephen Kotkin, Armageddon Averted: the Soviet Collapse, 1970-2000 (Oxford: Oxford University Press, 2001), 71-72.

350. Stephen F. Cohen, Reinterpreting the Soviet Experience (New York: Oxford University Press 1985), 126.

351. Yegor Ligachev, Inside Gorbachev's Kremlin (Boulder: Westview Press, 1993), 343.

352. Brown, 98.

353. Anthony D'Agostino, Gorbachev's Revolution (New York: New York University Press, 1998), 112.

354. Brown, 127.

355. Ligachev; 125; Brown, 127.

356. Howard Selsam, Socialism and Ethics, (New York: International Publishers, 1943), 92-99. Lenin held that the class values of the working class--solidarity, unity, cooperation, comradeship, etc., would become universal as socialist society became universal. The needs of the working class "create for it an ethics that is at one and the same time a class ethics and a human ethics embracing actually or potentially all men."

357. Jerry Hough, Democratization and Revolution in the USSR, 1985-1991 (Washington DC: Brookings Institution, 1997), 192-196.

358. Ligachev, 132, 189.

359. Ellman and Kontorovich, "The Collapse of the Soviet Union and the Memoir Literature," Europe-Asia Studies, 49, no. 2 (March 1997): 265.

360. Robert Kaiser, Why Gorbachev Happened: His Triumphs and His Failure (New York: Simon & Schuster, 1991), 156.

361. Anthony Jones and William Moskoff, Koops: The Rebirth of Entrepreneurship in the Soviet Union (Bloomington: Indiana University Press, 1991), xv.

362. Jones and Moskoff, 78.

363. Victor Perlo, "The Economic and Political Crisis in the USSR," Political Affairs, 70, (August 1991): 15.

364. Gregory Grossman, "The Second Economy: Boon or Bane for the Reform of the First Economy?" in Economic Reforms in the Socialist World (London: Macmillan, 1989), 83.

365. John B. Dunlop, The Rise of Russia and the Fall of the Soviet Empire (Princeton: Princeton University Press, 1993), 5.

366. Brown, 166.

367. Anders Aslund, Gorbachev's Struggle for Economic Reform (Ithaca, New York: Cornell University Press, 1989), 32.

368. Ligachev, 318.

369. Hough, 154.

370. David M. Kotz and Fred Weir, Revolution from Above (New York: Routledge, 1997), 97.

371. Nina Andreyeva, "I Cannot Forgo My Principles," in Alexander Dallin and Gail W. Lapidus, eds., The Soviet System: From Crisis to Collapse (Boulder, San Francisco and Oxford: Westview Press, 1995), 288-296.

372. Leading proponents of this view are: Mikhail Gorbachev, Memoirs, 252-254; Anatoly Chernyaev, My Six Years with Gorbachev (University Park, Pennsylvania: Pennsylvania State University, 2000), 153-160; Roy Medvedev and Giulietto Chiesa, Time of Change (New York: Pantheon, 1989), 189-206; Robert Kaiser, Why Gorbachev Happened (New York et al.: Simon and Schuster, 1991), 204-213; Yitzhak M. Brudny, "The Heralds of Opposition to Perestroika," Ed A. Hewett and Victor H. Winston, eds., Milestones in Glasnost and Perestroika (Washington, D. C.: Brookings Institute, 1991), 153-189; Anthony D'Agostino, Gorbachev's Revolution (New York: New York University Press, 1998), 191-197; David M. Kotz and Fred Weir, Revolution from Above (London and New York: Routledge, 1997), 67-68; Joseph Gibbs, Gorbachev's Glasnost (College Station: Texas A&M University Press, 1999), 66-73.

373. Medvedev and Chiesa, 190.

374. Brudny, 167.

375. Kaiser, 204.

376. Andreyeva, passim.

377. Kaiser, 204.

378. Andreyeva, 290-293.

379. Kaiser, 204.

380. Andreyeva, 294-295.

381. Gibbs, 67.

382. Stephen F. Cohen, "Introduction," to Ligachev, x, xxxii.

383. Gorbachev, 252.

384. Medvedev and Chiesa, 192.

385. Andreyeva, 296.

386. Gibbs, 67.

387. Ligachev, 301.

388. Valery Boldin, <u>Ten Years That Shook the World: The Gorbachev Era as Witnessed By His Chief of Staff</u> (New York: Basic Books, 1994), 168.

389. Gibbs,68.

390. Medvedev and Chiesa, 193.

391. Ligachev, 302.

392. Ligachev, 304-308.

393. Ligachev, 308.

394. Medvedev and Chiesa, 193.

395. Medvedev and Chiesa, 194-196.

396. Kaiser, 213.

397. Medvedev and Chiesa, 196.

398. Chernyaev, 154.

399. Medvedev and Chiesa, 196.

400. Kaiser, 213.

401. Gibbs, 71.

402. Medvedev and Chiesa, 196.

403. Chernyaev, 156.

404. Ronald Grigor Suny, <u>The Soviet Experiment</u> (New York, Oxford University Press, 1998), 461.

405. Ligachev, 152.

406. Hough, 106.

407. William Taubman, <u>Khrushchev: the Man and His Era</u> (New York: W. W. Norton & Co., 2003), 587, 782. Alexander Yakovlev was a link between the Khrushchev and Gorbachev eras on the proposal to divide the Party, according to this biography, which seems likely to be the

standard scholarly work in English for some time. Taubman interviewed Yakovlev, author of the party-splitting proposal to Gorbachev. Having worked in Moscow under Khrushchev in 1962, Yakovlev described to Taubman the CC Secretariat's resistance to Khrushchev's division of the Party into industrial and rural segments. Taubman states that, at the October 1964 Plenum that endorsed Khrushchev's forced retirement, certain leaders characterized the party's division as "the worst confusion our Soviet state has known since it was created."

408. Brown, 106.
409. Mikhail Gorbachev, Memoirs (New York: Doubleday, 1995), 282.
410. William E. Odom, The Collapse of the Soviet Military (New Haven: Yale University Press, 1998), 209.
411. Brown, 101; Gorbachev, Memoirs, 605.
412. P. Fedosyev, ed., What Is Democratic Socialism? (Moscow: Progress Publishers, 1980), 18.
413. Norman Markowitz, "On Holz's Defense of Leninism," Nature, Society and Thought 6, no. 3, 354.
414. Brown, 42, 328.
415. Odom, 115.
416. Ligachev, 15.
417. Andrew Murray, Flashpoint: World War III (London: Pluto Press, 1996), 42.
418. D'Agostino, 117-118.
419. D'Agostino, 119.
420. D'Agostino, 119.
421. Odom, 151
422. Odom, 137.
423. Mikhail Gorbachev, October and Perestroika: the Revolution Continues (Moscow: Novosti Press Agency, 1987), 66-67.
424. Odom,102.
425. Sarah E. Mendelson, Changing Course: Ideas, Politics, and the Soviet Withdrawal from Afghanistan (Princeton: Princeton University Press, 1998), 111. A strongly favorable assessment of Najibullah can be found in Philip Bonosky,

Afghanistan: Washington's Secret War(New York: International Publishers, 2001).

426. Mendelson, 122.

427. Mendelson, 117.

428. Vladimir Shubin, ANC: A View from Moscow (Bellville, South Africa: Mayibuye Books, University of Western Cape, 1999), 340-341.

429. V. I. Lenin, Questions of National Policy and Proletarian Internationalism (Moscow: Progress Publishers, 1970), 60.

430. David Lane, The Rise and the Fall of State Socialism (Cambridge: Polity Press: 1996), 124.

431. Ellman and Kontorovich, 134.

432. Ellman and Kontorovich, 145.

433. Ellman and Kontorovich, 188.

434. Ligachev, 339.

435. Ellman and Kontorovich, 2.

436. Ellman and Kontorovich, 150.

437. Ellman and Kontorovich, 189.

438. S. Frederick Starr, "A Usable Past," in Alexander Dallin and Gail Lapidus, eds., The Soviet System from Crisis to Collapse (Boulder: Westview Press, 1995), 14-15.

439. Anne White, Democratization in Russia under Gorbachev 1985-91: The Birth of a Voluntary Sector (New York: St. Martin's Press, 1999), 6-12.

440. Ellman and Kontorovich, 150.

441. Stephen F. Cohen, Bukharin and the Bolshevik Revolution (New York: Vintage, 1975), 36.

442. Yuri Andropov, "In Celebration of the Sixtieth Anniversary of the Union of Soviet Socialist Republics," A Reader on Social Sciences (Moscow: Progress, 1985), 381; John and Margrit Pittman, Peaceful Coexistence: Its Theory and Practice in the Soviet Union (New York: International Publishers, 1964), 85.

443. Yitzhak M. Brudny, Reinventing Russia: Russian Nationalism and the Soviet State (Cambridge: Harvard University, 1998), 17.

444. Odom, 407.

445. Ligachev, 143.

446. Terry Martin, <u>The Affirmative Action Empire: Nations and Nationalism in the Soviet Union, 1923-39</u> (Ithaca: Cornell University Press, 2001), 1.

447. Suny, 464.

448. D'Agostino, 178

449. Ellman and Kontorovich, "The Collapse of the Soviet Union and the Memoir Literature," 268-269.

450. Marshall I. Goldman, <u>What Went Wrong with</u> *Perestroika* (New York: Norton, 1991), 128-136.

451. Gregory Grossman, "Sub-Rosa Privatization and Marketization in the USSR," <u>Annals of the American Academy of Political and Social Science</u>, 507, (January 1990): 49.

Notes for Chapter 6

452. Graeme Gill, <u>The Collapse of a Single-party System</u> (Oxford: Oxford University Press, 1994), 78.

453. Stanislav Menshikov, <u>Catastrophe or Catharsis? The Soviet Economy Today</u> (London: Inter-Verso, 1990), 41.

454. Roy Medvedev, <u>Post-Soviet Russia</u> (New York: Columbia University Press, 2000), 47.

455. Carl A. Linden, <u>Khrushchev and the Soviet Leadership: With an Epilogue on Gorbachev</u> (Baltimore: Johns Hopkins, 1990), 235.

456. Seumus Milne, "Catastroika has not only been a disaster for Russia: a decade on, enthusiasm for the Soviet collapse looks misplaced." <u>The Guardian</u> (London), 16 August 2001.

457. John B. Dunlop, <u>The Rise of Russia and the Fall of the Soviet Empire</u> (Princeton: Princeton University Press, 1994), 94.

458. Archie Brown, <u>The Gorbachev Factor</u> (Oxford: Oxford University Press, 1996), 193.

459. Jerry Hough, <u>Democratization and Revolution in the USSR, 1985-91</u>(Washington D.C.: Brookings Institution, 1997), 502.

460. Anatoly Chernyaev, <u>My Six Years with Gorbachev</u> (University Park: Pennsylvania State University, 2000), 135.

461. Chernyaev, 299.

462. Vadim Volkov, <u>Violent Entrepreneurs: the Use of Force in the Making of Russian Capitalism</u> (Ithaca: Cornell University Press, 2002), 24. Volkov confirms that the bogus "co-ops," created by the ill-named 1988 Law on Cooperatives, led to explosive growth in private business enterprise and corresponding growth in violent business protection rackets. In 1992, with Yeltsin in power, the less well-known Law on Private Protection and Detective Activity actually legalized private protection rackets and "for several years formally sanctioned many of the activities already pursued by racketeering gangs...."

463. Hough, 503.

464. Hough, 260.

465. Robert Kaiser, <u>Why Gorbachev Happened: His Triumphs and His Failure</u> (New York: Simon and Schuster, 1991), 409.

466. Hough, 249.

467. William E. Odom, <u>The Collapse of the Soviet Military</u> (New Haven: Yale University Press, 1998), 439.

468. Chernyaev, 255.

469. Frances Fitzgerald, <u>Way Out There in the Blue: Reagan, Star Wars and the End of the Cold War</u> (New York: Simon and Schuster, 2000), 475.

470. Peter Schweizer, <u>Victory! The Reagan Administration's Secret Strategy That Hastened the Collapse of the Soviet Union</u> (New York: Atlantic Monthly Press, 1994), 14.

471. Odom, 474.

472. Hough, 432.

473. Hough, 502.

474. Pekka Sutela, <u>Economic Thought and Economic Reform in the Soviet Union</u> (Cambridge: Cambridge University Press, 1991), 5. Outside the Soviet Union, bourgeois economists stated bluntly that "socialist reform" economics aimed to incorporate capitalist elements into socialism until capitalism was fully restored. According to Sutela, "Seeing the inefficiency and indeed impossibility of such an [orthodox Communist, i.e., largely publicly owned and centrally planned] economic model, early reformers relaxed

some of the orthodox assumptions and tended to see the capitalist corporation as their model. Further along the road, more and more characteristics of capitalism were added to the normative image of efficient socialism until--by the late eighties--a transition to genuine capitalism was advocated and also practiced in such countries as Hungary and Poland." Dr. Sutela, a Soviet affairs specialist, worked for the Bank of Finland.

475. Chernyaev, 257.
476. Gill, 95.
477. Marshall I. Goldman, What Went Wrong with Perestroika? (New York: W. W. Norton, 1991), 193.
478. Brown, 184
479. Gill, 68.
480. Chernyaev, 173.
481. Gill, 74.
482. Chernyaev, 175.
483. Chernyaev, 179.
484. Yegor Ligachev, Inside Gorbachev's Kremlin (Boulder: Westview Press, 1992), 91-93.
485. Vitali I. Vorotnikov, Mi Verdad: Notas y Reflexiones del Diario de Trabajo de un Miembro del Buro Politico del PCUS (Havana: Casa Editorial Abril, 1995), 486.
486. Gill, 78.
487. Gill, 79.
488. Gill, 79.
489. Dunlop, 79.
490. David M. Kotz and Fred Weir, Revolution from Above (New York: Routledge, 1997), 102.
491. Dunlop, 81.
492. Dunlop, 79-81.
493. Dunlop, 106-7.
494. Kotz and Weir, 139.
495. Ligachev, 347.
496. Dunlop, 82.
497. Dunlop, 51.
498. Gill, 94-95.
499. Gill, 104.

500. Gill, 104.
501. Ligachev, 89.
502. P. N. Fedoseyev, ed., What Is Democratic Socialism? (Moscow: Progress Publishers, 1980), 127.
503. Gill, 115.
504. Gill, 115
505. Gill, 117.
506. Gill, 135.
507. Ligachev, 368.
508. Ligachev, 177-179.
509. Gill, 144.
510. Vorotnikov, 486.
511. Chernyaev, 189.
512. Chernyaev, 189.
513. Ligachev, xxiii.
514. Chernyaev, 270.
515. Ligachev, 44.
516. Valery Boldin, Ten Years That Shook the World: The Gorbachev Era as Witnessed by His Chief of Staff (New York: Basic Books, 1994), 258.
517. Boldin, 282.
518. Stephen Handelman, Comrade Criminal: Russia's New Mafiya (New Haven: Yale University Press, 1995), 311.
519. Stephen Kotkin, Armageddon Averted: the Soviet Collapse 1970-2000 (Oxford: Oxford University Press, 2001), ix.
520. Medvedev, 47.
521. Alexander Dallin and Gail W. Lapidus, eds., The Soviet System: From Crisis to Collapse Boulder, Colorado: Westview Press, 1995), 75.
522. Dunlop, 72.
523. Dunlop, 80.
524. Kaiser, 378.
525. Hough, 416.
526. George W. Breslauer, Gorbachev and Yeltsin as Leaders (Cambridge: Cambridge University Press, 2002), 170.
527. Boris Kargarlitsky, Restoration in Russia: Why Capitalism Failed (London: Verso, 1995), 83.
528. Goldman, 128.

529. Hough, 208.
530. Ligachev, 339.
531. Kotz and Weir, 80.
532. Hough, 343.
533. William Moskoff, <u>Hard Times: Impoverishment and Protest in the *Perestroika* Years. The Soviet Union 1985-91</u> (Armonk, New York and London: M.E. Sharpe, 1993), 28.
534. Moskoff, 43, 46.
535. Moskoff, 59.
536. Michael Ellman and Vladimir Kontorovich, <u>The Destruction of the Soviet Economic System</u> (Armonk, New York and London: M.E. Sharpe, 1998), 22.
537. Hough, 359.
538. Kaiser, 378.
539. Abel Aganbegyan, <u>The Economic Challenge of *Perestroika*</u> (Bloomington: Indiana University Press, 1988; <u>Inside Perestroika: the Future of the Soviet Economy</u> (New York: Harper and Row, 1989).
540. Michael Alexeev and William Pyle, "A Note on Measuring the Unofficial Economy in the former Soviet Republics," <u>William Davidson Institute Working Papers</u>, University of Michigan Business School, no. 436, table #6, (July 2001): 19. The table is presented here as presented by Alexeev and Pyle. It seems doubtful, however, that their method yields estimates accurate to a tenth of a percentage point. We believe the estimates should be understood merely as a reasonable indicator of the order of magnitude of the second economy in each republic and a reasonable indicator of its growth rate. Thus, in Estonia and Uzbekistan, the exceptional cases, the slight decline in share should be interpreted as an indicator of little or no change in the second economy's role in the total economy of those republics in the period under review.
541. Roy Medvedev, <u>Post Soviet Russia</u> (New York: Columbia, 2000), 170-171.
542. Steven L. Solnick, <u>Stealing the State, Control and Collapse in Soviet Institutions</u> (Cambridge: Harvard University Press, 1998), 116.
543. Handelman, 56.

544. Handelman, 71.
545. Hough, 130.
546. Anthony Jones and William Moskoff, eds., <u>The Great Market Debate in Soviet Economics, An Anthology</u> (Armonk, New York and London: M.E. Sharpe, 1991), ix.
547. Hough, 134.
548. Hough, 139.
549. Hough, 360.
550. Hough, 363.
551. Carolyn McGiffert Ekedahl and Melvin A. Goodman, <u>The Wars of Eduard Shevardnadze</u> (University Park: Pennsylvania State University, 1997), 4.
552. Chernyaev, 83.
553. David Remnick, <u>Resurrection: the Struggle for a New Russia</u> (New York: Vintage Books, 1997), 17.
554. Ligachev, 152.
555. Hough, 374.
556. Arch Puddington, <u>Broadcasting Freedom: The Cold War Triumph of Radio Liberty and Radio Free Europe</u> (Lexington: University of Kentucky Press, 2000), 291.
557. Dunlop, 90.
558. Dunlop, 90.
559. Dunlop, 91.
560. V. I. Lenin, <u>Selected Works</u>, 1, (New York: International Publishers, 1967), 625. "From their daily experience the masses know perfectly well the value of geographical and economic ties, and the advantages of a big market and a big state. They will, therefore, resort to secession only when national oppression and national friction make joint life absolutely intolerable and hinder any and all economic intercourse."
561. Geoffrey Hosking, <u>The First Socialist Society</u> (Cambridge: Harvard University Press, 1992), 473.
562. Kaiser, 315.
563. Brown, 280-282.
564. Hosking, 473.
565. Dunlop, 55.
566. Hough, 388.

567. Odom, 351.

568. Hough, 406.

569. Kotz and Weir, 266.

570. Mikhail Gorbachev, <u>Memoirs</u> (New York: Doubleday, 1995), 501.

571. Chernyaev, 148.

572. Fred Coleman, <u>The Decline and Fall of the Soviet Empire: Forty Years that Shook the World from Stalin to Yeltsin</u> (New York: St. Martin's Press, 1996), 312.

573. Chernyaev, 320, 327.

574. Chernyaev, 297, 298.

575. Chernyaev, 305.

576. Chernyaev, 356.

577. Anthony D'Agostino, <u>Gorbachev's Revolution</u> (New York: New York University Press, 1998), 310.

578. Hough, 428.

579. Hough, 439.

580. Hough, 455.

581. Hough, 429.

582. Dunlop, 196-197.

583. Odom, 320.

584. Hough, 431.

585. Dunlop, 217.

586. Dunlop, 253.

587. Amy Knight, <u>Spies Without Cloaks</u> (Princeton: Princeton University Press, 1996), 18.

588. Dunlop, 253.

589. Hough, 431.

590. Knight, 18.

591. Hough, 432.

592. Dunlop, 199.

593. Dunlop, 201.

594. Dunlop, 198.

595. Odom, 342.

596. Knight, 18.

597. Hough, 433.

598. Hough, 432.

599. Odom, 353,354.

600. Odom, 355.
601. Hough, 436.
602. Dunlop, 186.
603. Dunlop, 195.
604. Odom, 341.
605. Vladimir Shubin, <u>ANC: A View from Moscow</u> (Bellville, South Africa: Mayibuye Books, 1999), 390.

Notes for Chapter 7

606. Fedor Burlatsky, *Khrushchev and the First Russian Spring: the Era of Khrushchev through the Eyes of His Adviser* (New York: Scribners, 1992), 276.
607. Fedor Burlatsky, *Khrushchev and the First Russian Spring: the Era of Khrushchev through the Eyes of His Adviser* (New York: Scribners, 1992), 276.
608. Alexander Dallin, "Causes of the Collapse of the USSR," in Alexander Dallin and Gail Lapidus, eds., <u>The Soviet System from Crisis to Collapse</u> (Boulder: Westview Press, 1995), 686.
609. Fedor Burlatsky, <u>Khrushchev and the First Russian Spring: the Era of Khrushchev through the Eyes of His Adviser</u> (New York: Scribners, 1992), 276.
610. "Socialism in the Soviet Union: Lessons and Perspectives. From the Program of the Fourth Congress of the Communist Party of the Russian Federation," 20 April 1997 in <u>Nature, Society, and Thought</u>, 10, no. 3 (1997): 421.
611. Jerry Hough, <u>Democratization and Revolution in the USSR, 1985-1991</u> (Washington DC: Brookings Institution, 1997), 15.
612. Francis Fukuyama, <u>The End of History and the Last Man</u>, New York: Avon Books, 1992), xiii.
613. Vladimir Treml and Michael Alexeev, "The Second Economy and the Destabilizing Effect of Its Growth on the State Economy of the Soviet Union: 1965-1989," <u>Berkley-Duke Occasional Papers</u>, no. 36, (1993): 2.
614. Stephen F. Cohen and Katrina van den Heuvel, <u>Voices of Glasnost</u> (New York: Norton, 1989), 25.

615. Domenico Losurdo, "Flight from History? The Communist Movement between Self-criticism and Self-contempt," Nature, Society, and Thought, 13, no. 4, (2000): 507.

616. Stephen F. Cohen, "American Journalism and Russia's Tragedy." The Nation 2 October 2000, 23 December 2000, <http://www.thenation.com/doc.mhtml?I=20001002&s=cohen.

617. Leninism and the World Revolutionary Working-class Movement, (Progress Publishers: Moscow, 1971), 133.

618. John and Margrit Pittman, Peaceful Coexistence (New York: International Publishers, 1964), 69.

619. Albert Szymanski, "The Class Basis of Political Processes in the Soviet Union," Science and Society, 62, (winter 1978-79): 426-457.

620. Since we speak of both egalitarian and non-egalitarian aspects of Soviet society, perhaps a clarification is necessary. A number of things were true at once. Wage-leveling increased in Soviet industry starting with Khrushchev and served to reduce worker productivity incentives which in turn reduced overall Soviet economic growth rate, though there were other growth-inhibiting factors too. Nevertheless, the general egalitarianism promoted by Soviet policies was a positive achievement. Though inequality caused by the ill-gotten gains in the second economy increased over time, it remained paltry by capitalist and especially by U.S. standards. Similarly, the material privileges of top Party and state officials were a reality, but they too were modest compared to elite privileges in capitalist countries. Still, the inequality caused by illegal money-making and official privilege were politically objectionable from a Leninist standpoint and were politically unwise because they became an easy target for domestic and foreign anti-Communists.

621. Boris N. Ponomarev, Communism in a Changing World (New York: Sphinx Press, 1983), 78.

622. Gus Hall, Socialism and Capitalism in a Changing World (New York: New Outlook Publishers, 1990), 50-53.

623. Gus Hall, "Marxism-Leninism in the World Struggle against Opportunism," (speech at Political Affairs Forum, 28 February 1982) Political Affairs Reprint, 5.

624. Gus Hall, "The World We Preserve Must Be Livable," World Marxist Review, 35, no. 5 (May 1988): 22-23.

625. Bertell Ollman, "Market Mystification in Capitalist and Market Socialist Societies," in Market Socialism: the Debate among Socialists (New York: Routledge, 1998), 99.

626. David Laibman, "Editorial Perspectives, Socialism: Alternative Visions and Models," Science and Society, 56, no. 1 (spring 1992): 4.

627. Michael Ellman and Vladimir Kontorovich, The Destruction of the Soviet Economic System: an Insider's History (Armonk: M.E. Sharpe, 1998), 34-35.

628. Anders Aslund, How Russia Became a Market Economy (Washington, DC: Brookings, 1995), 13.

629. Treml and Alexeev, 25-26.

630. Bahman Azad, Heroic Struggle, Bitter Defeat (New York: International, 2000), 116.

631. Victor and Ellen Perlo, Dynamic Stability: the Soviet Economy Today (New York: International Publishers, 1980), 337.

632. Ronald L. Meek, Studies in the Labour Theory of Value (London: Lawrence and Wishart, 1973), 262.

633. Joseph V. Stalin, Selected Works (Davis, California: Cardinal Publishers, 1971), 324.

634. Maurice Dobb, Soviet Economic Development since 1917 (New York: International Publishers, 1968), 334; Meek, 282.

635. A. M. Rumyantsev, Categories and Laws of the Political Economy of Communism (Moscow; Progress Publishers, 1969), 225.

636. Anders Aslund, Gorbachev's Struggle for Economic Reform (Ithaca: Cornell, 1989), 4.

637. David M. Kotz and Fred Weir, Revolution from Above (New York: Routledge, 1997), 67.

638. Tatyana Zaslavskaya, The Second Socialist Revolution, an Alternative Soviet Strategy (Bloomington: Indiana University Press, 1990), ix.

639. Stalin, 368.

640. Yuri Andropov, "Speech at the CPSU Central Committee Meeting," June 15, 1983 (Moscow: Novosti Press Agency Publishing House, 1983), 22.

641. Michael Parenti, Blackshirts and Reds (San Francisco: City Lights, 1997), 60-61.

642. Arguably, Laos can be added to the list. Laos has a Marxist-Leninist government that seeks to maintain an orientation toward socialism, and over time, of course, it can develop into a socialist society. The development hurdles are enormous. Presently the country is characterized by the UN as among the "least developed" states, a status owing in part, no doubt, to savage U.S. bombardment during the Indochina War. By and large, since 1986, in step with its neighbor Vietnam, Laos, led by People's Revolutionary Party (LPRP), has pursued a renewal strategy to create a multi-tiered economy with a public sector, a foreign sector, and domestic private sector. Laos has sought partial integration into the world capitalist economy. See official website of Laos at <http://www.laoembassy.com>

643. Carl Riskin, China's Political Economy (Oxford: Oxford University Press, 1987), 290.

644. Al L. Sargis, "Ideological Tendencies and Reform Policy in China's Primary Stage of Socialism," Nature, Society, and Thought, 11, no. 4, (1998): 396.

645. Jose Bell Lara, ed., Cuba in the 1990s (Havana: Instituto Cubano del Libro, Editorial Jose Marti, 1999), 111, 87.

646. Evelio Vilarino Ruiz, Cuba: Socialist Economic Reform and Modernization (Havana: Editorial Jose Marti, 1998), 16-17.

647. Rajan Menon, "Post-Mortem: the Causes and Consequences of the Soviet Collapse," The Harriman Review, 7, nos. 10-12, (1994): 9.

648. Domenico Losurdo, "Flight from History? The Communist Movement between Self-criticism and Self-contempt," Nature, Society, and Thought, 13, no. 4, (2000): 498.

311

649. Stephen F. Cohen, Failed Crusade: America and the Tragedy of Post-Soviet Russia (New York: Norton, 2001), 208.

650. David M. Kotz, "Is Russia Becoming Capitalist?" Science and Society, 65, no. 2, (summer 2001): 157-181.

651. Roy Medvedev, Post Soviet Russia (New York: Columbia University, 2000), 51.

652. Ian Fisher, "As Poland Endures Hard Times, Capitalism Comes under Attack," New York Times 12 June 2002, 14 July 2002, <http://query.nytimes.com/search/article-page.ht ml?res=9F0DE5DF163CF931A25755C0A9649C8B63>.

653. G. A. Kozlov, ed., Political Economy: Socialism (Moscow: Progress, 1977), 80-81.

654. "Mr. X" George Kennan, "The Sources of Soviet Conduct," Foreign Affairs (July 1947): 566-82, quoted in Gregory Grossman, "Subverted Sovereignty: Historic Role of the Soviet Underground," in Stephen S. Cohen et al., eds., The Tunnel at the End of the Light (Berkeley: University of California, 1998), 24-50.

655. Azad, 179.

656. Kenneth Neill Cameron, Stalin: Man of Contradiction (Toronto: NC Press Ltd., 1987), 7.

657. Mikhail Gorbachev, October and Perestroika: The Revolution Continues (Moscow: Novosti, 1987), 26.

658. Hans Heinz Holz, "The Downfall and Future of Socialism," Nature, Society, and Thought 5, no. 3, (1992): 121.

659. Herbert Aptheker, "The Soviet Collapse and the Surrounding Capitalist World," Science and Society, 62, no. 2, (summer 1998): 284.

660. Michael Parenti, Blackshirts and Reds (San Francisco: City Lights, 1997), 77.

661. Parenti, 76-86.

662. Aileen Kelly, "In the Promised Land," The New York Review of Books 68, no. 19, (November 29, 2001): 45.

663. Stephane Courtois et al., eds., The Black Book of Communism, Crimes, Terror, Repression (Cambridge: Harvard University Press, 1999).

664. Yuri Krasin, The Dialectics of Revolutionary Process (Moscow: Novosti, 1973), 7.

665. Anthony Coughlan, "Social Democracy and National Independence," (unpublished article, May 1993), 4.

Notes for Epilogue

666. Karl Marx and Frederick Engels, <u>Selected Correspondence</u> (Moscow: Progress Publishers, 1965), 264.
667. "Social Dimensions of Globalization," ICFTU submission to the first meeting of the ILO World Commission on Globalization (25-26 March 2002) International Confederation of Free Trade Unions, Brussels, 2002, 1.
668. Fred Halliday, "A Singular Collapse: The Soviet Union, Market Pressure, and Interstate Competition," <u>Contention Magazine</u> (1992).
669. We have adapted and supplemented the explanations identified by Kotz and Weir, David Kotz and Fred Weir, <u>Revolution from Above: The Demise of the Soviet System</u> (New York and London: Routledge, 1997), 3-5.
670. Jack Matlock, <u>Autopsy on an Empire</u> (New York: Random House, 1995), 648.
671. See the summaries and critiques of Malia and Pipes in Walter Laqueur, <u>The Dream That Failed</u> (New York and Oxford: Oxford University Press, 1994), <u>passim</u> and Alexander Dallin, "Causes of the Collapse of the USSR," <u>Post-Soviet Affairs</u> 8(1992): 279-282.
672. Dmitri Volkogonov, <u>Autopsy for an Empire</u> (New York, London, Toronto, Sydney, Singapore: The Free Press, 1998).
673. Roy Medvedev and Giulietto Chiesa, <u>Time of Change: An Insider's View of Russia's Transformation</u> (New York: Pantheon, 1989).
674. Elizabeth Teague, "The Fate of the Working Class," in Robert Daniels, ed., <u>Soviet Communism from Reform to Collapse</u> (Lexington, Mass.: Heath and Company, 1995), 352-365.
675. Stephen White, "The Minorities' Struggle for Sovereignty," in Daniels, 216-229; Yitzhak Brudny, <u>Reinventing Russia: Russian Nationalism and the Soviet State, 1953-1991</u> (Cambridge, Mass., and London, England: Harvard University Press, 1998), and Helene d'Encausse, <u>The End</u>

of the Soviet Empire: The Triumph of Nations (New York: A New Republic Books, Basic Books, A Division of Harper Collins, 1994).

676. Anders Aslund, Gorbachev's Struggle for Economic Reform (Ithaca, New York: Cornell University Press, 1989), 4-5.

677. Michael Ellman and Vladimir Kontorovich, The Destruction of the Soviet System: An Insider's History (Armonk, New York, and London, England: M. E. Sharpe, 1998), 17.

678. Ellman and Kontorovich, 30-40.

679. Anthony D'Agostino, Gorbachev's Revolution (New York: New York University Press, 1998), 272-273, 285, 296.

680. New York Times (February 26, 2001).

681. Andre Gunder Frank, "What Went Wrong in the 'Social' East?" Humboldt Journal of Socialist Relations 24, no. 1 and 2: 179-184.

682. Manuel Castells and Emma Kiselova, The Collapse of Soviet Communism: A View From the Information Society (Berkeley: University of California Press, 1995), 3.

683. Laqueur, 58-59.

684. Peter Schweizer, Victory: The Reagan Administration's Secret Strategy that Hastened the Collapse of the Soviet Union (New York: Atlantic Monthly Press, 1994); Sean Gervasi, "A Full Court Press: the Destabilization of the Soviet Union," Covert Action 35(Fall, 1990): 21-26.

685. Peter Schweizer, Reagan's War [Bound galley copy] (New York: Doubleday, 2002), 3-4.

686. Frances Fitzgerald, Way Out There in the Blue: Reagan, Star Wars and the End of the Cold War (New York et al.: Simon & Schuster, 2000).

687. Fitzgerald, 474.

688. Ellman and Kontorovich, 57.

689. Ellman and Kontorovich, 59.

690. Leon Trotsky, The Revolution Betrayed (New York: Merit Publishers, 1965), 252-254.

691. David Kotz and Fred Weir, Revolution from Above: The Demise of the Soviet System (New York and London: Routledge, 1997.

692. Jerry F. Hough, <u>Democratization and Revolution in the USSR, 1985-1991</u> (Washington, D.C.: Brookings, 1997).
693. Steven L. Solnick, <u>Stealing the State: Control and Collapse in Soviet Institutions</u> (Cambridge, Mass. and London, England: Harvard University Press, 1998).
694. Bahman Azad, <u>Heroic Struggle Bitter Defeat: Factors Contributing to the Dismantling of the Socialist State in the USSR</u> (New York: International Publishers, 2000).
695. Ellman and Kontorovich, 27.
696. Solnick, <u>passim</u>.
697. Azad, 115-118, 120, 129-134.
698. Azad, 162.
699. See the "Conclusion" for a full discussion of these positions.
700. Karl Marx and Frederick Engels, "Manifesto of the Communist Party," in <u>Selected Works</u> (Moscow: Foreign Languages Publishing House, 1962), 53.
701. C. B. Macpherson, <u>The Real World of Democracy</u> (New York and Oxford: Oxford University Press, 1972), <u>passim</u>.
702. E. Ambartsumov, F. Burlatsky, Y. Krasin, and E. Pletnyov, <u>Real Socialism...for a working class estimate</u> (reprint from <u>New Times</u>) (New York: New Outlook Publishers, [1978]), 10.
703. For a good summary of studies of Soviet political institutions, see Albert Szymanski, "The Class Basis of Political Processes in the Soviet Union," <u>Science & Society</u> (Winter, 1978-79): 426-457.
704. Stephen Cohen, <u>Failed Crusade: America and the Tragedy of Post-Communist Russia</u> (New York and London: W. W. Norton, 2000), 41.
705. Archie Brown, <u>The Gorbachev Factor</u> (Oxford, England: Oxford University Press, 1996).
706. Robert V. Daniel, "Was Communism Reformable?" <u>The Nation</u>, 3 January 2000, 26.
707. Euvgeny Novikov and Patrick Bascio, <u>Gorbachev and the Collapse of the Soviet Communist Party</u> (New York: Peter Lang, 1994), 39-44.

708. Anthony D'Agostino, <u>Gorbachev's Revolution</u> (New York: New York University Press, 1998), <u>passim</u>.

709. "1992 Castro Interviewed on Soviet Collapse, Stalin," <u>El Nuevo Diario</u> [Managua] (3 June 1992).

Index

C

Cameron, Kenneth 33, 238
capitalism 1, 6–8, 9–11, 13, 18,
    20, 21, 31, 38, 62, 64, 65,
    69, 84, 85, 88, 102, 105,
    108, 113, 133, 134, 143,
    151, 154, 162, 170, 176,
    177, 180, 201, 202, 204,
    205, 227, 228, 229, 231,
    234, 242, 245, 246, 247,
    248, 252, 253, 254, 263,
    264, 266, 269, 272, 273
Carr, E. H. 7, 21
Carter, Jimmy 91
Casey, William 92
Castells, Manuel 261
Castro, Fidel 11, 275
Chechens 210
Chernenko, Konstantin 58
Chernyaev, Anatoly 20, 136, 150,
    171, 175, 206
Chikin, Valentin 147
Chile 62, 176
China 6, 39, 51, 156, 233, 244,
    245, 246, 249
Churchill, Winston 145
CIA 8, 44, 66, 92, 121, 122, 260,
    261
civil society 161, 195
class struggle 12, 13, 20, 21, 29,
    31, 33, 40, 54, 82, 120, 134,
    155, 157, 158, 227, 229,
    233, 237
Cohen, Stephen F. 10, 20, 23, 43,
    126, 136, 144, 190, 232,
    266
Cold War 1, 7, 9, 10, 25, 39,
    55, 134, 167, 249, 251,
    259–261
collapse, Soviet 2, 5, 9, 10, 12, 14,
    84, 176, 179, 189, 219, 226,
    226–228, 230–232, 234,
    236, 239, 244, 260, 262,
    266, 267, 272–274
Congress of People's Deputies
    148, 174, 178, 180, 181,
    182, 183, 192, 195, 197,
    216, 260, 273
Conquest, Robert 33
cooperatives 124
corruption 13, 41, 45, 50, 56, 61,
    63, 78–82, 90, 91, 93, 98,
    101, 104, 111, 113, 119,
    135, 144, 190, 191, 228,
    230, 232, 249, 258, 260,
    265
Coughlan, Anthony ix, 252
coup of August 1991 219
CPSU (Communist Party of the
    Soviet Union or Bolshevik
    Party) 15, 25, 28, 40–42,
    48, 49, 54, 57, 62, 81, 94,
    101, 112, 114, 119, 132–
    137, 139–141, 149–151,
    154, 155, 156, 158, 160,
    163, 164, 167, 170, 173,
    173–175, 178, 181–193,
    195, 196, 197, 200, 202,
    203, 207, 210, 216, 219,
    222, 226, 227, 228, 230,
    233, 236, 242, 263, 264,
    266
Cuba 5, 6, 39, 42, 156, 157, 213,
    233, 244, 245, 249, 265
Czechoslovakia 154, 179, 180,
    185, 207

D

D'Agostino, Anthony 1, 97, 166,
    220, 273
Dallin, Alexander 1
Daniels, Robert V. 133
Davidow, Mike 11, 87, 103, 119

318

S

Sachs, Jeffrey 62
Sagdayev, Roald Z. 94
Sakharov, Andrei 11, 41, 119,
    182, 194, 195, 196, 208
Sarkisyants, G. S. 65
Schweizer, Peter 92, 261, 262
second economy x, 13, 17, 57, 61,
    63, 64, 65, 66, 69, 70, 71,
    72, 73, 74, 75, 76, 77, 78,
    80, 81, 82, 83, 84, 85, 91,
    98, 105, 107, 108, 111, 124,
    125, 128, 129, 138, 139,
    158, 161, 170, 173, 190,
    192, 197, 198, 200, 201,
    227, 228, 229, 230, 237,
    238, 240, 266, 270, 274
separatism 6, 113, 137, 162, 166,
    167, 173, 187, 195, 206,
    207, 222, 236. *See* National-
    ism
Serbia 179
Shakhnazarov, Georgy 81
Shaposhnikov, Marshal 221
Shatalin, Stanislav 204, 205
Shatrov, Mikhail 41, 119
Shcherbitski, Vladimir 110
Shenin, Oleg 216
Shevardnadze, Eduard 101
Shmelev, Nikolai 150
Shubikin, V. 41
Simis, Konstantin 69
Slovo, Joe 11
Sobchak, Anatoly 187
social democracy 38, 113, 150,
    177, 234, 268
Social Democracy 20
socialism x, 2, 5, 6, 7, 9, 11, 12,
    13, 17, 18, 19, 20, 21, 25,
    27, 28, 29, 34, 36, 38, 39,
    40, 41, 45, 49, 52, 57, 58,
    62, 63, 64, 65, 66, 67, 73,
    76, 77, 80, 81, 82, 83, 84,
    88, 90, 91, 100, 102, 104,
    105, 106, 107, 108, 111,
    112, 113, 114, 118, 120,
    123, 124, 126, 132, 133,
    134, 136, 137, 140, 141,
    142, 143, 144, 147, 151,
    152, 158, 162, 171, 173,
    174, 176, 177, 178, 179,
    180, 183, 185, 192, 194,
    198, 214, 222, 227, 229,
    230, 231, 232, 233, 234,
    236, 237, 238, 239, 240,
    241, 242, 243, 244, 245,
    247, 248, 249, 250, 251,
    252, 253, 254, 258, 259,
    260, 261, 263, 265, 266,
    267, 268, 269, 271, 272,
    273, 274, 275
social reformism 150, 231
Sokirko, V. 82
Solnick, Steven L. 263
Solzhenitsyn, Alexander 50
Soros, George 204
South Africa 43, 213
sovereignization 208, 209, 210
Soviet economy 10, 36, 37, 43, 47,
    61, 65, 66, 72, 78, 92, 108,
    110, 170, 171, 184, 198,
    240, 241, 261
Soviet foreign policy 54, 100, 154,
    155, 156, 157, 174, 178,
    214, 215, 227
Soviet Union (USSR) x, 1, 2, 3, 4,
    5, 6, 7, 8, 9, 10, 11, 12, 15,
    16, 20, 21, 22, 25, 30, 31,
    35, 37, 38, 39, 40, 41, 42,
    43, 44, 47, 48, 52, 54, 55,
    57, 62, 64, 65, 66, 74, 76,
    78, 84, 88, 91, 92, 93, 94,
    97, 100, 102, 123, 128, 139,

Weir, Fred 263

Western Europe 5, 30, 97, 101,
        239

White, Anne 162

working class 4, 5, 6, 9, 12, 17,
        40, 42, 62, 82, 143, 145,
        163, 170, 183, 185, 186,
        194, 197, 230, 232, 234,
        235, 255, 269, 272

Y

Yakovlev, Alexander 106, 116,
        131, 136, 175, 178

Yanaev, Gennadii 216

Yazov, Dmitrii 217

Yeltsin, Boris 11, 97, 101, 104,
        114, 118, 167, 171, 172,
        173, 182, 185, 195, 196,
        204, 208, 219, 222, 263

Yugoslavia 51, 145, 179, 214, 248

Z

Zaikov, Lev 110

Zakharov, Vasily 118

Zaslavskaya, Tatyana 41, 107, 243

Zhdanov, Andrei 25

Zhukov, Georgy 33, 50

Zinoviev, Grigory 18

Zyuganov, Gennady 89